QUAKERS IN SOUTH CAROLINA

Wateree and Bush River, Cane Creek, Piney Grove and Charleston Meetings

The Rev. Silas Emmett Lucas, Jr., Editor

Southern Historical Press, Inc.
Greenville, South Carolina

Copyright 1991
By: Southern Historical Press, Inc.

All rights reserved. No part of this publication may be reproduced, stored in a retrieval system, transmitted in any form, posted on to the web in any form or by any means without the prior written permission of the publisher.

Please direct all correspondence and orders to:

www.southernhistoricalpress.com
or
SOUTHERN HISTORICAL PRESS, Inc.
PO BOX 1267
375 West Broad Street
Greenville, SC 29601
southernhistoricalpress@gmail.com

ISBN #0-89308-450-6

Printed in the United States of America

Table of Contents

	Pages
1. Quaker Records from *Historic Camden, S.C* by Kirkland and Kennedy, 1905.	1-43
2. Quaker Records from *The Annals of Newberry* (County, S.C.) by O'Neall and Chapman, 1892	46-84
3. Quaker Records from Hinshaw's *Encyclopedia of American Quaker Genealogy*, Vol. I: North Carolina, 1936, 1991	87-143
4. Index	144 ff.

Introduction

The material appearing in this volume has been taken from three major sources, viz: "Historic Camden, S.C." by Kirkland and Kennedy, published in 1905, "The Annals of Newberry (County, S.C.)" by O'Neall and Chapman, published 1892 and from Hinshaw's "Encyclopedia of American Quaker Genealogy, Vol. I, North Carolina," 1936. The material appearing in the first two titles consists of considerable early records pertaining to many of the pioneer Quaker families that settled in South Carolina, many of whom intermarried with other pioneer families and were assimilated into other religious denominations, while still others left South Carolina and moved to Tennessee, Ohio, Indiana and other states. Many South Carolina families, prominent and otherwise will be surprised to find that they have Quaker roots. Because of the valuable information found in the Camden and Newberry books, we have also reprinted the Minutes from Hinshaw's N.C. volume listing marriages, deaths, births, etc. for not only Bush River but also Cane Creek, Piney Grove and Charleston Monthly Meetings in South Carolina but also that of the Wrightsboro, Georgia Meeting. This consolidated title will provide a veritable storehouse of information not found elsewhere in one volume.

Quaker Records from *Historic Camden, S.C.*

CHAPTER III.

PINE TREE HILL.

"Rest there, old fathers, in thy quiet graves."
—*J. Belton O'Neall.*

Mention has been made in the preceding chapters of the first settlements in the vicinity of Camden, but under this heading something more particular will be undertaken in regard to that obscure subject. There are few data to go upon, except such as may be extracted from original grants and ancient deeds, exhumed from musty trunks and the tomes of the State House. Few chronicles did those first comers leave behind, other than a cleared field or a deed of land.

That district for some miles above and below Camden, on both sides of the river, was early known as "The Waterees," a name which was sometimes used to designate Fredricksburg, the township on the eastern side. According to the petition of Thomas Brown, the Indian trader, his family was among the few inhabitants, in 1735, residing in "that remote part of the country."

So far as careful research reveals, the very first landowner in the vicinity of Camden was one James Ousley, who obtained a precept for 300 acres on the western side of the river, nearly opposite Camden, on January 17, 1733. Near the same site came Thomas Hanahan, August 16, 1735. The land of James Ousley passed to the Quaker, Nebo Gaunt, then to Joseph Kershaw, and now forms a part of the "Westerham" plantation of Henry Savage.

After close scrutiny of the township grants for evidence of the first settlers on the Camden side, none earlier can be found than February 8, 1737, on which date a group of families obtained precepts for land in Fredricksburg Township. Fifty acres being allotted for each member of a family, the number of individuals may be inferred from the number of acres granted to the head. The following may therefore be cited as the original prospectors of Camden:

Adam Strain	200 acres	4 in family
David Alexander	100 acres	2 in family
James McGowan	300 acres	6 in family
Hugh McCutchin	100 acres	2 in family
Michael Harris	50 acres	1 in family
William Seawright	250 acres	5 in family
Robert Seawright	50 acres	1 in family
		21

The unnamed family, mentioned in the Council Journal of 1736 as murdered by the Indians on Pine Tree Creek, belonged, no doubt to this little colony. We can but marvel at their hardihood in bringing wives and children into such surroundings.

Of these seven families, William Seawright and Robert Seawright settled in Belmont Neck, just south of Mulberry; Hugh McCutchin, Michael Harris, and James McGowen about seven miles southeast of Camden, on waters of Swift Creek; Adam Strain and David Alexander cannot be precisely located, but were probably within hailing distance of some of the others.

It is six years later before the records show any other arrivals in Fredricksburg, after which there is a small annual accession. A list of these comers, down to 1750, has been made up after much exploration of the old grant books, and is here presented as matter of curiosity:

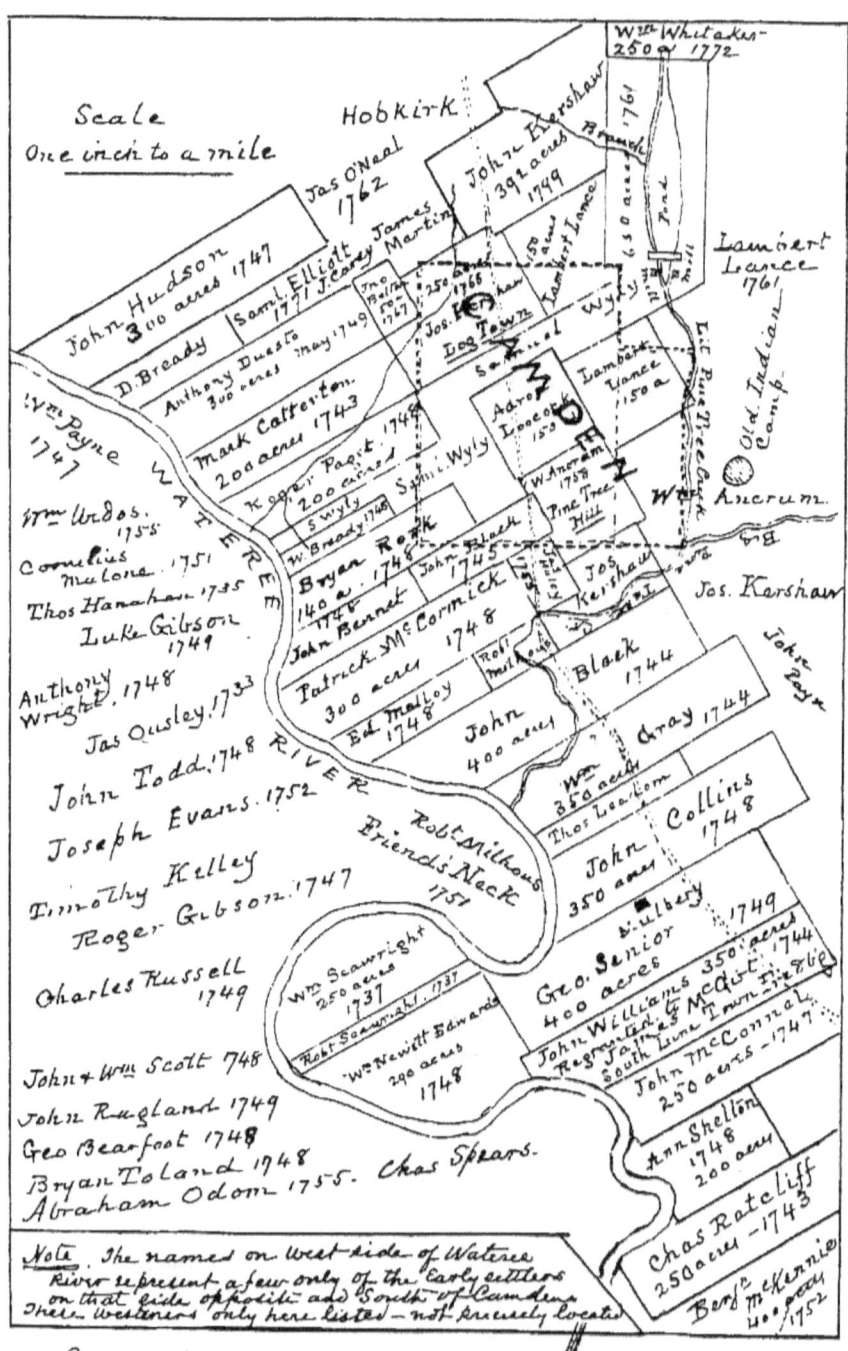

DIAGRAM No. 9.

PINE TREE HILL.

Thomas Bryan,	100 acres, February 7, 1743.
Charles Ratcliff,	250 acres, February 7, 1743.
Mark Catterton,	200 acres, February 7, 1743.
John Williams,	350 acres, March, 1744.
John Black,	400 acres, October 6, 1744.
William Gray,	350 acres, October 6, 1744.
Michael Branham,	200 acres, October 6, 1744.
Ann Duyett (widow),	300 acres, November 2, 1746.
John Hope,	350 acres, November 2, 1746.
Benjamin McKinnie,	600 acres, November 2, 1746.
John Hudson,	500 acres, February 7, 1747.
John McConnel,	250 acres, May 15, 1747.
Edward Malloy,	150 acres, January, 1748.
Thomas McCormick,	*450 acres, January, 1748.
Patrick McCormick,	300 acres, January, 1748.
Paul Harlestone,	140 acres, January, 1748.
Thomas Leadom,	100 acres, January, 1748.
William Bready,	50 acres, January, 1748.
Daniel Bready,	100 acres, January, 1748.
Bryan Rork,	140 acres, January, 1748.
Roger Paget,	200 acres, February, 1748.
John Collins,	350 acres, February, 1748.
Ann Shelton,	200 acres, February, 1748.
Anthony Duesto,	500 acres, February, 1748.
Alexander Rattray,	500 acres, February, 1748.
William Newitt Edwards,	290 acres, February, 1748.
John Bennet,	100 acres, March, 1748.
Daniel McDaniel,	500 acres, June, 1748.
Samuel Neilson,	400 acres, November, 1748.
William Kelley,	550 acres, December, 1748.
George Senior,	400 acres, May, 1749.
Samuel Buxton,	50 acres, August, 1749.
Thomas Harper,	50 acres, October, 1749.
John Maddox,	300 acres, October, 1749.
William Guess,	200 acres, October, 1749.
Edward McGraw,	100 acres, October, 1749.

*Granted in 1768 to John Weatherspoon.

To illustrate this chapter, comparison has been made of the plats annexed to the original grants in Fredricksburg Township, found in the State archives. These have been fitted together, and the accompanying Diagram No. 9 constructed according to scale.

These settlers, with but few exceptions, located adjacent to the river, their lands joining one to another for some six miles above and the same distance below Camden. But three of the whole list, viz.: John Black, Bryan Rork, and Roger Paget, owned a foot within the present corporate limits, and that barely within the southwestern corner. They seemed to be attracted by the immense fertility of the river bottoms, and to ignore the uplands, except spots for their houses above freshets. Most of them resided so near the swamps that we can imagine they must have suffered seriously from malaria, disposing them to sell out to subsequent colonists, and accounts no doubt for the disappearance of most of their names from this locality.

Immediately west of Camden, between it and the river, located Anthony Duesto, Mark Catterton, Roger Paget, William Bready.

To the north of them, above the Indian mound, were Daniel Bready, John Hudson, Thomas McCormick, Samuel Buxton, Samuel Neilson, Michael Branham, Thomas Harper.

Just south of Camden came Bryan Rork, John Black, John Bennet, Patrick McCormick, Edward Malloy, whose name is still perpetuated by *"Malloys Pond";* William Gray, Thomas Leadom.

Around Mulberry: John Collins, George Senior, William Newitt Edwards, William Seawright, Robert Seawright, and John Williams, whose tract was acquired by James McGirtt in 1752.

On Town Creek were John McConnel, Ann Shelton,

Charles Ratcliff,* Thomas Bryan, Ann Duvett, Benjamin McKennie, ALEXANDER RATTRAY, William Guess.

John Hope had the courage to take his abode on the sandy and secluded wilds of Gum Swamp, northeast of Camden. A few other settlements of this date outside of Fredricksburg will be noted. In February and March, 1748, Edward Howard and James Gamble took grants at the mouth of "White Oak Creek"; Oliver Mahaffy and Michael Brannon, in 1749, on "Grannys Quarter Creek," and John Ragland, the same year, near the creek which bears his name. All of these streams had received their titles as far back as the dates of these grants.

On the western side of the river, opposite, were an almost equal number of settlers, among whom may be mentioned: Anthony Wright, whose name is preserved by "Wrights Branch," ROGER GIBSON, Luke Gibson, William Paine, William Harrison, Nathaniel Hill, Charles Russell, Richard Gregory, Thomas Paget, William Scott, Roger Roberts, John Arledge, John McKenzie, and some others.

In the above enumeration the names of Alexander Rattray and Roger Gibson have been "writ large," for the reason that from them alone of the number have we derived a contemporary narrative of the experiences of pioneer life. The following documents, extracted from the ancient State records, speak more graphically of the times than could be expressed in volumes of description:

Affidavit of Alexander Rattray† before Governor Glen, May 24, 1751: "That he has lived for Ten years

---

*On the plat attached to grant of fifty acres to Charles Ratcliff, dated April, 1745, is represented a stream marked "Sims Creek," which seems to correspond with Town Creek; also a mill dam, and house of one G. Davis. This was in all probability the very first attempt at a mill in these parts.

†Indian Book, Vol. 2, p. 65. State Records.

past near the Wateree River, and is at present captn. of the company there, in which there is one hundred men; that the country thereabouts was pretty well settled, and there would have been many more Inhabitants, had it not been for the Constant alarms from the Cherokees almost every year since he has been there. That at present the fear of the People in those outposts is so great that all the familys have left their habitations, and betaken themselves to Forts with their wives and children, and their most valuable effects. That numbers of them must lose their crops notwithstanding he takes all manner of care to Preserve them by sending parties of men from Plantation to Plantation, and so while one party works the other party guards them."

Roger Gibson to Governor Glen:*

Wateree, May ye 9th, 1751.

I am informed this day by some my Company just returned from the Congarees that the Inhabitants of 96, Seludy and upper inhabitants are fled to the Congaree Fort† for safety because of the Cherokees and Norw'd Indians who have killed several white People, and as my Company is the nighest to the enemy of all the Wateree Inhabitance‡ we are in most danger, and is at present altogether unprovided with ammunition, the people being mostly new settlers here, within these two years my Company having advanced from 35 to 83. We would therefore pray your Excellency to grant us such a supply of ammunition as may Enable us to defend ourselves and familys against these Heathens who Theateneth our Present Destruction. Without it (if attackt) we must fall a sacrifice to their Heathen Fury.

*Indian Book, Vol. 2, p. 51, State Records.
†The present site of Columbia.
‡As previously stated, Gibson was settled on west side of river, opposite Camden. Rattray was on Camden side.

One hundred wt. of Powder, one of Bulletts, and 100 lb. wt. of swan shot would supply our Present necessity.

ROGER GIBSON.

In another letter of July 22, 1751, this same Gibson complains to Governor Glen of the hardships of his men, and their poor pay: "My men also complain that the pay allowed them is too Little, that to Ride in the Heat, and often sleeping wett by Day and Night in the wilderness, 120 miles from their familys, having their Provisions to provide, and too farr to carry, their Horses Tyring and themselves often taken sick and no proper means to help them, as also Day and Night in danger of their Lives, requireth a better reward than £14 per month."

We now come to an important epoch in our story, the advent of the colony of Irish Quakers, in 1750-51, to whom, in all the sketches of Camden heretofore written, from 1816 downward, is attributed the foundation of Camden. But as demonstrated above, they were greeted by not a few white faces already on or near the spot, and while they were the most notable body among the early immigrants, they must share the credit for the origin of Camden with those who preceded and followed. As will be seen, it was not a Quaker who in fact located Camden, or even its antecedent, "Pine Tree Hill."

This band of Quakers most probably came by way of the river, as did most of the pioneers, and landed near the site of Camden, for we find them, soon after, distributed equi-distantly above and below this point. The precise date of their coming is not known by a twelvemonth. We should say, however, it was in the fall of 1751, for the earliest grants discovered to any of their number are those to Josiah Tomlinson, October 25, 1751, in West Wateree, and to Robert Milhouse, November

20, 1751, in "Friends Neck," also in West Wateree, a part probably of the Baum plantation.

How much we should like to know about them! But there are few authentic facts to relate, picked out of old records by slow and tedious process. Their very names are but partly known, and some of these have only been identified by the probate of some antique document wherein the witness, being a Quaker, *affirmed* instead of swearing, which was against their tenets. By similar roundabout means others have been ascertained, and thus we are enabled to make up the following imperfect roll:

Robert Milhouse, who has been accredited as the leader of the colony; Samuel Milhouse; Henry Milhouse; John Milhouse and Abigail, his wife; Daniel Mathis and Sophia, his wife; Joshua English; Robert English; Thomas English; Jonathan (or John) Belton; Abraham Belton, who, however, did not come out until probably as late as 1770; Joseph Evans; Robert Evans; John Wright; Samuel Kelly and Hannah Belton, his wife; Timothy Kelly; Walter Kelly; Samuel Russell; Josiah Tomlinson; William Tomlinson; John Furnass; Nebo Gaunt; Zebulon Gaunt; Zimri Gaunt; Samuel Wyly and Dinah Milhouse, his wife; James Adamson and John Adamson, who are classed as Quakers by Colonel Shannon, but by Doctor Boykin said not to have been of that persuasion, though connected by marriage with the Milhouses.

The following named, while they cannot be positively rated as Quakers, were probably such, judging from the date of their grants, their names, the adjacency of their locations to others of the sect, and various circumstances:

Anthony Wright; Samuel Thomas; Samuel Buxton;

James Haley; Thomas Moon; Cornelius Melone; William Widos; Timothy Plunkett; Timothy Morgridge; Archibald Watson; Bryan Toland; John Tod; John Cook; Jonathan Christmas; Moses Downing; Ann Dunsworth; Thomas Finin; Philip Fain; David Courson; John Cain, and others who might be added to this list, with names suggestive of Quakerism.

Strangely, it was some eight or ten years after the arrival of these Quakers before a single one of their number, or as to that, any other person, obtained a grant for any land now within the boundaries of Camden (aside from the small area already mentioned as falling within the tracts of Black, Paget and Rork). We are informed by Colonel Shannon, in his sketches of old Camden, that Daniel Mathis located with his family in that quarter of the town lying between the Courthouse and the Cemetery, although the records show no grant or conveyance to him of a foot of land anywhere. The statement, however, may be true, as his son Samuel was the first white male born on Camden soil. He may have occupied a spot of land, without grant, and omitted to obtain or record his papers.

Samuel Wyly, surveyor and merchant, of whom much has been said in the Indian chapter, acquired the tracts of Bryan Rork, Roger Paget, and William Bready, lying to the southwest of Camden, just beyond the Cemetery, now the Smyrl place. His dwelling must have been beyond the town limits, for although his son, Samuel, was born in 1756, yet Samuel Mathis, born four years later, is accredited as the first male native to Camden. He went first to Williamsburg, and came to Fredricksburg in 1752, a year later than his other "Friends," but from that time to his death, sixteen years after, he was the most prominent member of the colony, and his store its chief center and nucleus, until the coming of Joseph

Kershaw. The business of Wyly & Co., conducted by his sons, existed during the Revolution.

North of Wyly, between the river toll-bridge road and the Indian Mound, John Belton, surveyor, located, purchasing the tracts of Mark Catterton, now part of the Cureton place. The branch which rises at the southern foot of Hobkirk Hill, and flows through the northwest corner of Camden, and down through these lands to the river, originally called Harolds Branch, became known as Beltons Branch, a name which it should retain, though now almost obsolete.* Josiah Tomlinson purchased the adjoining tract of Anthony Duesto. These lands were conveyed in 1776 by John Belton to his younger brother, Abraham Belton, who, it is related, selected a situation for his home near the Indian Mound, upon the swamp edge, where he lost eight sons from malarious effects.

The Adamsons settled north of the Beltons, acquiring the lands of Daniel Bready, John Hudson, Michael Branham, and others, the property being still known as the Adamson place, subsequently owned by the Curetons and Dunlaps, now of Witte. The military tendency of the Adamsons would indicate that they were not of the persuasion of Friends, though they may have been of the "fighting" variety. The brave exploits of James Adamson in the Indian wars have been recounted. John Adamson was a valiant Royalist during the Revolution.

The Milhouses made choice of the lands around Mulberry, two miles south of Camden, purchasing from the

---

*This branch in olden days did not enter the river, as it does now, but made a great detour to the east and emptied into Pine Tree Creek just below the bridge on the Charleston road. Mr. W. W. Lang, when he became owner of the property, cut a channel and diverted it to the river as it now is. Its old course is marked by what is called "Baitman's Ditch."

first owners, John Collins, George Senior, and James McGirtt, who had acquired the John Williams tract. Robert Milhouse, for the purpose of a mill, obtained a grant of fifty acres on Pine Tree Creek, just below Camden, where now is Carrison's Mill, which is known to have been a mill site prior to 1780. The first mill, which was burnt by Lord Rawdon in 1780, was in all probability built by Robert Milhouse. Its site was on the creek, a few hundred yards north of the present one, and the trace of the old canal which led to it may still be seen. Robert Milhouse died in 1755. His son, or nephew, of the same name, died in 1771, at Camden, where he owned a tannery. The family gradually disappeared from these parts, and removed, it is said, to the Edisto, in Barnwell County, where descendants lived in recent years. We find the name in Camden so late as 1798. Their lands were purchased by the Kershaws and Canteys, and later by John Chesnut.

Thomas and Robert English settled west of the Milhouses, on Town Creek and Swift Creek. Joshua English selected Spears Creek, on the west side of the river, some thirteen miles south of Camden. He became a great landowner, and is said to have had grants for 70,000 acres. In the Revolution he was a Royalist, and letters of Lord Rawdon addressed to him were found in his old homestead, now destroyed. The letters, in recent years, were lost or mislaid.

Others of the Quakers settled in West Wateree, such as the Gaunts,* Kellys, and Evanses. Indeed quite half of their number seem to have taken post on that side. Their Meeting-House and Graveyard they established on the eastern side, on a spot within our present

---

*Nebo Gaunt became owner of the Camden Ferry, known in early times as Gaunt's Ferry. It was purchased by the Kershaws, and in the deed Nebo is designated as a "millwright."

Cemetery inclosure and within the limits of Camden. Samuel Wyly, in 1759, made conveyance to them of four acres, for this purpose, of which the following is a copy:

"*This Indenture,* made the sixth day of September, in the year of our Lord one thousand seven hundred and fifty-nine, and in the Thirty-third year of the Reign of our Sovereign Lord George the Second, of Great Britain, France and Ireland, King, Defender of the faith and so forth,

"Between Samuel Wyly of Fredricksburg Township in Craven County, in the Province of South Carolina, Esquire, of the one part and Timothy Kelly, Samuel Milhous and John Milhous of Craven County and Province aforesaid, of the other part, *witnesseth*

"That the said Samuel Wyly for and in consideration of the yearly Rents and Covenants hereinafter Reserved and contained on the part of the said Timothy Kelly, Samuel Milhous and John Milhous as Trustees for the People called Quakers in Craven County aforesaid, to be paid, observed and performed on the part of whatever Trustees shall be hereafter appointed and Nominated by the said People called Quakers,

"Hath Demised, granted and to farm Lett unto the said Timothy Kelly, Samuel Milhous and John Milhous for the use and in trust for the aforesaid People called Quakers in Craven County aforesaid,

"A Tract of Land containing Four Acres, situate, lying and being in Fredricksburg Township aforesaid and butting and bounding Southwestwardly and Northwestwardly by the said Samuel Wyly's Land, to the Southeast by Land granted to John Black, and to the Northeast by land not yet laid out (as by Platt hereto annexed may appear)

"Together with all and Singular the Houses, Buildings, woods, wells, waters, ways, paths, passages, easements, profits, Commodities, advantages, Hereditaments and appurtenances whatsoever, to the said Tract of land belonging or in anywise appertaining or accepted, Reputed, Deemed, taken, known and enjoyed, held, occupied, Leased or Demised as part, parcel or member of the same or of any part thereof,

"*To have and to hold*, the said Tract of four Acres of Land together with their and every of their Rights, members and appurtenances, unto the said Timothy Kelly, Samuel Milhous and John Milhous in Trust as aforesaid or unto whatever Trustees shall be appointed by the said people called Quakers as aforesaid from the day next before the day of the date of these presents, for and during and untill the full end and expiration of the term of Nine hundred and ninety-nine years thence next ensuing and fully to be completed and ended.

"Yielding and paying therefor yearly during the said term unto the said Samuel Wyly his heirs and assigns, the rent of one Pepper Corn, in and upon the first day of August every year if the same shall be lawfully Demanded.

"And the said Samuel Wyly for himself, his Heirs and Assigns, Doth covenant and agree to and with the said Timothy Kelly, Samuel Milhous and John Milhous, or with any other person or persons which shall be hereafter appointed as Trustees by the said people called Quakers That they the said Timothy Kelly, Samuel Milhous and John Milhous or other the Trustees appointed by the said people as aforesaid shall and may by and under the yearly rent and covenants herein reserved and contained peaceably and quietly have, hold, occupy, possess and enjoy the said Tract containing four acres of

Land, and all and singular the premises herein mentioned with the appurtenances in trust for the aforesaid people called Quakers, for and during the said term hereby granted, without Lett, Trouble, Hindrance, Molestation, Interruption and denial of him the said Samuel Wyly his Heirs and Assigns or of any other person or persons claiming or to claim by from or under him.

"And, moreover, the said People called Quakers shall have power to nominate and appoint other Trustee or Trustees in place and room of the said Timothy Kelly, Samuel Milhous and John Milhous at the time of their or either of their Deaths or at such other time as the said people called Quakers shall choose in order that the number of Trustees may be always kept up.

"In witness whereof the said parties to these presents their seals and hands have Interchangeably sett the day and year first above written.

Sealed and delivered in presence of	Samuel Wyly (Seal)
John Gray	Timothy Kelly (Seal)
John Kennedy.	Samuel Milhous (Seal)
	John Milhous (Seal)

"Endorsement

"At a meeting of the within named people called Quakers, held on the within mentioned premises the 23d day of the 10 month called October 1776, Have chosen and appointed William Tomlinson and Samuel Russell Trustees in the room of Timothy Kelly and Samuel Milhous Deceased, Two of the Trustees within mentioned. In witness whereof they have sett their hands and seals the day and year above mentioned.

Witness	Samuel Russell (Seal)
Zn Gaunt,	William Tomlinson (Seal)
Nebo Gaunt	
Zimri Gaunt."	

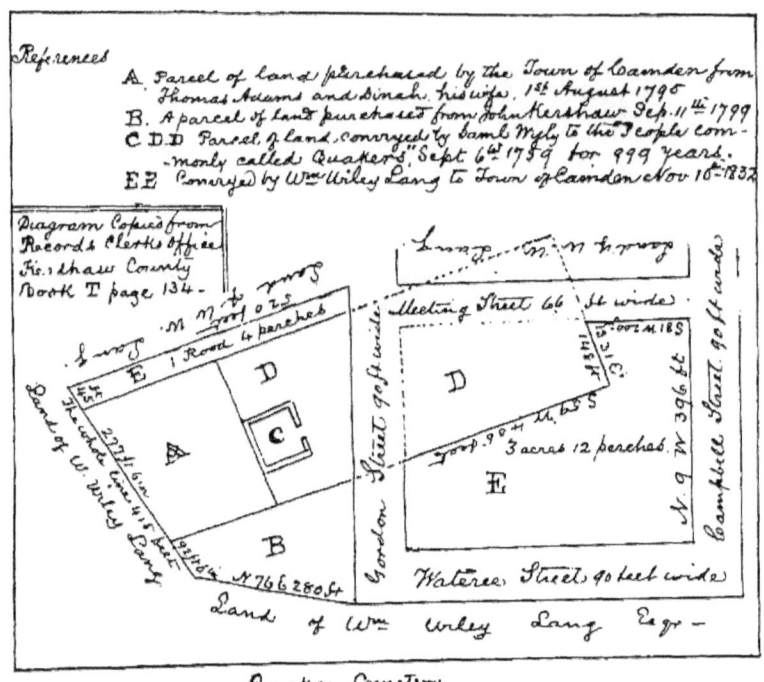

DIAGRAM No. 10.

Upon this four-acre tract, near its western end, was erected the Meeting-House, probably had been erected some time prior to the date and execution of the above deed, which mentions "Houses, Buildings." To its site Meeting street directly leads, probably so named from that circumstance. Around or beside the House, a small plot, surrounded by a ditch, was reserved for the burial of Quakers, indicated by the letter "C" in the annexed Diagram No. 10. The House and ditch have long since been obliterated, but their location might be very nearly fixed by survey.

The Quaker graves, too, have been encroached upon, but some of them, evidently ancient, may still be traced, marked by a mere arching of bricks. This plain people eschewed all forms and display, and did not indulge in monuments. With them the spirit was all in all. To their reserved half acre the lines of Wordsworth would have been truly applicable:

"Here's neither head nor foot stone, plate of brass,
 Cross-bones nor skull—type of our earthly state—
 Nor emblem of our hopes; the dead man's home
 Is but a fellow to that pasture field.
 The stone cutters, 'tis true, might beg their bread,
 If every English churchyard were like ours."

The Quaker lot was enlarged from time to time, until it has expanded into our present Cemetery, where all sects are interred. When we come into these precincts on memorial days, where the beauties of spring seem more ineffable than elsewhere, these few Quaker mounds deserve attention. Their tenants were the ancestors of our place, those who first "with the olive branch of peace and industry, made the lands of our district smile with examples of thrift and economy." We may well take pride in them, these disciples of George Fox, of whom Cromwell said: "They are a people whom I cannot win with gifts, honors, offices, or places." Odd though they were, no people were ever more staunch and incorruptible.

Judge O'Neall, himself a full-blood Quaker of Camden stock, has described some of their customs from his own observation, in his Annals of Newberry, and from him we quote:

"The meeting for worship was every Sunday at eleven o'clock. At that hour all entered the house and sat covered and in silence for an hour, unless the Spirit moved some Friend to speak. Any Friend may speak under the influence of the Spirit, but in general, only those speak in public whose gifts have been approved. If prayer be made, then the Friend who prays uncovers himself, and kneeling down utters the petitions which the Spirit prompts. The congregation rise and the men are uncovered during the prayer. As soon as it closes all take their seats covered."

In 1806 he witnessed the marriage of Robert Evans (who went to Newberry from Camden) and Keren Happuch Gaunt. As to the Quaker marriage he says: "A pair of young people about to marry are said to pass meeting by their purpose being announced at one monthly meeting, when a committee is appointed to inquire if there be any objections. At the next, if their report be favorable, Friends assent to the marriage, and on the succeeding fifth day (Thursday), it takes place, by the man and woman standing up and holding one another by the right hand and repeating the ceremony. The man says about as follows: 'I take this my friend to be my wedded wife, whom I will love, cherish and her only keep, until it shall please the Lord to separate us by death.' The woman says: 'I take this my friend to be my husband, whom I will love, honor and obey, until it shall please the Lord to separate us by death'."

The Quaker sect, after planting their settlements, received few accessions, and were steadily disintegrated or merged by marriage into other denominations. Another cause of their decline, as expressed by Colonel Shannon, was the "advancing civilization of slavery." Says O'Neall: "In the beginning Friends were slaveowners in South Carolina. They, however, soon set their faces against it, and in their peculiar language, they have borne their testimony against the institution of slavery as irreligious. Such of their members as refused to emancipate their slaves, when emancipation was practicable in this State, they disowned. Samuel Kelly, who was the owner of a slave or slaves in 1762, when he came from Camden, refused to emancipate his, on the ground that he had bought and paid for them; they were therefore his property; and that they were a great deal better off as his property. He was therefore disowned. His brother's children manumitted theirs."

A wise people in their day and generation! Their wisdom now shines like Portia's "good deed in a naughty world." Had all the colonists been as they were it is obvious their descendants would have escaped much of the calamities that befell them.

Again we draw from Judge O'Neall's storehouse of facts. Says he: "But it will be asked what became of the Friends? Between 1800 and 1804 a celebrated Quaker preacher, Zachary Dicks, passed through South Carolina. He was thought to have also the *gift of prophecy*. The massacres of San Domingo were then fresh. He warned Friends to come out from slavery. He told them that, if they did not, their fate would be that of the slaughtered islanders. This produced in a short time a panic, and removals to Ohio* commenced, and by 1807 the Quaker settlement had, in a great degree, changed its population. Newberry thus lost, from a foolish panic and a superstitious fear of an institution which never harmed them or any other body of people, a very valuable portion of its white population."

Whether this spirit of exodus infected the Camden Quakers we have no means of knowing, for alas, we cannot boast for our locality such an annalist as O'Neall. We learn more from him about the four Quakers whom he mentions as having gone from Camden to Newberry, than we know of all those who remained with us. We give here a short summary of what he tells of these four.

Samuel Kelly settled in West Wateree, north of Camden. He was from Kings County, Ireland, and his wife, Hannah Belton, of Queens County, a sister of John Belton. Samuel and Hannah removed to the large Quaker colony on Bush River, in Newberry County, about 1762. Their daughter, Anne Kelly, married Hugh O'Neall of Newberry, a Quaker, and their son, John Belton O'Neall, the distinguished jurist, was born April 10, 1793. John Furnass and Robert Evans went to Newberry from Camden (or what was soon after to be Camden) about the same time as did Samuel Kelly.

It seems quite warrantable to say that John Wright was originally one of the Camden colony, for he appears as witness on a deed of Mary and Robert English, dated May, 1760, and proven by him before Samuel Wyly, at Pine Tree Hill. He became, however, a resident of Bush River, Newberry. He lived to be aged, and, before his death, gathered around him his descendants, their husbands, wives and progeny to the number of one

---

*Ohio, the first State formed, in 1803, out of the Northwestern Territory, from which slavery had been excluded by the Ordinance of 1787.

hundred and forty. His two daughters, Charity Cook and Susannah Hollingsworth, were gifted with speech, Charity especially. She became a notable preacher, although mother of a large family, and in her mission work traveled through the States extensively and twice visited England. Her husband was not unlikely of the Camden family of Cooks; and to her with much probability may be attributed the following unique example of eloquence from the sermon of a Quakeress, extracted from the *Charleston Courier* of 1807:

"*A Quaker Woman's Sermon.*

"Dear Friends: There are three things I very much wonder. The first is, that children should be so foolish as to throw up stones, brickbats and clubs into fruit trees to knock down the fruit; if they would let it alone, it would fall of itself.

"The second is, that men should be so foolish and even wicked as to go to war and kill one another; if they would only let one another alone, they would die of themselves.

"And the third and last thing, which I wonder at most of all, is that young men should be so unwise as to go after the young women; if they would only stay at home, the young women would come after them."

Companion settlers with the Quakers, though not members of the sect, coming between 1750 and 1755, were several with names familiar to us, such as: John Cantey, 1752; Francis Lee, 1752; Richard Kirkland and Joseph Kirkland, 1752; Joseph Mickle, 1753; John Drakeford, 1754; William Boykin, 1755; and the catalogue could be greatly extended, did time and space permit.

It would perhaps be a matter of interest to many to

know the connections of our Camden families of today with the old Quakers. To trace these in all their ramifications would doubtless be too tedious for most readers, so that we will only attempt here to point out some of the leading lines of Quaker descent.

Daniel and Sophia Mathis left, so far as known, four children, Samuel, Israel, Mary, Sarah. A daughter of Samuel married Dr. Joshua Reynolds of Camden, their descendants being represented here (by Miss Sophia Zemp) and in other parts of the State. Sarah married Col. Joseph Kershaw. Israel practiced law at Camden in partnership with his brother, Samuel, until about 1810, when he moved to Sumter County. Mary married Capt. William Nettles. Of Samuel more will be told in the next chapter.

The Lang family, also the descendants of Dr. E. M. Boykin and Burwell Boykin, trace to Samuel Wylie and Dinah Milhouse through their daughter, Sarah Wylie, who married William Lang in 1775.

From John Belton, who married Mary, a sister of Joshua English, through their daughter, Martha, who married Maj. Joseph Mickle, are descended the families of John, Joseph and Robert Mickle, and of James Lyles. John Belton died in 1790. We are not quite sure Mary Belton was sister to Joshua English. She may have been a niece.

From Abraham Belton, who married Elizabeth Alexander before coming to America, through their daughters, Rebecca, who married Everard Cureton, and Ann, who married John Doby, are descended the families of Cureton and Doby. Abraham Belton died in 1826, aged seventy-eight.

From an old family Bible we gather something of the lineage of Joshua English, who married Elizabeth, daughter of Lieut. James Adamson. Of their children,

James married Nancy Darrington, whose daughter, Sarah, married James C. Doby. Sarah English married James Kershaw and, so far as known, left no descendants. Elizabeth English married Thomas Hopkins, whose daughter married Lemuel Boykin. Harriet English married a Singleton. Mary English married Austin F. Peay. From another son, Joseph English, who married Harriet Fitzpatrick, is descended Beverley M. English, of this county. Joshua English Sr. died in 1795.

Robert English (brother of Joshua) married another daughter of Lieut. James Adamson. Being a Royalist, he was banished from the colony at the end of the Revolution, and settled in the West Indies. His daughter married Isaac Lenoir, and to them trace the families of Lenoir and descendants of Benjamin Haile (the second).

John English (a younger brother of Joshua) in 1800 married Elizabeth Tucker, descendants unknown.

From Thomas English, who as early as 1761 settled on Town Creek, probably is descended the extensive Shannon family, through the marriage of Charles J. Shannon with Martha Allison English. It is possible that this Thomas English may have been the father of Joshua, Robert, Mary, John, and progenitor of the entire English family. We have been unable to obtain sufficient data to unravel this branch of English ancestry.*

The coming of Joseph Kershaw to Fredricksburg, in 1758, marks another stage in the evolution of Camden.

---

*Thomas English, son of the first Thomas, married Miss Allison, daughter probably of that Andrew Allison, one of his Majesty's Justices of the Peace for Craven County, and before whom, in 1763, Thomas DeLoach makes affidavit as witness to execution of a paper by Abraham Odam and Cibbie, his wife. This old document found among papers of Dr. E. M. Boykin—Mouzon's Map, 1775—shows that Allison's lands were in West Wateree, on Cornals Creek, Richland County.

He found the country dotted with inhabitants along the riverside, and here and there on the creeks, but the area which is now Camden was unoccupied woods, except, perhaps, the spot in the southwest corner, where the Mathis family alone resided. He came up from Charlestown, with the purpose, it would appear, of establishing a country branch of the mercantile firm of that city, composed of William Ancrum, Lambert Lance, and Aaron Loocock. Soon after, he himself became a member of the firm, the local branch going under his name and management, as Kershaw & Co.

The other partners never became residents of Fredricksburg, and it is not known that they ever came up except to visit or prospect. But just after the time of Kershaw's arrival we find the territory now covered by Camden being granted in blocks to the individuals of this firm. On the plat attached to the original grant of 150 acres to William Ancrum, dated June 12, 1758 (see Diagram No. 9), is marked PINE TREE HILL. This settles beyond dispute that what we now call the Magazine Hill was the original Pine Tree Hill. The name must have been given at the time of the grant, which affords the first recorded mention of it so far discovered. By whom was it bestowed? It seems reasonable to attribute it to Joseph Kershaw, who was the local head of the business there established by him, and as appears by later documents, which will be cited, the land on which it stood was partnership property, though granted to one member, William Ancrum.

The name was probably suggested by that of the adjacent creek, and the hill was no doubt covered with a growth of sturdy primeval pines. The store here situated is mentioned in the old Charlestown papers as "Pine Tree Store." The firm continued to secure grants of many surrounding tracts of land, through Kershaw, who displayed great energy, and built up an extensive and prosperous trade.

Just where the store of Samuel Wyly was situated nothing has been found to determine. He became, however, quite a landowner, for in 1761 he obtained a grant of 650 acres, covering all the central part of Camden, including the present DeKalb Mill site and lake, and extending in a narrow strip to the river (see Diagram No. 9). But this body of land, too, the next year was purchased by Kershaw & Co. The diagram shows that so early as 1761 a mill was situated on this tract, just where it exists today, rebuilt, of course, on the pond which we call the "Factory Pond."

In 1766 Lambert Lance withdrew from the firm, conveying his interests to Ancrum and Loocock, who were then, it seems, the moneyed members. Just before this time the Chesnut family* came to Pine Tree Hill—John and James, with their mother and stepfather, Jasper Sutton. John entered the store of Kershaw & Co. as an apprentice, where he must have been very efficient, for after a brief service he became a partner.

In ante-bellum days there existed an official memorial of the origin of Camden, in the shape of the municipal seal, which, unfortunately, disappeared during the military occupancy of the Council Chamber by Federal officers in 1865. No document has been discovered showing an impression of this old device, which, it will be conceded, from the description, was appropriate, and evinced a commendable pride in our past. We are informed by the minutes of Council, wherein the loss is recounted, that it represented (undoubtedly an emblem of primitive Camden) "A Pine Tree on a Mound."

*For a full account of the Chesnut family see Chapter XIX.

CHAPTER IV.

CAMDEN.

For just ten years did the name Pine Tree Hill endure, from 1758 to 1768. So little disposed do the first settlers seem to have been to congregate, that during that decade there were not probably more than a dozen families within a radius of a mile around the present center of Camden. There is no evidence of the existence of the slightest division into streets or lots. However, tracts in the outlying district were being constantly occupied by newcomers.

As has been heretofore stated, the very first mention of the name of Camden is found in the Act of Assembly bearing date April 12, 1768, which provides for a court to be established at Camden, "lately called Pine Tree Hill." The bestowal of this name has always been assigned to Joseph Kershaw, and no doubt rightly. The same year he became the owner of a tract of 250 acres, which now constitutes the northern section of Camden, but which was not within the limits of the first town. This tract he named "Log Town." (See Diagram No. 9.)

The common statement that Camden was laid out into lots and streets by Kershaw in 1760 rests upon no proof, and seems improbable. The name certainly does not antedate 1765, and, as pointed out in the first chapter, the earliest recorded plan of the town cannot be given a date earlier than 1774. This plan, shown in a preceding diagram (No. 3), was the work of John Heard, deputy surveyor, and may be termed official. Kershaw

Lord Camden.

ILLUSTRATION D.

may have, before that, established a plan of his own, but there is no trace to be found of any such.

We are impressed by the rapid course of events as we review the past. Scarce had the feeble village of Camden begun to form, when the Revolution burst upon it. Indeed it was born of revolutionary spirit, and also of the spirit of law. The neglect of the Royal Board in London to heed the demand for courts in the interior of the province, and the consequent disorders, was a potent cause of dissatisfaction. The name of Camden makes its appearance with the establishment of a Courthouse. Just three years after it was built Justice Drayton and a grand jury there assembled, in November, 1774, announced the principles upon which the Revolution was fought.

The name has also another high association. It was given in honor of one of those four British champions of colonial rights, Camden, Chatham, Burke, and Fox. Here would seem an appropriate place to recall briefly the career of the statesman and jurist whose name and fame belong to us.

Charles Pratt was born in 1713, at Careswell Priory Devonshire, England. His father, Sir John Pratt, was an eminent lawyer. He left his family, however, in reduced circumstances. Charles attended Eton, and was a schoolmate of the great Pitt, of whom he was, throughout life, a personal and political ally. He was a finished classical scholar.

In 1735 he entered upon the legal profession. For many years he was without practice, the only knocks on his door being those of duns. In 1741 he wrote that he was "so poor that I have scarce money enough to bear me in a summer's ramble." But after nine years waiting an opportunity came in a case which befell him, the defense of a printer for breach of privilege of Parliament. In this he made a reputation and received popular demonstrations. He thereafter advanced with rapid strides.

In 1757, Pitt, having reached the premiership, appointed him attorney-general, and he won a seat in Parliament. His decision, as Chief Justice of the Common Pleas, against the odious "general search warrants," in the case of the celebrated John Wilkes, which, on account of the principles of personal liberty involved, had aroused the deepest feeling, was received by the population of London with a shout "heard with dismay at St. James."

In Parliament, July, 1765, he made that imperishable utterance against the declaration of the right to tax the colonies, a few sentences of which may not be out of place:

"I shall not criticize the strange language in which your proposed declaration is framed, for to what purpose, but loss of time, to consider the particulars of a bill, the very existence of which is illegal—absolutely illegal—contrary to the fundamental laws of nature, contrary to the fundamental laws of this constitution—a constitution grounded on the immutable laws of nature—a constitution whose center is liberty, which sends liberty to every individual who may happen to be within its ample circumference. Nor, my Lords, is the doctrine new; it is as old as the constitution; it grew up with it; indeed it is its support; taxation and representation are inseparably united. God hath joined them; no British Parliament can put them asunder. My position is this—I repeat it—I will maintain it to my last hour—taxation and representation are inseparable.

"There is not a blade of grass growing in the remotest corner of this kingdom which is not—which was not ever—represented since the constitution began; there is not a blade of grass which, when taxed, was not taxed by the consent of the proprietor.

"The forefathers of the Americans did not leave their native country, and subject themselves to every danger and distress, to be reduced to a state of slavery; they did not give up their rights; they expected protection, not chains, from the mother country."*

After this speech, the ministry, it is said, because of his great popularity, appointed him Baron Camden. The title was derived from the estate, Camden Place, whereon he resided, which had formerly belonged to the antiquarian, William Camden, and had been acquired by the Pratt family. The name Camden had no general notoriety whatever, until rendered famous by being attached as a title to Charles Pratt in 1765, and hence it is safe to conclude that it could not have been applied to our town until after that.

It may be excusable to explore somewhat further towards the source, and relate something about that William Camden, the old author with whom or whose family the name originates. In the South Carolina College Library, at Columbia, is a genuine and ancient "volume of forgotten lore," published A. D. 1610, being the second edition, the first having appeared in 1586. The title page reads as follows, and speaks for itself:

Britain
A Chronographicall
Description of the Most
Flourifhing Kingdomes, England
Scotland and Ireland, and the

---

*The degree of feeling in Carolina over the odious Stamp Acts may be inferred from these indicative circumstances: The *South Carolina Gazette* of October 30, 1765, appears in *mourning,* with the announcement of the arrival of STAMPS in Charlestown. In the issues immediately following are bold headings: "NO STAMPS TO BE HAD."

Ilands adioyning, out of the depth of
Antiqvitie
Beautified with Mappes of the
feverall shires of England
Written firft in Latine by William Camden
Clarenceaux K. of A.
Translated newly into English by Philemon Holland
Doctour in Physic
Finally revised, amended and enlarged with sundry
Additions by the Author

Londoni
Impensis Georgii Bishop
& Ioannis Norton
M D C X.

From the preface to this most quaint and curious production, wherein the author sets forth the difficulty of his task, we quote the following expressions, to which all who may have essayed even the humblest historical subject, will cordially subscribe:

"A painfull matter, I affure you, and more than difficult, wherein what toyle is to be taken, as no man thinketh, fo no man believeth but hee that hath made the triall."

In the year, we might almost say the day, of the birth of the town of Camden, on February 13, 1768, Samuel Wyly died, and was laid in the Quaker burial square. His death is announced in the *South Carolina Gazette* of March 17, 1768, as having occurred at "Pine Tree Hill," by which it appears the new name had not come into use, although, as we have seen, not a month later, on April 12th, the Act of Assembly mentions Camden as "lately called Pine Tree Hill." We should therefore be justified in fixing the christening of Camden between February 13, and April 12, 1768.

The materials for anything like a picture of the first six years of Camden are scant indeed. It seems to have been but a mere "neighborhood," without definite boundaries. The building here in 1771 of a Courthouse (located where it now stands), serving for a large district, known as "Camden District," now subdivided into nine counties, must, of course, have created an epoch, and together with the two stores of Kershaw & Co., Wyly & Co., and the Quaker Meeting-house, have been a powerful magnet for residents.

At this time, beside that of the Quakers, there was a Presbyterian church at Camden.* The system of parish government was in force, and elections of members of the House of Commons by the inhabitants were held under auspices of the Wardens of the Church of England. The Parish of St. Mark, in which Camden was situated, was very extensive, and there was then but one such church in its borders. We can but wonder at the isolation of the people at that day, which is strikingly depicted in the presentment of the grand jury at the first term of Court at Camden, November 5, 1772, wherein they set forth as a grievance:

"The Parish of St. Mark, in our District, being so extensive that the numerous inhabitants are deprived of the comfort of the Preaching of the Gospel and divine service, some of the Inhabitants being one hundred and Forty miles distant, and consequently subject to many

---

*Joseph Kershaw in his will (1788) devises as follows:
"To the Presbyterian Congregation the lots No. 287 and 288, with all my right title and property to that part of Church street laying south of the lot given to that Congregation prior to the town of Camden being laid out into lots as far down as Wateree street, not doubting but that ground will hereafter be vested in that Society by law and that Church street will not extend further south than the Meeting House ground."

evils too notorious to be overlooked in a Christian part of the world." They also mention "many villainies and Roberies committed."

The wild state of the country is thus picturesquely presented at the Camden April term, 1773:

"The want of Law to encourage the killing and destroying of Beasts of Prey, such as Wolves, Tygers, Bears &c., which, it is found, grow very numerous and of course detrimental to the inhabitants." Presentment is also made of "idle and disorderly vagrants constantly hunting in the woods and destroying Deer for their skins, especially when they do it in the night by fire light, whereby great numbers of cattle are destroyed, and the lives of the people endangered."

Among the subscribing jurors we find such names as: James Cook, Joshua English, John Witherspoon, Robert Carter, George Sanders, Glass Caston, John Chesnut, James McGirtt, Thomas Sumter, Robert Belton, James Cantey, Moses Gordon, John Gamble, Jasper Sutton, John Cantey, Joseph Kirkland.

In the *South Carolina Gazette* of December 10, 1772, Chief Justice Gordon and Justice Murray give an interview, just after return from the Camden Circuit, and express themselves as:

"Astonished with the views of a fine country, of whose value and importance they before had very inadequate Ideas, and highly satisfied with the reception they everywhere met with, as well as the general conduct of the Inhabitants, who, in those parts where they are termed in a great measure uncivilized, only want good Schools and School Masters, Churches and Ministers, and fit Magistrates to render them as valuable a people as any upon Earth."

The dissolution of the partnership of Ancrum, Loocock, Kershaw & Chesnut, in 1774, marks another important incident in the little community of Camden. In November of that year the property of the concern was offered for sale. It was only partially disposed of and another sale was made in April, 1777. This step was probably caused by the approach of the Revolution. A body of land containing 1,743 acres, which covered a great part of Camden, the DeKalb Mill tract, and the mills on the creek just south of the town, were purchased by Thomas Jones of Camden, for the aggregate amount of £26,605, equal to $133,025.00.* These transactions are of record in our Clerk's office. Jones, however, would seem to have been but a nominal bidder, for a few days later he transfers the property for the same figures, which appear quite huge for the times, to Joseph Kershaw. Thus in 1777 Kershaw became the owner of well-nigh the whole of Camden and adjacent lands. There is no record of any mortgage to secure the price, and that he should have been able to meet such a sum is an indication of prosperity in business.

As Aaron Loocock figures as one of the original owners, if not residents, of Camden, the following old letter written by him to Joshua English, discovered by chance, may be thought worthy of insertion:

Grandby Decr 8th 1774.

Joshua Inglish:

SIR: I have had not an opportunity of saying much to you, when I saw you last at Camden, about my planta'n at friends neck, which I hope it will not be Inconvenient for you to manage in the same manner and on the same footing as Coln. Thompson does for the People in Town who cannot be on the spot themselves—

---

*These figures are probably to be measured by a colonial standard, and not sterling.

so shall depend on your advice and assistance, now and then when it suits you to take a ride to Mr. Powers—whom I have a good opinion of on answer—he is to have two shares for himself and one negro—and as I have bought Mr. Hopes stock of Hogs—have also agreed to give him a quarter of the Increase of them supporting them 200 head—for his taking care of them—and as I have a great oppinion of the article of Madder, will soon become as much Planted and full as profitable as Indigo, I have offered him fifty pounds to plant out and take care of some plants I intend sending up, not to exceed Two acres. I must beg you to go to Mr. Powers and tell him to fitt Scipio out with his waggon and as many horses as he can bring down, to my Plantation at Goosecreek, he is to bring down Roger Rees and his wife and some Little furniture they have. He lives on Mr. Kershaw's place at the mouth of Pine Tree Creek. I have engaged him to plow at Goosecreek—he must also call at the store, and bring down Two plows and 4 large Iron forks or drags—for digging Madder with—w'ch are in the new store—shall send up by the waggon as many negroes as will make up 20 working hands w'ch is all I intend this year—here is a negro wench, Phillis, who will be sent over to Camden by the first waggon—she is to go to the Plantation and is wife to Ben the Baker—if anything be wanted for the Planta'n you may order it to be got at the store, or if you will be kind enough to write me, will send it from Town. I hope to be up in February or March—so for the present remain

Sir your most humble servant
AARON LOOCOCK.

To
Mr. Joshua Inglish
    at his Plantation
        Waterees.

CAMDEN.   39

While it is certain that Camden at the time of the Revolution was a very small community, it is now possible to name but a few of its few residents, among whom may be mentioned: The families of Joseph and Eli Kershaw; Samuel, Israel and Mary Mathis; John Cantey; the Wylys; William Lang; Joseph Clay; James Brown, Jasper Sutton, and the Chesnuts, John and James; Adam Fowler Brisbane; William Nettles; the Milhouses; the Adamsons; the Postells, and one P. Morong, in Log Town; Thomas Jones; Thomas Charlton; James Carey; John Cook; Richard Wadison; James Martin; Richard and William Tomlinson; probably John Belton; William Murrell, a schoolteacher; Bettie, a dealer; Murchison, a tailor; Thompson, a blacksmith; and one Castelo, a shoemaker. As to some of these we cannot be entirely certain, but all were in or near Camden, and of course there were others now unknown to us.

Having brought the meager narrative up to the Revolutionary period, before embarking into that broad field, we shall attempt here to record a brief memorial to the "first white person born in Camden," one well worthy a tribute on his merits, aside from the circumstance of his birth. The inscription upon his gravestone, in the old Quaker ground, reads as follows:

"The remains of SAMUEL MATHIS, son of Daniel and Sophia Mathis, Born 22nd March, 1760, Died 26th Sep. 1823, aged 63 years 6 mo., 4 days. The Departed was the first white person born in Camden. Naturally active and enterprising, and living in an age of extraordinary events and revolution, he passed through many chequered scenes which taught him this important truth: 'That all is vanity which is not honest, and that there is no solid wisdom but in early piety'."

The excellence of the character of Samuel Mathis is

also attested by another tablet to his memory, erected in 1849 on the wall of the Methodist Church, to which the Town Council contributed, in these words:

"Sacred to the Memory of SAMUEL MATHIS, the first male born in the town of Camden. He was an exemplary and useful citizen, and filled many offices of honor and trust, the duties of which were discharged with punctuality and fidelity. For many years he was an active and zealous member of the Methodist Episcopal Church of this place, and departed this life in the full assurance of a blessed immortality. Born 22nd March 1760, Died 26th Sepr. 1823."

It will be noticed that the epitaph and tablet differ slightly in stating, the former, that he was the "first white *person* born in Camden," the latter, "the first *male*." It may be inquired by some how the statement can be true that he was born in Camden, and it be also true that there was no Camden until 1768? Both assertions may be reconciled upon this ground, that Samuel Mathis was the first white person born within that area included in the limits of Camden, defined and named a few years after his birth.

Although full-blooded Quakers, he and Samuel Wyly, who was four years his senior, joined the patriot ranks in the Revolution, and were captured at the fall of Charleston in May, 1780. The story of the cruel murder of Wyly by the British at Camden is told in a subsequent chapter. Young Mathis, being then but twenty, after his return home took care of the affairs and family of Joseph Kershaw, who had married his sister, Sarah, at the country place, Burndale, having been driven from the Camden home by the British. Here he struggled with the problems of the plantation, and kept a minute diary of his doings, fragments of which have luckily been discovered, and will be found in another part of this volume. In the midst of his plantings of corn, cabbage, peas, and potatoes, and worries with the slaves, he records the sound of musketry and cannon on Hobkirk Hill. When the British evacuated Camden, and his sister could spare his protection, he joined Marion's men.

Immediately after the war was over he opened a store in Camden. But in 1790 his name is found among the lawyers of the Camden bar, where for twenty years or more he was engaged in numerous and important cases.

He returned, however, to the mercantile profession, and in the *Camden Gazette* of June 20, 1816, we find the following advertisement:

Samuel Mathis & Co.
They have added to the stock which S. Mathis had, a considerable number of other useful and handsome
Goods
All which they are willing to exchange for Gold or Silver current Coin or good Bank Bills of any of the Banks of South Carolina, or the Bills of those Gentlemen in Camden, who issue Bills (while those Gentlemen support their credit as well as they have done). And they solicit the favor of their friends, acquaintances and all others to call and let them have a little of their loose cash, and not to pass by on the other side of the way (where nobody lives) as many do. They request the custom of the Planters, Farmers, and Mechanics, Lawyers, Doctors and Divines, &c., &c. And particularly invite the Ladies to call and see their Goods. They will think it no trouble, but a pleasure to wait on them, even should they buy nothing, and hope it will be full as profitable and cost less than seeing the Panorama lately exhibited.

Camden June 20th 1816.

The "Co." above was one John Cessford Ker, of Charleston. In December, 1816, Mr. Mathis again advertises on his own hook a "small stock of goods *at the upper end of Camden.*" This location was probably near the southwest corner of DeKalb and Broad streets, where he then owned two lots. The following combination of articles advertised is rather heterogeneous (only a few here given):

"Copperas	Tin Cups	Bibles
Saltpetre	Tin Pans	Testaments
Pepper	Coffee Pots	Dictionaries
Alspice	Candlesticks	Almanacs
Ginger	Pepper Boxes	Hymn Books and
Brimstone	Dippers &c.	other Books."

The benevolence of this good man is bespoken by the two following clippings from the Camden papers of 1817 and 1820. They cannot now but excite a smile:

"CUTTINGS to Plant, of the Tree called the *Balm of Gilead*, to be had of Samuel Mathis, gratis.
"March 6, 1817."

"The
Sacred Songster
of Pilsbury
Sold for the benefit of the Widow, by
Samuel Mathis.
Camden, May 18, 1820."

The exemplary life of this honest and pious man is so well vouched for that nothing is lacking on that score. In 1790 he married Margaret C. Miller, a daughter of Andrew and Elizabeth Miller. The last named, by a second marriage, became Elizabeth McNair, and died at

Camden, 1831, aged eighty-four. A memorial stone to her, in our cemetery, was erected by her children, Elizabeth McLeod, Mary C. Taylor, Margaret C. Mathis, Thomas H. Miller, and John B. Miller. A daughter of Samuel Mathis, Sophia Elizabeth, married Dr. Joshua Reynolds, of Camden, and their daughter was the first wife of the late Dr. F. M. Zemp.

Quaker Records
from
The Annals of Newberry

NO. 5.

The Quaker settlement was on Bush River and the Beaverdam. It extended from three to four miles on each side of the river. A line drawn from the Tea Table Rock, by the place once owned by Wm. Miles, now the property of Mathias Barr, to Goggan's old field, now Washington Floyd's, would be about the northwest limit. The settlement was prolonged down the river to the plantation, formerly the property of Col. Philemon Waters, now of Chancellor Johnston. No finer body of land can be found in South Carolina, than that embraced within those limits.

When the settlement commenced, or whence came the great body of settlers, it is out of my power to say with certainty. Certain it is that Wm. Coate, before '62, lived between Spring Field and Bush River, and that Samuel Kelly, a native of King's County, Ireland, but who came to Newberry from Camden, settled at Spring Field in '62, John Furnas at the same time, and adjoining, made his settlement. David Jenkins, about the same time, or possibly a few years before, settled on the plantation where major Peter Hare resides. Benjamin Pearson and Wm. Pearson lived on the plantation, once the property of John Frost, now that of Judge O'Neall, as early as '69. Robert Evans, who settled the place now owned by Sampson Marchant, came also from Camden, probably between '62 and '69. John Wright, Jos. Wright, Wm. Wright, James Brooks, Joseph Thomson, James Patty, Gabriel McCoole, John Coate, (Big) Isaac Hollingsworth, Wm. O'Neall, Walter Herbert, Sr., Daniel Parkins, Daniel Smith, Samuel Miles, David Miles, William Miles, Samuel Brown, Israel Gaunt, Azariah Pugh,* William Mills, Jonathan and Caleb Gilbert, John Galbreath, James Galbreath, James Coppock, John Coppock, Joseph Reagin, John Reagin, Abel and James Insco, Jesse Spray, Samuel Teague, George Pemberton, Jehu Inman, Mercer Babb, James Steddam, John Crumpton, Isaac Cook, John Jay, Reason Reagen, Thomas and Isaac Hasket, Thos. Pearson, the two Enoch Pearsons, Samuel Pearson, Nehemiah Thomas, Abel Thomas, Timothy Thomas, Euclydus

---

* The ancestor of Senator Pugh, of Ohio.

Longshore, Sarah Duncan, Samuel Duncan, and John Duncan, were residents of the same tract of country before or during the revolution, and were Friends or were ranked as such by descent.

The Friends had three places of meeting, one, the oldest and principal, at Bush River, where their house of worship still stands, neglected, but not desecrated. Within the grave yard, south of it, sleep hundreds of the early settlers of Bush River. Often have I seen more than five hundred Friends, women and children, there gathered together to worship God in silence, and to listen to the outpouring of the spirit, with which some of the Friends, male and female, might be visited. In imagination, often can I see the aged form of the elder David Jenkins, sitting immediately below the preacher's bench, on the left of the southern entrance to the men's meeting, leaning on the head of his staff, his large protruding lower lip, the most remarkable feature of his face. Alongside of him might be seen the tall form and grey hairs of Tanner Thomson, as he used to be called. Scarcely could the sacred stillness of Friends' meeting keep him from snapping his thumb and finger together, as if feeling a side of leather. Just here I recall the person of Isaac Hollingsworth. His was a stalwart form, more than six feet high. He sits the picture of firmness, and ever and anon, throwing up the ample brim of his flapping beaver, he looks as if he was restless for execution. He it was of whom youngsters, who did not know the meaning of "turning out of meeting" used to suppose the duty was demanded of leading an erring member to the door, saying to him, as he applied his foot to the seat of honor: "Friends have no further use for thee." A little further to the right or lower down, might be seen the pale features of that excellent man, Joseph Furnas! Near to him was to be seen the tall, erect form, florid complexion, clear, blue eye, ample forehead, and grey hair of John Kelly, Sr. ; just alongside of him might be seen Isaac Kirk. Friend Kirk, as he used to be called, was a true Quaker. He was plain and simple as a child, kind and forbearing in every thing. No better heart was ever covered by a straight-breasted coat. He had his peculiarities : one, that in reading, he read as if he was singing the passages—another, that when talking to any one his foot had always to be in motion. It was, therefore said, when he called on a debtor to dun him, his mission was known by his kicking the chips, sticks, and stones all around. In this vicinage might be seen the person of Samuel Gaunt, dressed with all the precision of a Quaker, but neat as a pin. A little above him might be seen the tall form and gray hairs of James Brooks. A little lower might be seen the brothers, Abijah, Hugh, William, John, Henry, and Thomas O'Neall. Some description of some of these may be afterwards attempted, but here will not now be given.

In the women's meeting, on the preacher's bench, under their immense white beavers, I recall the full round faces and forms of the sisters, Charity Cook and Susannah Hollingsworth. Both wives, both mothers of large families, still they felt it to be their duty to preach "Jesus and him crucified." The first, Charity Cook, was indeed a gifted woman. She traveled through the States extensively. Twice visited England and Ireland. When her husband drove his stage wagon into Rabun's creek, at a time when it was high, drowned two horses, and only escaped drowning himself by riding a chunk to land, she swam to the shore, and thus saved herself. Her sister, Susannah Hollingsworth, was not so highly gifted. Henry O'Neall, and other young Friends, used to affirm, that when Aunt Suzey, as she was called, began to pray, they could always keep ahead of her by repeating the words she was about to say. Just below the preacher's bench, the once round and graceful form (afterwards bent by 82 winters) of Hannah Kelly once Hannah Belton, a native of Queen's County, Ireland, might be seen. No more intelligent, kind, or benevolent face ever met the upturned gaze of her juniors. Well might it be said of her, that she was indeed "a mother in Israel." Her eye of blue, her long straight nose, high cheek bones, and clear Irish complexion, can scarcely ever be forgotten by those who saw her. Their other places of meeting were Rocky Springs, now a Baptist meeting house, and White Lick, on the land where Robert Burton now lives. They were much junior to that of Bush River, and therefore they are not necessary to be further described.

Every thing relating to Friends *here* is now a novelty. Their very dress, the broad-brimmed, low-crowned hats, straight-breasted, collarless coats; breeches without suspenders, and of the plainest color, is strange to us *now*, but was and is defended upon the ground that they seek no change— it is comfortable, and as they found society dressed in the time of George Fox, so it is with them now. The dress of the females, was equally plain, and defended on the same ground. White beavers, with the mere indentation for a crown, with a brim around it of full six inches every way, secured on the head by a plain white ribbon passing through loops, or perfectly plain silk bonnets called hoods; caps as plain as possible; long-waisted gowns or wrappers and petticoats, constituted the *tout ensemble* of a Quaker lady's dress. Their language 'thou,' to a single person, or 'you' to more than one, was grammatical, and free from all personal idolatry, and therefore they used it. It is true, that it was corrupted, and 'thee' the objective instead of the nominative case of the personal pronoun was used.

They met to transact business and worship on the fifth day (Thursday,) weekly, and on the seventh day, (Saturday,) monthly. There were also quarterly and yearly meetings of delegates. The meeting for worship was every first day (Sunday) at 11 o'clock. At that hour all entered the house, and sat covered and in silence for an hour, unless the spirit moved some Friend to speak. Any Friend may speak under the influence of the spirit, but in general only those speak in public whose gifts have been approved. If prayer be made, then the Friend who prays, uncovers himself, and kneeling down, utters the petitions which the spirit prompts. The congregation rise and the men are uncovered during prayer. As soon as it is closed, all take their seats covered. At the end of the hour, the elder members grasp one another by the hand, walk out and every body starts for home.

Just here, I may be pardoned for stopping and relating an anecdote. John Wright, the father of Charity Cook and Susannah Hollingsworth, was a very aged man at the time of which I am about to speak, but principally accustomed to walk to and from meeting. He was living with his daughter, Susannah Hollingsworth; something prevented her from going to meeting; she induced the old man to ride her mare. This he did; but after meeting, he walked out of the meeting house, and home as usual. As he entered the door, his daughter said to him, "Father, where is the mare?" "Dads me, Sue, I forgot her," was the old man's prompt reply. This old gentleman before his death, assembled his sons, his sons' wives, his daughters, his daughters' husbands, his grand children, and their respective wives and husbands, and his great grand-children. When all were assembled, they numbered one hundred and forty-four. Did he not deserve well of the Republic? Where can such a family now be found?

A pair of young people about to marry are said to pass meeting by their purpose being announced at one monthly meeting, when a committee is appointed to inquire if there be any objections. At the next, if their report be favorable, Friends assent to the marriage, and on the succeeding fifth day (Thursday) it takes place by the man and woman standing up and holding one another by the right hand, and repeating the ceremony. The man says about as follows: "I take this my friend to be my wedded wife, whom I will love, cherish and her only keep, until it shall please the Lord to separate us by death." The woman says: "I take this my friend to be my husband, whom I will love, honor and obey until it shall please the Lord to separate us by death." I may not be accurate in the words. I am sure I am in substance, although I never saw but two marriages of Friends, one of Robert Evans and Keren Happuch Gaunt in 1806; and the other of Joseph Stanton and Sarah Hollingsworth in 1807. As soon as the ceremony is repeated, they sit down; a Friend, most generally the clerk of the men's meeting, reads a certificate of the marriage, which is signed by Friends present. The meeting then proceeds, as usual, to its close. I ought to have mentioned before, that there is a clerk of both the men's and women's meeting. Every thing of importance is regularly entered upon their books, such as business transactions, marriages, births and deaths. Every child born of parents who are Friends, is by descent a Friend. The same result follows, if the mother alone be a Friend. No beggar or pauper was ever known among Friends. They take care of all such. Their meeting of Sufferings provides for these and all other wants.

The Quaker community of Bush River was a most interesting one. Small farms, enough and to spare, among all, was its general state. Hard working, healthy, yet an honest, innocent and mirthful, though a staid people, make up altogether an interesting picture. It is true, among them were many hickory, or formal Quakers; now and then some wet, or grog-drinking Quakers; and now and then some cheating Quakers. But these are now no more—of each I would only say, *"requiescat in pace."* The only valid objection which I know to the practice of Friends is, that they do not generally sufficiently attend to the religious education of their children and the reading of the Scriptures. In this respect, there are, I know, many, very many illustrious exceptions; and I believe their rules require the Scriptures to be read, and their children to be religiously instructed. In other points, I think no religious community can present better claims for respect, and even the admiration of men.

In the beginning, Friends were slave owners in South Carolina. They however, soon sat their faces against it, and in their peculiar language, they have uniformly borne their testimony against the institution of slavery, as irreligious. Such of their members as refused to emancipate their slaves, when emancipation was practicable in this State, they disowned. Samuel Kelly, who was the owner of a slave or slaves in '62, when he came from Camden, refused to emancipate his, on the grounds that he had bought and paid for them: they were therefore his property; and that they were a great deal better off as his property, than they would be if free. He was therefore disowned. His brother's children manumitted theirs. Some followed them to Ohio; others have lived *here* free, it is true, but in indigence and misery, a thousand times worse off than the slaves of Samuel Kelly and their descendants. For the far-seeing old gentleman took good care in his last will, that the bulk of his slaves who were left to his widow, should not be emancipated, by giving her the power to dispose of them at her death, provided it was to some member of or among his family. Friends are opposed to war; they therefore hold everything which appertains to it to be contrary to their discipline. Hence, Generals Greene and Brown were disowned. Still, however, they never entirely forgot their duty to their country. I have before me now the soldier's song, on the receipt of the Quaker's present of 10,000 flannel shirts, to the army marching from England into Scotland, against the Pretender:

> "This *friendly* waistcoat keeps my body warm,
> Intrepid on the march and free from harm,
> A coat of mail, a sure defender,
> Proof against the Pope, the Devil, and Pretender.
> The Highland plaid of no such force can boast!
> Armed thus, I'll plunge the foremost in their host,
> With all my force, with all my strength, with all my might,
> And fight for those whose creed forbid to fight!"

After the bloody battle of Guilford, gladly did Friends obey the call of him, whom, although disowned, they gloried in claiming as a Quaker, Nathaniel Greene, and rushed in throngs to take charge of the wounded Americans and Britons!

Between '97 and '99, Abijah O'Neall and Samuel Kelly, Jr., bought the military land of Jacob Roberts Brown, in Ohio; the great body of it was in Warren County, near Waynesville. Abijah O'Neall visited, located the land, and in '99, in the language of Samuel Kelly, Sr.:

> "Beyond the mountain and far away,
> With wolves and bears to play,"

he commenced his toilsome removal to his western home. When about starting, he applied to Friends for his regular certificate of membership, &c. This they refused him, on the ground that his removal was itself such a thing as did not meet their approbation. Little did they *then* dream that in less than ten years they would all be around him in the then far West!

Abijah O'Neall was about five feet eight inches high, stout, round-shouldered, light brown hair, eyes grey, nose Roman, mouth protruded slightly, his face had the appearance of great firmness. Such was his character. He came up to the Latin description, "*ver bonus tenax propositi.*" Every body knew this, as may be better illustrated by a little anecdote:

a young man boarding with him, disposed to play off a joke on an old family negro, who had been manumitted, but who still lived with Miss Anne, (as he called Mrs. O'Neall,) seized the old man on his way to mill, and said to him, "Jack, I'll carry you off and sell you." "You can't do dat," said Jack; "de bery Bije (the usual abbreviation of the name Abijah) can't do dat." He had some strange peculiarities. For many years before his death, he would not sleep on a feather-bed; he must have a straw bed. Again, he cut his hair as close as possible, and had at least two windows in the crown of his hat. This was to keep his head cool. He drank neither tea nor coffee. He was a surveyor, and after he went to Ohio spent much of his time in the woods as such, and as a hunter in the pursuit of game. He believed firmly that this State would, in time, become as sterile as the deserts of Arabia. Such at least were his words in 1810, when I last saw him.

But it will be asked, what became of the Friends? Between 1800 and 1804, a celebrated Quaker preacher, Zachary Dicks, passed through South Carolina. He was thought to have *also the gift of prophecy.* The massacres of San Domingo were then fresh. He warned Friends to come out from slavery. He told them if they did not their fate would be that of the slaughtered Islanders. This produced in a short time a panic, and removals to Ohio commenced, and by 1807 the Quaker settlement had, in a great degree, changed its population. John Kelly, Sr., Hugh O'Neall, John O'Neall, Henry O'Neall, James Brooks, Isaac Kirk, Walter Herbert, William Wright, Samuel Gaunt, William Pugh, and Timothy Thomas alone remained. Land which could often since, and even now after near forty years cultivation in cotton, can be sold for $10, $15 and $20 per acre, was sold then for from $3 to $6. Newberry thus lost, from a foolish panic and a superstitious fear of an institution, which never harmed them or any other body of people, a very valuable portion of its white population. But they are gone, never to return! It is our business to repair the loss, by better agriculture, more attention to the mechanic arts, and more enterprise. Thus acting, our wasted fields will yet blossom like the rose, our streams will resound with the music of machinery, and our hills will be vocal with the songs of industry and peace.

I.

THE FRIENDS AND THEIR MIGRATION TO OHIO.

The readers of the Annals of Newberry will be glad to find, I think, the following supplementary chapter to Judge O'Neall's work, contributed by Mr. David Jones, of Ohio, a relative of Lambert J. Jones, Esq., of Newberry. The chapter is strictly supplementary and not a continuation in time of the former work:

"I have read one very interesting narrative or history of Newberry District written, as I have been informed, by the late John Belton O'Neall, a resident of said district, from birth until death, embracing a period of more than sixty years, during a long portion of which he held the office of Supreme Judge of the State. Having learned that another history of said district is in preparation by Mr. John A. Chapman, I will furnish, at his request, some account of the most prominent families who left there near the beginning of this century, and contributed to the peopling of three counties, namely, Miami, Warren and Clinton, in the State of Ohio.

"I feel interested in the task because my parents and maternal grandparents came from there, bringing those grand traits of the pioneer, namely, industry, enterprise, fortitude and indomitable courage. I know that the present inhabitants of Newberry District will not feel dishonored when they learn something of what has been wrought by her emigrant citizens and their descendants.

"In O'Neall's history we are told in part of the Friends, or Quakers, who resided in the district, the exodus of whom and others between the years 1800 and 1810, reflexively decimated the district. He says, also, that they held a large quarterly meeting on Bush River, where he had often seen more than five hundred Friends assembled.

"There must have been some great moving cause or causes that induced such an exit in so short a period. O'Neall ascribes it to their repugnance to the 'peculiar institution' of the South, together with frightful predictions of war and carnage made by an itinerant minister of this church, named Zachary Dicks. During the year 1803 this minister made a visit to Wrightsborough monthly meeting, in Georgia, an integral part of Bush River quarterly meeting. He there told the Friends of a terrific internecine war not far in the future, during which many men like those in the Apocalypse would flee to the mountains and call on those mountains to hide them. With reference to the time of fulfilment, he said the child was then born that would see it; thus intimating the time, not as immediate, but not very far off. He also advised them to leave there, which they did. Forty-eight years after came the predicted war. I heard this account more than forty years ago from a man who was at the meeting. From Wrightsborough, Z. Dicks went to Bush River meeting, held in a well made house erected only five years before with the full calculation of a long continued occupancy. I give his first words there as related by a dear aunt of mine who was present, and was just blooming into womanhood: 'O, Bush River! Bush River! How hath thy beauty faded away, and gloomy darkness eclipsed thy day!' Going into particulars, he depicted the silence and loneliness that would attend that house after its abandonment by those who had erected it; that herbage would ere long grow in its now well beaten paths. I did not understand that he advised removal here as at Wrightsborough, but only foretold it. Indeed, it did not suffer during the war like the other place, for I have learned no hostile troops came near it.

"Friend Dicks must have been at this time rather elderly, for I am informed that not long before the Revolution he had been at Guilford, North Carolina, and foretold that war. Pointing to the walls of the meeting house he said its floors and walls would be stained with human blood. This was literally fulfilled, for, after the bloody battle of Guilford, the Friends carried the wounded soldiers, both British and American, into the house and performed for them the part of the good Samaritan; the stains of whose blood, though faded, were on its walls many years afterwards. To those who are skeptical as to Z. Dicks' prophetical attainments, I will only say that he was at least a 'good guesser.' Whatever effect his (Dicks) visit may have had in causing the Friends' removal, other causes co-operated. Those living east of the Alleghanies had looked upon them as a barrier against savage invasion, and also as one against removing to an unexplored and unknown savage wilderness. Such had been the view until the arrival of the time thus described by the poet, when,

> " 'Boone had with bold adventurous tread,
>   Beyond the mountain barriers prest;
> And saw a richer landscape spread
>   In the broad valley of the West.
> Fiction had lent her magic hand
> To paint that second Fairy land;
> For it was drawn a clime as fair
>   As youthful fancy's brightest dream;
> And all who heard might justly deem
> Another Eden blooming there.'

"Allowing much for exaggeration, the description was still tempting enough, with the first-named cause, to produce the exodus which began soon after Dicks' visit. I must remark, however, that this exodus was far from being confined to the Friends. The Barretts, Elmores, Halls, Dennys, Campbells, Laytons and others, who removed during that period, were not members of the Friends' Church, and many of them were not of any. The first removal, as well as I can find, took place some months after Dicks' visit there. This was John Jay, the only Jay mentioned in the Annals, though with him came seven sons and three daughters. They came to Miami County, I think, during the autumn of 1803. They found Friends from Guilford, North Carolina, who had come the year before, and as all belonged to the same yearly meeting, namely, Guilford, North Carolina, the matter of removal seems to have been well understood between them. The same may be said of Wrightsborough Friends in Georgia, for they came in great numbers, leaving the parent meeting in the same condition as that of Bush River.

"I will now give an account of some of the most prominent persons who came from Newberry and settled in the three counties previously mentioned. Many of those emigrants being unknown or forgotten by the author of the Annals of Newberry, are not mentioned by him, and we need not wonder, for he was a boy at the time of their emigration. The traits of some, however, are given with almost surprising accuracy; and could he have known their subsequent lives it would no doubt have given him much satisfaction, and would have been a supplement to the Annals.

"The first I'll mention is Thomas Pearson, 'Little Old Tommy,' who lived to the greatest age of any who came from Newberry, besides being the oldest emigrant to his township and, as near as I can learn, county. Born in 1728, he was older than the Father of his Country, a fact which seemed to attach additional importance to him. In early life he lived in Philadelphia, following the trade of saddler and harness-maker. Years before, and during the Revolution, he and his family resided in Newberry District and had their full share of its honors. Once, when a captive, his enemies required his service in saddlery and harness work, regardless of his lack of tools. He answered them by saying that 'Neither wise men nor fools can work without tools,' the piquancy of which caused them to laugh and excuse him. He appears to have occupied the first seat in the 'Common Meetings' of Friends. A granddaughter of his told me that once during the solemn quiet of a meeting a partially insane woman came in with fruit in her apron and going up to him said, 'Here, Mr. Pearson, I'll give you the apples if you will preach to-day:' Being a harmless person they got rid of her in a quiet way; but whether or not they regarded her interruption as a rebuke upon their silent worship I was not informed. I think it was in 1805 or 1806, that Father Pearson left Newberry with a numerous retinue of children, grandchildren and one great-grandchild. Coming directly to Miami County they pitched their tents in proximity to the Jays and Jenkinses, who had preceded them. It was not many years before his many descendants were settled comfortably around him and he saw teeming fields, in place of dark, tangled forests. His wife died, and, though in advanced age, he took another. A few years more and his walk became tremulous, his eyes grew dim, and his hearing blunted. The writer saw him in 1820, when he had Old Dodson's Three Warnings:—'he was lame, and deaf, and blind.' He could walk only with support on both sides, could hear only by loud speaking in his ear, both day and night were alike to him. In this lamentable condition we may well suppose time hung heavy on his hands. Upon asking what time it was, if answered ten o'clock, he would say and repeat, 'Ten o'clock, ten o'clock,' striving, but in vain, to impress it upon his memory, for it would not be long before he repeated the question. The author, child as he was, pitied him whose lamp of life, so nearly gone out, seemed to be leaving him rather impatient. At this time the great human butcher, but now a captive of Europe, whose

> " 'Evil deeds were writ in gore,
> Nor written thus in vain;
> Whose triumphs told of fame no more,
> Or deepened every stain;'

was languishing like Prometheus upon his sea-girt rock, saying sorrowfully to his followers: 'I once dictated to four or five secretaries at once; I was then Napoleon; I am now no longer anything; my senses, my faculties, forsake me; I no longer live, I only exist.' How much the weight of blood upon his soul distressed Napoleon, we cannot know; but we do know he had his sight and hearing, which old Thomas Pearson had not. In natural ability they bear no comparison, neither did they in ambition. The first died in the calmness and quiet of Christian resignation; the second a few months after with his spirit deliriously engaged in the strife of battle and the rage of tempests around him.

"A short time after the above-described sight of Old Thomas, the author heard a grandson of his announce his death and burial, which elicited but little remark, seeming to be acquiesced in because of his relief from his lamentable condition. Of some of his relatives I will write hereafter, but will now take up the names seriatim of persons, of whom I know something, mentioned in the Annals of Newberry, on pages 31, 32 and 33,* who emigrated to Ohio.

"David Jenkins and family came to Miami County, Ohio, in 1805. He had married Martha Evans a few years after the Revolution and brought several children with him. He made a good selection of land which he cultivated to advan-

---

* Part I., 28, 29 and 30.

tage. He built a hewed log house of good size, which is considered the oldest one in his (Monroe) Township. He reared two sons and four daughters, not one of whom, I think, was born in Ohio. They all did well except one son, who became intemperate. A very quiet and unassuming little man, he performed his part well and died in good old age about the year 1842.

"Benjamin Pearson, a relative of Old Thomas', emigrated about the same time as David Jenkins, being nearly his age. He was the father of seven sons and two daughters, but few of whom were born in Ohio. They all married to good advantage; all prospered and lived to good age, but none of them are now living.

"Of William Pearson but very little is now known, and his descendants do not appear to have belonged to the Friends.

"Robert Evans, at least one of that name, went with his family to Tennessee. His brother Joseph, not mentioned in the Annals, came with his family to this county. Being of an enterprising turn, he purchased land on the west fork of Stillwater River, located a village, West Milton, there in 1807. This site was a good selection, being seventy-five feet above low water mark; in proximity to several perennial springs that poured over precipices nearly, or quite, fifty feet perpendicular, affording ample power for the propulsion of machinery. Evans built, I think, the second mill on Stillwater, the first being by Frederick Yount, from North Carolina. The scenery here was grand and almost inspiring. The towering, umbrageous forests; the magnificent cascades; the slopes and grassy banks of Stillwater, might make it seem to the imaginative beholder as the place where the queen Violenta led her *fairy troupes* in their mazy moonlight dances. On the first sale of lots the buyers were few and the prices low. Two boys rode two steers to the sale, which would have seemed singular at Newberry. Evans started the first store and postoffice on the place and continued them until after the war of 1812, when he went to Cincinnati to engage in greater business. About 1828 he returned to Milton; opened a store which he continued a number of years, dying of abdominal dropsy in 1837; having, a number of years before, lost his right among Friends. Father Evans' four daughters and son were, as near as I can learn, born on Bush River. They were well educated and highly accomplished, but, like their father, left the Friends. The eldest daughter was such an admirer of Paradise Lost that, 'tis said, it induced her father to name his village after its illustrious author. Evans was a man of more than ordinary ability, who, it was said, could see as far into a trade as any man. He was a full-handed man in Cincinnati, but the shrinkage of currency and of values after the war of 1812, so reduced him as to cause his return to Milton. His family was for years what might be called 'Quaker Aristocrats,' when disowned. He possessed much courage, decision and fortitude. Whilst sitting at his bedside one night during his last sickness, at his request I read a newspaper article on the machinery propelling powers of animal magnetism. When done he said, 'Young people will live to see wonderful things in mechanical and physical science, which I have not seen.' A prediction fully realized. Not one of his descendants now lives in this county, but a grandson is a millionaire in St. Louis, Missouri.

"John, Joseph and William Wright, next mentioned in the Annals, settled and died, I think, (except John, who died in Newberry,) in Clinton County, Ohio, in Indiana and Illinois. Two other brothers not mentioned, namely, Thomas and Isaac Wright, came West also, where, in 1834, the author saw Isaac, his great uncle. He was then a little, old, dingy man and said to be intemperate.

"James Brooks must have died in early times, but two sons who came with him, Nimrod and John, were practical farmers, both rearing many children and living to good age.

"Joseph Thompson came with a number of children, some of whom were married, and settled in the region called Ludlow's Creek, a tributary of the Stillwater. He did not, however, live long at his new home, but his children did. One of his sons was a preacher, though never recommended, awhile among the Friends, and next among the New Lights, or Christian Church. But few of them belong now to the Friends.

"James Patty must have been the father of James, David and Charles Patty, who came also from Newberry, as did three married sisters. The author well knew the last three

Pattys, but not the first; so he must have died not many years after arriving. James Patty had a large portion of 'suaviter in modo,' and perhaps much 'fortiter in re.' Such were his pleasantness and equanimity that

> "'Along the cool, sequestered vale of life
> He kept the noiseless tenor of his way.'

"His marriage with Anna Brown at Bush River not long before their removal is said to have been partly caused by the jocular recommendation of some, or one of the young folks. James was not acquainted with her, but had seen her at church and noticed that she limped a little in her walk. After hearing her fitness for him described he answered with characteristic gravity: 'Who is this Anna Brown? Is she the girl that when she walks goes *one pound ten?*' After marriage he found that she would *'Storm like March, but not weep like April.'* It seemed through their whole marital life that he was as proper a mate for her as Socrates was for Xantippe. On one occasion I heard of when she and her husband went to a magistrate's office to sign a deed of land conveyance; she was asked in private by the magistrate, as the law required, if she did this signing under her own will, or under fear of her husband. 'No,' said she, almost indignant, 'I ain't afraid of Jimps.' 'That's one time,' said Squire T., laughing, 'that I know she told the truth.'

"She, however, like others had good qualities. She brought him four sons and five daughters, only two of whom are now living. The sons were of more than ordinary ability, and three of them followed professions, all showing that they had not received bad maternal training. One anecdote of James Patty is similar to that of John Wright told in the Annals. For many years he rode a mule to West Branch, whose hybrid neighings or brayings often broke upon the stillness of the meeting. Forgetting the mule once he walked home and when told of it was taken aback; but whether he said 'Dads me, Anna!' or 'O pshaw!' I am not informed. In conclusion, his whole life was economical, quiet and peaceful. He died in 1833 and his widow about the year 1846.

"Gabriel McCoole, with his five sons and two daughters, came here, I think, in 1806. His wife dying some years after, he spent his last days among his children and grandchildren. He was a highly conscientious and good old man, but his sons partook far more of the ways of the world. One of them, Thomas, who was married to a daughter of old 'Tanner Thompson,' [see Annals] in Newberry District, had a bankering as well as an aptitude for office. He served for many years as Squire, in what was called the 'Creek Nation,' composed mainly of Newberry people and their descendants. If he did not exhibit the wisdom and legal acumen of a Hale he tried to the dignity of a Mansfield. Many of the suits which he decided were unique in their character; two of which I will briefly relate. One F. Jones, not a Newberry but Georgia Jones, the laziest man 'in all creation,' had rented a small farm to W. Friend, reserving a small house in which he lived, and a favorite apple tree. Their residences were near together and for a time things went well. After awhile Jones, who, though too lazy to work, was not too lazy to get mad, became offended at something, and as Friend's geese had eaten a few of his reserved apples lying under the tree, he sought satisfaction by suing him, Friend, for damages. Spectators, as well as witnesses, attended the trial, which, being managed by the parties, was rather devoid of declarations, replications and argued technicalities, resting entirely upon its proved merits. When the one-sided and almost infinitesimal testimony was ended, Squire McCoole put on his dignity and slowly patting the floor with his foot to keep time, thus gave his decision: 'I hardly know how to apply law to this case, so I will just strike at *Justas*. I decide that W. Friend pay F. Jones six and one-fourth cents damage, and each party pay his own costs.' The guffaws of the spectators can be better imagined than described. The defendant was well pleased. He, having made little or no cost, had little or none to pay, while the plaintiff had several dollars. He, the plaintiff, was the only one there that could see nothing to laugh at. Could any one have decided that case better than did old Squire McCoole?

"The other case was between a German and a Tennessean. It was hard to tell which of them was most tricky. Lawyers managed the case, and, of course, there was much wordy warring. One of them being more prolix than pointed, the magistrate's patience gave out and he stopped him short with,

'Well, Samuel, I guess you've spoke about long enough; I guess I'll have to give judgment against you.' 'Why,' said Samuel in much affected surprise, 'haven't I proved thus and so?' 'Yes,' answered the Squire, 'you've proved it, but I don't believe your witnesses.' The discomfited attorney felt about small enough to crawl into an auger hole. Squire McCoole's decisions were believed to be generally correct and were but seldom reversed through a long official course. His chirography was almost unreadable and may have resembled Senator Choate's, whose writing was said to look like the marks made by a spider, after crawling out of an inkstand.

"Squire McCoole reached good old age and died in Iowa but a few years ago. I may mention that Gabriel, his father, died on Stillwater not far from the year 1828. None of his other sons merit being mentioned.

"John Coate is next mentioned in the Annals, but I think John' is a mistake. Marmaduke Coate, with six sons, came here among the earlier emigrants. His sons, Moses, Henry and Samuel, having married at Newberry. His other sons, John, James and Jesse. married here. They all became prosperous farmers, reared numerous families, some dying at advanced age; all dying in membership with Friends. Henry Coate became a most useful and efficient blacksmith, making sickles for many years, supplying that desideratum to the farmers of Stillwater Valley. He amassed a handsome estate and left it to his children. Old Marmaduke, the father, did not live many years after coming here; so, little is known about him, but of his numerous descendants it may be said: They are an honor to Miami County and do no discredit to Newberry District.

"Big Isaac Hollingsworth comes next, who is so graphically, though briefly, described on pages 32 and 33* of the Annals. He possessed great physical strength and unbounded courage During the Revolution when a British officer approached his corn crib he was forbidden entrance. The officer drew his sword and threatened. Big Isaac went to him, took the sword from him, saying: 'Thus far shalt thou go, but no farther.' The officer succumbed. Once, when he was about starting to meeting, a poor Irishman accosted him desiring employment.

---
* Part I., 29, 30.

Isaac having nothing else for him to do set him to moving a pile of stones. On returning from meeting and finding the job done he had him to move the stones back. After which he paid him. While on the road to Ohio he was one day sitting upon a log while his horses were eating. A man came along and asked him where he was moving. 'I am not moving,' said Isaac, 'I am sitting still.' 'Well, where are you bound then?' 'I am not bound at all,' said he, 'I am a free man.' The discomfited man passed on. When reprimanded by his daughter for his uncourteous answers he naively answered that he did not know that it was any of that man's business where he was going. Five daughters and three sons, six of whom were married, accompanied him, making quite a company. All of them, except two daughters and with husbands, settled near him in Miami County. There amongst wolves, deer and other wild animals, they built their rude cabins in the

"'Dark, mephitic tangled woods.'

"Those woods or forests they began to level; to build cabins for shelter and clear the lands for cultivation. Log rollings, which I need not describe, became common. The practice of wearing suspenders, vulgarly called gallowes, was then coming into vogue among the young men. Big Isaac looked upon this innovation as savoring of pride, and as he possessed 'fortiter in re' without 'suaviter in modo,' when he met the young men at log rollings or stable raisings, with suspenders unprotected by coat or jacket, he would, when opportunity offered, thrust his forefinger under one of them and giving a jerk the button had to fly. It was useless for the boys to get angry on such occasions, so their plan was to watch and avoid him. Yet with all his exterior rudeness he had a good and tender heart; more internal than external piety. This I have learned from his children. He used to say that his crops never grew better than when Susie, his wife, (mentioned on pages 33 and 34* of the Annals) was away from home preaching. By which it seems he gave her all necessary assistance. He died of pleurisy in 1809, aged about 61; and though having enjoyed but three years residence, the opening in the forest, the buildings and fences long remained as the work of his hands.

---

* Part I., 31, 32.

"His second son Joel merits a place in Newberry history. Born in that district in 1778 he married there and came to Ohio with two children. Possessing the size, strength and courage of his father, he had more suaviter in his deportment, making himself agreeable to every one. Of his five stalwart sons, none were quite equal to him, and the man was not known who could break him down at the handspike. The forest soon showed his power and industry, for it melted away, succeeded by teeming fields of grain and grass. Being of an adventurous spirit he made frequent voyages to New Orleans on flat-bottomed boats loaded with pork and flour, for himself and neighbors. These enterprises were attended with much hardship and danger, yet Joel appeared to delight in them. During the year 1830 he, with his wife, returned on a visit to Newberry and hunted up their friends and relatives yet living. Boating and clearing having measurably ceased, Joel's rather restless spirit induced him to move again and settle in the Indiana forests. There he cleared another farm and lived until near his 80th year, when one day being engaged in butchering and rendering lard, he fell upon the floor and died, perhaps of heart disease. I believe he is the only Newberry man emigrant that met with instantaneous death. His elder brother William and younger brother John had left Ohio long before he did and the deaths of the three occurred within three months of each other, the news of which was received by their only surviving sister all in one day.

"Of Isaac Hollingsworth's daughters, namely, Rachel, Ruth, Keziah, Sarah and Susanna, the four first were married at Bush River, and the last, Susanna, in Ohio. She married Elisha Jones, a twin brother of Elijah Jones mentioned on page 115 of the Annals. As Elisha moved to Ohio in 1805, Susanna the following year, and they married soon after, it looks as if they might have made the marital agreement in Newberry District. They settled on land joining their father's, and being young, courageous and industrious, a farm was opened and plenty was smiling around them. Nearly eleven years of married life had passed and they had become the parents of five children, when a terrible event occurred, which no human prescience could discern, nor human power avert. They each had a saddle which hung together against the wall.

One night they awoke and saw a bright spot on Susanna's saddle. They first thought a hunter was passing with a torch; but the bright spot did not move and a visit to the window disclosed no torch. What could this mean? they wondered. Not long afterwards, about 10 o'clock in the morning, a small cloud was passing southeastward. Its ominous rumblings were heard while passing and it went over the house. Susanna had stepped to the open door with something in her hand, when a tremendous peal was heard, not only there, but far over the country, and she fell lifeless on the floor.

> "'The fiery bolt from upper air,
> Attendant of the rain,
> Which oft assumes the Ash to tear
> And Oak to rive in twain;—
> Descending from its lofty height,
> To kill instead of save,
> With speed of thought and matchless might,
> Had hurled her to the grave.'

"This occurred in 1817, not far from the time of her brother-in-law, Elijah Jones' death. On the 66th anniversary of Susanna's funeral, two surviving children, too young to have retained her image, went to her grave to drop their tears there and etch anew the moss-grown inscription on her tombstone. I may further add that she was the youngest daughter of Susanna Hollingsworth mentioned in the Annals, and that I, the author, am her youngest child. Further, I may mention the remarkable fact that the brother, Joel, and the sister, Susanna, met instantaneous deaths. Newberry, I believe, furnishes no more such examples.

"Before Isaac Hollingsworth's family is dismissed I must give a short after-biography of his wife, my most revered maternal grandmother. Left a widow, as before stated, in 1809, at the age of 54, she lived among her children the remainder of her life. She made religious visits after her husband's death, one of which was, I think, to Newberry, others to the East. Possessing an excellent memory and having long experience, she was an excellent conversationalist. With great interest have I heard her tell the fearful tales of the Revolution in Newberry District; of Hal Foster, the desperate Tory and criminal, who, refusing to heed the warning her father had given, was shot through the head after peace was made. Her piety, equanimity and kindliness, particularly towards her grandchildren, were such that they loved her with the most ardent affection, believing that no grandmother could be better. One Sunday evening in July, 1830, she went on horseback from her daughter's residence to that of her son-in-law, his wife being dead. On the way she said to her accompanying young grandson: 'I am going to thy father's just to die.' This was said with as much calmness of feeling as though she had said I am going there to live. The next day she was taken ill. To her son Joel who visited her she said 'I am going, but not as speedily as I could wish.' Death came to her as a friend. Near the close of the week she died and was buried on the following Sunday. Her sister, Charity Cook, mentioned in the Annals, traveled extensively in the ministry. She once crossed the Atlantic, visiting the Friends' churches in England and Ireland. In the last country she had an interview with the Irish giant, Patrick O'Brien, who respectfully received her testimony. She died in 1820, but the particulars thereof are unknown. Another sister, Kirial Hanks, not mentioned in the Annals, a widow, came here with three sons and two daughters. Her second son, James, became a school teacher and most efficient surveyor. Her eldest daughter, Mary, possessed more than ordinary ability; was useful in the church, but was the only one of the children not disowned.

"Judge O'Neall appears to have forgotten Big Isaac Hollingsworth's brothers, namely, James, George and Nathan, who went also to Ohio; the two first bringing families. Their descendants were strong, hardy and adventurous, spreading themselves over portions of Ohio, Indiana and Iowa. Of all the Newberry emigrants none were equal to the Hollingsworths in physical strength and none excelled them in courage. Being of peaceable natures they sought no quarrels, and being of superior prowess, quarrels were not sought with them. I do not know of any criminal record that has the name of a Hollingsworth upon its pages; which is honorable to them, though many are not now members of the Friends' Church.

"William O'Neall, whose name in the Annals follows that of Isaac Hollingsworth, was a Quaker minister somewhat advanced in years when he left Newberry. He seems to have dropped the O' from his name, for, in Ohio, he and his decendants have Neall as their surname. Two sons, James and Mahlon, came with him and James became a preacher at an early age, living and dying a very humble and pious man. William was employed to teach some of the earliest schools; but really was better qualified to preach the gospel than to teach the sciences, as the following anecdote will show: A young full grown man took a sum in long division to him which he had worked out, desiring to know if it was done correctly. After examining it the teacher handed it back, saying with serious candor: 'Well, Jonathan, it looks very pretty, but I really don't know whether it is done right or not.' His school government was not, like that of Richard Clegg, of Newberry, sustained by the birch, but by pleasantness and kindness, by which he generally succeeded. It indeed took a hard-featured boy to violate the rules of so old and good a teacher. Once, however, they trespassed so far upon his forbearance that he told them 'if they did not behave he would bring Granny tomorrow.' This seems to have had the desired effect, for one of the offenders said many years afterwards, 'I thought if Granny had to come and see my misbehavior I'd quit right off.' This good old man, it was said, was once accosted by a presumptuous skeptic who said: 'Mr. Neall, I am an unbeliever in the Bible, but can deliver as good a discourse as you, and if you do not believe me just listen and I'll convince you.' The old man assenting, he took his place and spoke his piece. Asking what he thought of it, the answer was: 'What thee has said is good enough, but it has come through a very dirty channel.' He died at an advanced age more than sixty years ago.

"In following the Annals I mention only those with whom I've had personal or second-hand knowledge, and whose life here was worthy of a brief notice.

"Samuel, David and William Miles, relatives, were worthy, industrious and prosperous farmers, who lived to good age, leaving behind them a numerous and enterprising posterity, many of whom are living in other and newer States.

"Samuel Brown was a rather elderly man when he left Newberry. He was a man of more than ordinary ability, but rather too much governed by strong impulses that sometimes caused him trouble. He left, when removing, a son, Joshua, who departing from Quaker habits and teachings, went to Charleston and became quite rich by privateering during the last war with England. Being elated with riches, he treated his venerable father, who in after years returned to Newberry- and then went to see him, with such coldness and neglect that it greatly wounded the old man's heart. Returning to Ohio, he was said to have spoken condemnatorily of the manner by which his son had obtained his wealth; uttering the trite but rather vulgar expression 'that what comes in over the devil's back generally goes out under his belly.' In after life this was fulfilled, the sheriff selling even his bed to pay his creditors. He brought another son, Samuel, to Ohio, who also caused more sorrow than joy to him. He was the father of Anna Brown, mentioned before as the wife of James Patty. He died in 1827 at an advanced age.

"William Mills lived and died a plain farmer in Warren County, Ohio. Charles. Mills, not mentioned in the Annals, was educated at Newberry by John B. Mtichell and Richard Clegg. Coming to Ohio, he made school teaching the principal business of his life for a period of forty years. He was a good penman or scribe, and was remarkable for his success in school government, causing his scholars to both respect and fear him. Some of his scholars were children of parents who had gone with him to the Newberry schools, and who always showed willingness to employ him in teaching. In his latter days he used to speak with pleasure of the positions his many pupils occupied in different communities. He died in Indiana some twenty years ago, remembered with the kindest regards by his few living scholars, whose hair is now whitened by age.

"James, John, Benjamin and Samuel Coppock emigrated from Newberry, with many more of that name, and settled in Miami County. Many of them did not retain their Society rights, but were nevertheless good citizens. Moses, son of James, was a very solid and useful member of the Friends' church, dying at an advanced age a few years ago.

"Abel and James Insco were brothers. Abel was son-in-law of Thomas Pearson mentioned near the first of these memoirs. He was remarkable for stuttering, and doubtlessly caused many a laugh at Newberry, as he afterwards did in Ohio. I've heard it told that while living at Newberry he was at a corn-shucking where a man who had been caught stealing a turkey kicked his dog. Not liking it, he said to the man, 'I don't even allow thee to say, tut, tut, tut-turkey to my dog.' I was told that at another corn-shucking, or husking, a man who had offended him accused him of having given him a blow and threatened prosecution. To this Abel replied whenever accused : 'Sh sh-sh-show the wound.' The men who were carrying away the shucks in the dark were much amused, and as no one saw him strike and he wouldn't own it, the matter had to drop. Abel more than fifty years ago died childless, and James' children being all girls the name Insco is now possessed only by his grandson, Insco Yount, and which being his first name, will at his death become extinct.

"The Annals mention Jesse Spray, which may be a mistake. I well knew old Samuel Spray, who lived in another county. He was a minister who lived in the time of the Revolution, and one whom I have heard preach. His daughter Dinah, who was born in the South, was rather eminent as a minister, and often traveled as such. Both father and daughter have for many years been dead.

"Samuel Teague was not originally a Quaker. He was reared near Black Jack, in Newberry District. Being a lad during the Revolution, he had escaped conscription by the Whigs, but was exposed to the cruelties of Tories. One day they were seen approaching the house, when a puncheon was lifted and he was hidden under the floor. The Tories came in and by their terrible demonstrations so frightened his sick father that he rose from his bed and ran across the adjoining lot. The Tories shot him down, hacked him over with their swords and so stripped the house of everything in the clothing line that Samuel had to take the shirt from his back to bury his father in. Truly, those were the times that tried men's souls. Samuel Teague, to avenge the murder of his father, to serve his country, or both, afterwards enlisted in the service of the patriots, but to what extent I have never learned ; but presumably until the end of the war. He married and lived at Newberry until the exodus, when with a considerable family he came to this (Miami) county. He purchased and cleared land successfully and became an efficient and useful citizen. He joined the Friends, I think, some time before leaving Newberry. He was a Quaker in the strictest sense of the word, hardly tolerating singing. One day as he was husking corn under his crib-shed, assisted by two Newberry boys named John Turner and Elisha McCook, he was asked if McCook, who was a good singer, might not give them a song. Consenting rather reluctantly, McCook did his best, acquitting himself well. When finished and asked if that was not good singing, he replied, 'Perhaps it was if there is such a thing as good singing.' It was said he could have obtained a pension in his latter days, but he would not apply for one. He was very useful in his church, lived to advanced age, leaving a numerous train of descendants, his children all keeping their rights in the church, though none of them are now living.

"Three Pemberton brothers, namely, Isaiah, Robert and John, came from Newberry to Miami County, perhaps being sons of George, mentioned in the Annals. They opened farms and reared families some of whom yet live. John in after life went into a state of 'melancholia.' Concluding he was useless to the world and had better leave it, he sent for James Hall, a once Newberry neighbor, but not a Quaker, and asked him if he did not think that he (John) had better commit suicide. Hall, who, though illiterate, had common sense, encouraged him in the project. Well, how had it better be done? Would not drowning in Ludlow Creek, which was near, be the best way of accomplishing it? 'Yes,' replied Hall, 'and I'll go down with you and if necessary help you do it.' Having arrived at the creek, Pemberton stood hesitating upon the bank, when Hall shoved him in. He would not drown, however, but came out with a good wetting and, what was better, an entire cure of his suicidal desires. He lived many years afterwards, but in a state of semi-dementia, an object of pity to those who saw him.

"The Inmans, several in number, settled near the above named creek and were plain, unpretentious farmers.

"James Steddam must have settled in Warren County, and must have died long ago. His two sons, John and Samuel, not mentioned in the Annals, settled there and became two of the most prosperous farmers in the county. They lived to good age and left behind them numerous and worthy posterity. John Crumpton, or properly Campton, and Isaac Cook appear to have settled in the adjoining county of Clinton, and, like the others, were industrious, prosperous and efficient church members.

"John Jay merits special mention, the removal of whom and family was more loss to Newberry than that of any other. He was married during the Revolution, and his seven sons and three daughters were born and, in part, married there. Courage, industry, enterprise and thrift were characteristics of the entire family. He and his sons were remarkable for rearing and training horses. No other seven brothers drove as many fair horse teams as they; could crack their whips as loud and haul as heavy loads. In those early days grain, flour, pork and merchandise were transported on wagons and often long trips had to be made. Their names were Jesse, Samuel, Walt D. (always called Denny), Thomas, John, William and James. All lived to advanced age except Thomas, who died soon after the birth of his fourth child. Five of them lived on lands adjoining and reared such families that they long had the name of the 'Jay Settlement,' a name that carried with it the idea of industry, enterprise, success and independent fortune, coupled with such honesty, probity and morality as made them a blessing to the country. John, the father, died in their midst in or about 1828, having lived to see his good example followed by both his sons and daughters, all retaining their rights in church and some being pre-eminent in it. Walter Denny, the third son, was a most remarkable man. One who knew phrenology said he had a head much like that of Napoleon Bonaparte, and in many traits he resembled him. In planning and carrying on difficult enterprises he showed large combination and concentration, qualities essential for a general. He also showed indomitable courage with prudence, hardly knowing what fear of men was. These, together with great activity and push, which made him succeed in his enterprises, would have made him a formidable leader of armies had he turned his mind that way. Indeed, he was past middle life before, as he himself said, he had been completely changed from a state of nature to one of grace. A part of his sons attained to eminence in the college and pulpit. He was the first man that refused to furnish whiskey at his log-rollings, having seen evil grow out of it. And when some of his invited neighbors told him that they would not help him without it, he replied, 'They might stay away, for he and his horses would try to do the rolling without them.' So they had to succumb.

"In the year 1850, after an absence of forty-seven years from Newberry, he, together with this writer, returned to it. He sought out the few of his old acquaintance living. Amongst these was Judge O'Neall, who, though a number of years his junior, had gone to the same school taught by John B. Mitchell and Richard Clegg. They had a long, pleasant talk over the scenes of their early days and other matters, during which Denny asked the Judge this question: 'Does thee remember when thee and my brother Sam spent nearly all an afternoon in trying to divide twelve by four, and then didn't get it done?' The Judge, who was then quite a boy, and who, like brother Sam, was a tyro in figures, did not remember it. O'Neall, like many others when divested of official robes, exhibited that vein of humor and facetiousness to his old schoolmates which runs through much of his writings. He told of two tom-cats that fought over the mouth of a poorly covered dry-well and both fell into it. The owner of the well descended to help them out; but the belligerent felines not only resented his proffered help, but ran repeatedly up its sides, falling back upon his neck and shoulders, scratching him severely. He quickly got out of the well, but how the cats escaped I did not learn. Another story he told, which, if comical, was almost tragical. A warlike family of many years back, perhaps the Jess Dorvis one, of which I've heard my father tell, often had family battles, the father leading one side, the mother on the other and the children dividing. One day, after a set-to in which, as usual, they were only bruised and blood-stained, the chivalrous husband proposed that they finish after the manner of 'the honorable code.' 'You take this gun,' said he, 'and I'll take that; you get behind this post; I will get behind that yonder, and we will shoot whenever one of us can see enough of the other.' The wife agreed; they took their places, and when she peeped around the post her husband fired and she fell. He and the boys promptly dug a grave, but when they went to take her to it they found she had risen and gone into the house. To ease their disappointment the father said, 'Never mind, boys; I'll fetch her sure next time.' She was wounded near the eye, but not fatally. The Judge told this with such an air of *nonchalance* that even old Quaker Denny was almost amused by it. Denny, while at Newberry, also made visits to his old church sisters, the widows Hawkins and Pugh, the latter being seventy-five years old and eleven years his senior. These, with Nancy O'Neall, whom he also visited, were the only survivors who attended Bush River meetings when he did. He and myself were guests of L. J. Jones the most of the time when at Newberry; and perhaps L. J. Jones and his lady may remember how, to show his activity, he would skip upon their porch floor, letting himself clear down on one foot with the other thrust out; then, rising half way up, would reverse them and sink upon the other, continuing the exercise until he had set them all to laughing. This feat I have never seen performed by any other one. In Ohio those who saw it called it the Quaker dance. He could take a wagon whip, throw himself on his back, or spring astride of the ridge-pole of his wagon, and crack it round his head, following the tune of 'Yankee Doodle.' We may well suppose his horses knew what the cracking of his whip meant. It was said that he could come nearer hitting all four of them at once than any other teamster, and his team never failed to pull its best when he required it. Though his business brought him often in the company of rude and immoral men, his candor and courage preserved him from imposition. Once when a bullying fellow threatened to whip him he replied, it is said, 'Well, if thee will whip me thee must, but I'll keep the mosquitoes from thee while thee's at it.' That was enough; the man let him alone. He had been a most incessant laborer, and it might almost have been said of him, as the poet said of Charles XII. of Sweden :

> "'A frame of adamant, a soul of fire ;
> No dangers fright him and no labors tire.'

Not the fire of unhallowed ambition and war, but the baptismal fire of the Prince of Peace. Highly conscientious, he never swerved from walking in the path of apparent duty; he never departed from plain apparel or language; and whatever enterprise of a public nature received his sanction also received his support. His vigor at the time of his Newberry visit, though he was sixty four years old, was such that, though he walked all day, ascending and descending the mountains, he was not weary. He had given up labor shortly before that time and after his return to Ohio lived at his ease, often visiting other meetings until his death, which happened near 1870. Though he had more of Luther's firmness than Melancthon's mildness, he was well fitted to accomplish what he did during a life of over eighty years. That he had faults, is true; and who has not? But they were nearly hidden by his virtues, and I feel warranted in saying that I would have trusted his word, his honesty, probity and reliability as far as those of any man I ever knew. I admire him as a man the like of whom I never saw before and will never see again; not seeking

"'The boast of heraldry, and the pomp of power,'
* * * * * *
But 'down the sequestered vale of private life
Pursuing the noiseless tenor of his way.'

Such was Walter Denny Jay, an honor to Newberry, his native county, and to Miami, his adopted one. Well might we inscribe upon his tombstone:

"'Requiescat in pace!'

"Thomas and Isaac Hasket left Newberry during or about 1806. They were carpenters, as Hugh O'Neall informed me, and built the Bush River meeting-house in 1798. Thomas, of whom I knew but little, went to Indiana, but Isaac to Ohio. He was born in 1778, married at Newberry, and took his wife, Rebecca Evans, and their first child to Miami County on horseback. He was a large and strong man, but very modest and diffident. One anecdote of him shows that, though a serious young man, he could be jocular. One morning while at mill, perhaps Hugh O'Neall's, he was standing by an out-door fire, when David Jones, uncle to L. J. Jones, and myself, came also to the fire. In crossing the mill-pond he had fallen into it and was dripping wet. Wishing to be funny and make the best of it, he said to Isaac, 'Mr. Hasket, you see, I'm a Baptist; but I suppose you're a Quaker.' 'Yes,' said Isaac, 'I believe in going to the fire this cool morning, but thee believes in going into the water.' Friend Hasket, young and sturdy, went to work with his axe, felled the forest, and soon had fields in cultivation. He helped to build the West Branch Quarterly meeting-house in 1808, just twenty years after building the one at Bush River. The West Branch house, built of brick, by the Newberry Friends mainly, still stands, having been lately renovated, while the parent one, I learn much to my regret, has been demolished. Friend Hasket prospered, and reared five stalwart sons, none of whom ever thought of being broken down at a handspike lift. He was a very worthy and upright man, respected by all who knew him. He died in 1848.

"Thomas Pearson, following Hasket, has already been written about. The two Enoch Pearsons next mentioned were born in 1760 and 1761. One was the son of Thomas, the other was his nephew. They brought, or came with, many children, not one of whom is living. Three other Enochs came, which, with one born here, made six. They were designated thus: Preacher Enoch, Blacksmith Enoch, Lame Enoch, Pony Enoch, Nuck Enoch and Teent Enoch. All are now dead. Preacher Enoch was a man of high standing, both at Newberry and West Branch. He was a son of Thomas. He visited as minister once, if not more, North Carolina yearly meeting and the remnant of Bush River Friends. He traveled much. His sons, Robert, Thomas and Isaac, were worthy and useful men. He died in 1850, and the Blacksmith in 1860.

"Of the Thomases who emigrated, several are not mentioned. They were Abel, Isaac, John, William and Nehemiah. They came with considerable families and formed a settlement for a while called Thomastown. They were plain, modest, clever and moderately successful farmers, which about comprises their history. The same may be said of the Duncans, who came here with them, who died in early times, not leaving many children.

"The elder David Jenkins, next mentioned, was the man to whom my father, Elisha Jones, an orphan nine years old, was apprenticed in 1795. Baal Butler, a Quaker of some note, was the guardian who bound him until his eighteenth year.

"Barclay Benham and another Friend with two initials, B. D., in his name, seem to have escaped the author of the Annals. Their descendants are in Indiana, Clinton County and elsewhere, so I know but little about them. It was said that David found a joint-snake at Newberry which, on being switched, flew to pieces, afterwards becoming united. The present inhabitants ought to know if such an incredible thing ever happens there.* David removed to Ohio with Elisha Jones in 1805, who, though out of his apprenticeship, had continued with him and learned the chairmaker's trade. Settling with his family near the Great Miami, he cleared a farm, where he died nearly forty years afterwards. David Jenkins, Jr., went to Ohio a young man full of expectation and promise. He became school teacher and magistrate, holding the last position, I believe, until his death. He twice at least returned to Newberry, the last time during the winter of 1839. His long continuance in office made him about as good a judge of law as the Troy attorney, and his decisions were seldom reversed. He was so useful in his township that the people could hardly do without him. His death occurred many years ago, but at what time I have not learned.

"Two Wallace Joneses, father and son, emigrated from Newberry about the year 1806. The son was born in 1773, but the time of the father's birth I cannot learn. The most that need be said of him is, that he reared a family and died in 1823. Wallace, Jr., possessed much skill and courage. Not born a Friend, he was in early life not governed by their principles, and so at times violated one command of the Decalogue. One night when at a neighbor's where he should not have been, the wronged husband unexpectedly came upon him. While the man was jerking down his gun the guilty one rushed into the yard, hurrying across it. The man fired, but, it being dark, missed him. Wallace, fearing nothing but the loaded gun, now empty, turned round and coolly said: 'You are a d——d poor marksman when you can't hit a man ten steps off.' It is not reported that he stayed till the gun was reloaded, nor that he went there afterwards. He became a military officer, and continued such until he emigrated, when he took his uniform with him. His four sons and two daughters were nearly all, if not quite, born in the district, which some of them remembered. Being a carpenter and mechanic in wood, his services were sought after and he did well at his

---

* NOTE.—The compiler of these Annals when he was a boy often heard such stories told of the joint-snake, but the stories were never true. The joint-snake, poor fellow, is like other snakes. If he is ever broken up into two or more pieces, he never becomes whole again.

trade. His wife, the daughter of James Patty, was a mild, forbearing Quaker, and her influence, together with that of her neighbors, caused him to become seriously concerned for himself, and he at length applied to the Friends for membership among them. They, according to custom, appointed a committee to visit, learn the sincerity of his heart, and report accordingly. During their conference they asked him what he had done with his uniform. Forgetting himself, he answered, in his old strain, 'I've sold it to Sam Edwards (his Newberry nephew), and I reckon he thinks he'll play h—l with it.' Whether the committee smiled or frowned at this expression I am not informed; but they reported favorably. He was accepted as a member, becoming a very consistent and useful one. His brusqueness and comicality, however, never entirely left him. Once, after reading at West Branch church a marriage certificate which was to be signed only by the groom and bride, he forgot to read the one to be afterwards signed by the witnesses. Discovering his mistake, he exclaimed: 'I'll be whipped if I haint forgot the last of it!" and then read it amidst the tittering of the large congregation. After sitting down with the married couple, together with a large number of guests, to a sumptuous repast, and thinking there was useless delay in giving the signal to 'fall to,' he exclaimed: 'I wish somebody would tell us to go to eatin', for I am tired of settin' idle so long.' This provoked another titter, but every one knew what allowance to make for Uncle Wallace. We went back to his native Newberry, I think, in 1836, but found only few of his old neighbors and acquaintances living. Returning to Ohio, he lived until, I think, 1854, when he peacefully passed away, having, notwithstanding a few peculiarities, lived a very correct, useful and conscientious life. His second son, John, born in 1798, became when young a minister of some note and traveled in other lands. During 1831 he returned with an approving mission to Newberry, where at Bush River meeting-house (where he had gone when quite a child) he preached to a large congregation of willing listeners. Judge O'Neall, who remembered him of old, I learned, attended his meeting, and after its close invited him to his house. Seeing John's timid hesitancy, the Judge became earnest and told him he would almost consider it an 'open affront' if he did not go home with him.

This expression caused compliance, and no doubt the visit was mutually satisfactory. John traveled considerably in the ministry after that trip, removing to Missouri long afterwards, where a few years ago he died. A grandson of his elder brother, Philemon, is an active surveyor and lawyer, being now prosecuting attorney of Miami County.

"I must not omit to write of Samuel Reagan, called Blacksmith Sammy by way of distinction from younger ones of that name. He came here, I think, in 1806, with five sons and one daughter. Four sons were born in this county, in all nine, who grew up to respectability and married here. Only three and his daughter Rachel, who married Isaac Pearson of Newberry, retained their rights among the Friends. Samuel bought and settled on good land, having a large spring, on which he cleared a large farm and raised an abundance of fruits, particularly cherries. He was a most skillful and useful mechanic in both iron and wood, not ceasing work until compelled by age. Regular in attendance at meeting, he was almost as regular in nodding, if not sleeping, when there, attributable, perhaps, to his almost ceaseless activity. The time of his death I know not, though it happened many years ago.

"Tanner Thompson, the leather man, I think came here and died a great many years ago. I knew several of his sons, but their lives do not warrant particular notice.

"I have given a short biography of those of whom I had personal knowledge, mentioned on pages 31 and 32 of the Annals, besides some not mentioned there. On page 33 first comes the name of Joseph Furnas. Perhaps he was the father of Robert and Thomas W. Furnas, whom I well knew and who emigrated from Newberry with a considerable number of children. The old man must have died not long after his emigration. He must have had other sons whom I never knew, for there is a long list of Furnases, all related. A granddaughter, Sarah, traveled in Egypt, Palestine, and about all the countries of note in the old and new worlds. A short time ago she published at West Milton her 'Ten Years' Travel,' as interesting a work of its kind as I have ever read. Robert Furnas lived in Warren County, dying there many years ago a plain old Quaker; while his brother Thomas W. lost his right, became a politician, and was several times sheriff of Miami County.

He had a wonerfully active son, perhaps the most fleet-footed man in the country. His son Robert, I have heard, went to California* and became its governor.

"John Furnas, born at Newberry in 1798, became wealthy, reared a numerous family, did much public business, besides going to the Legislature. A man of irreproachable life, and member of the Christian Church, he was in the fullness of his years not very long ago gathered in the garner of the great hereafter as a shock of corn fully ripe. The few Furnases of whom I have written may serve as specimens of the race; a race of whom the present inhabitants of Newberry need never feel ashamed. The Kellys and Kirks, I think, settled in other counties, and little is known about them.

"Samuel Gauntt never came here. James Brooks I think I mentioned before. Of the O'Nealls I have seen John and Henry many years ago living among my Newberry relatives in Green County, Indiana. John was a plain old Quaker professor, but Henry seemed to be more of a politician than churchman. Thomas taught school in Miami County nearly seventy years ago. His wife, the daughter of old Thomas Pearson heretofore mentioned, died about that time, which caused the breaking up of his family. When and where he died I know not.

"Of the women who emigrated to Ohio mentioned in the Annals on pages 33 and 34 I have already written. One sister of Charity Cook and Susannah Hollingsworth, named Kesiah and not mentioned, deserves to be. She was born in 1763 and married a man named Hanks. After becoming the mother of three sons and two daughters her husband died leaving to her the support of their minor children. She brought them to Ohio with her relatives, among whom they were divided until maturity. The eldest daughter, Mary, became a woman of uncommon sense and ability. Coming to the wilderness at the age of fourteen she soon accustomed herself to all its conditions, making the best of whatever happened to her. While living with her uncle, Big Isaac Hollingsworth, she learned the art of making corn mush, which I think needs no describing. It was said that when her uncle found a lump of dry meal in his mush encrusted in a covering of dough, he would take it in his spoon and dash it across

---

* Nebraska, instead of California.—[J. A. C.]

the table at her, which, if it hit her on the face, was not pleasant. Remonstrance she knew was useless, as the old man was immovable in his way of thinking and doing. So her only remedy was to stir the mush better in the future. In after life she was a very useful member in the female part of the Friends Church, who, as my readers may not know, had a department to themselves. She died in Iowa a few years ago. Her brother, James, was born in 1796, and was about ten years old at the time of their removal. He had uncommon mental ability, easily became a scholar and school teacher. He learned trigonometry and became one of the most efficient surveyors in Miami County. Liking the employment he followed it until age rendered its abandonment necessary. His conversation was always moral, instructive and entertaining. He possessed the philosophy of contentment and was satisfied with the realization of Agar's prayer, 'Give me neither poverty nor riches,' etc. If he had possessed the energy and push of some of the Newberry emigrants he would have made his mark in the world. But these he had not, and made what the world calls a failure; but perhaps stands as high in the estimation of his Maker as though he had filled great earthly positions. He died several years ago in Iowa. His brothers and other sister need no particular notice.

"There were many Halls and Pennys went from Newberry; also Barrets, Elmores, Laytons, Campbells and others, of whom some were very worthy, but need not further notice.

"The school teachers who taught the Ohio emigrants must next be noticed. They were Richard Clegg, John B. Mitchell and James Howe. I have often heard my father speak of going to Richard Clegg's school in Newberry District. From his description and that of others I infer that he in part answered the description given of one in Goldsmith's Deserted Village:

" 'A man severe he was and stern to view.
* * * * * *
Well had the boding tremblers learned to trace
The day's disasters in his morning face.'

An Englishman with native domineering spirit, to which intemperance was added, one could hardly have expected him to be much different from what he was. The previous history of this man is given in a book called The Permanent Documents, pages 128, 129 and 130. It is the seventh chapter of the 'Drunkard's Looking Glass' written by Judge O'Neall, who kindly gave me the volume when at his home. He, Richard Clegg, reached Ohio, I think, not far from 1819, though I've no certain account. He resumed his old practice of school teaching and continued it till age compelled its abandonment. One remarkable thing is, that he taught in Ohio some of the children whose parents he had taught in South Carolina. Not one remembers him with reverence. Stern and irritable they feared but loved him not. It is said that he once when old fell asleep in his chair when a coal of fire was laid upon his head. When wakened by its burning not a scholar would tell who did it and Poor Richard had to bear it. It does not appear that he drank much liquor here, perhaps because hard to get, or perhaps because forbidden by his employers. He died in poverty more than fifty years ago, and his silly wife, Creese or Creesy, went to the poor house where in blindness she died. Richard is represented as having married this silly woman while he was silly from the effects of liquor, and however much he regretted it he could not undo it when sober. Their children partook somewhat of their mother's silliness and their father's improvidence, though not of his intemperance, and never amounted to much. Such are some of the fruits of intemperance. Richard has wealthy and respectable relatives in Dayton who avoided the rock on which he split.

"John B. Mitchell also taught many of the Newberry people who came to Ohio. I remember in my youth seeing a long well written manuscript, which my father told me was written by Mitchell for him. It was called the 'Advantages and the Disadvantages of the Married State.' I did not learn that Mitchell was its author. It was an Allegory, the scenes of which were laid in ancient days, old Babylon being mentioned in it. His concluding advice, beginning with 'From thy old friend John B. Mitchell,' showed him to be a man of fine thoughts and profound religious convictions, which, with his learning, made him a proper instructor for young people.

"It appears that James Howe taught a school or two here as far back as 1808 or 1809. I have seen a birth record, of my parents married here in 1806 and their eldest child born here in 1807, of incomparable beauty of penmanship. I was told this writing was done by James Howe, and as the next birth of 1809 was not his writing it would seem that he soon returned to Newberry where he died.

"In closing these brief memoirs of the emigrants from Newberry, far the most of whom I knew personally, besides a great many more not mentioned, I must say with sorrow that but one of those early emigrants is living. This one is Benjamin Pearson, born in 1805 and brought here in 1808. He is bowed with age, and only remembers crossing the Ohio on the way here. Those heroic adventurers left the balmy South, the land of the chestnut, the cedar and the pine; crossed the Alleghanies and entered the 'dark mephitic, tangled woods' of the far-off Northwest, whose giant oak, towering hickory, majestic walnut, spreading beech and lofty poplar, &c., frowned upon them and seemed to forbid their ingress. But with heads to plan and hands to execute, the forests disappeared, the wild beasts fled, waving fields of grain arose, dwelling houses, churches, villages and towns were built, all by the courage, industry, skill and labor of the brave people of the South. Should the question be asked, what county or district in the United States has furnished the most men, women and children to people the great Northwest? the answer must come from all the knowing ones that to Newberry District, South Carolina, belongs this great honor.

"DAVID JONES.

"WEST MILTON, OHIO, August, 1889."

I well remember the John B. Mitchell mentioned by Mr. Jones in the foregoing. He moved into Edgefield County, where he lived to be quite an old man. He was a Methodist and a local preacher, and I used to see him at Zoar church at love feasts and class meetings, for in my boyhood the class meeting was a regular institution of the church, and should be yet, I think. The last time I remember to have seen Mr. Mitchell was at a Baptist camp meeting at Mount Enon, where he preached and related some remarkable experiences he had then recently had. In a dream or a vision he thought he had passed into the other world, where he saw many of his old friends and neighbors; some in the good world and some in the other, and some in neither, but midway between the two, seemingly hesitating as to which they should at last gravitate.

This camp meeting was held some time between 1835 and 1840, but in what year I do not remember. But I very well remember seeing a young man, who had been at school at Mount Enon with me in 1835 and 1836, but was then in the South Carolina College, parade the camp ground, dressed in old style, with knee-breeches, silk stockings, with buckles in his shoes and ribbons and buckles at his knees, and coat and vest of the antique Revolutionary cut. His father was a staid, well-to-do farmer who lived near by, a member of the church, and you can well imagine how supremely disgusted he was at the exhibition.

Mr. Mitchell died not a great while afterwards, probably in that same year. He was then very feeble, both in mind and body. After a long and useful life he quietly fell asleep. His remains lie buried, I think, but I am not sure, at Zoar church. He has descendants, great-great-grandchildren, now living in that neighborhood, in Edgefield, and others in Georgia, mostly Methodists.

In regard to the O'Neall family I am able to give the following additional information which I learn from a letter received from G. T. O'Neall, of Waynesville, Ohio, written October 2, 1889.

Henry O'Neall, a native of Newberry, was the father of fourteen children, twelve of whom lived to rear families. One of his daughters, Rhoda, married Lewis Chapman, youngest son of Rev. Giles Chapman, and was living in Missouri in the year 1884, in her 82nd year. Elizabeth married John Bays, and was living in Warren County, Illinois, in her 72nd year; and Rebecca, who married Jno. T. B———, was living at the same time near Newberry, Indiana, in her 64th year. These are all the children of Henry O'Neall who were living at the above date.

The Hon. John H. O'Neall is the son of Henry Miles O'Neall, and the grandson of Henry, and was born near Newberry, S. C. He and his sisters were left orphans at an early age, and he became the ward of Judge John Belton O'Neall. About 1840 his grandfather Henry removed both him and his sisters to Southern Indiana, Davis County, where he has since remained. He is a lawyer and politician of prominence, was a member of the last Congress, and was, I think, re-elected last fall.

Quaker Records
from Hinshaw's
Encyclopedia of American
Quaker Genealogy

BUSH RIVER MONTHLY MEETING
Newberry County, South Carolina

During the last half of the eighteenth century four principal centers of Quakerism arose in South Carolina and one in Georgia. These were in Kershaw, Marlborough, Newberry and Union Counties, South Carolina, and in Columbia (now McDuffie) County, Georgia. The earliest of these settlements appears to have been in Kershaw County, S. C., about 1750. Fredericksburg Monthly Meeting, also called Wateree, was set up in this county about 1755 or earlier. The monthly meeting was laid down about 1782, and the meetings for worship disappeared not long afterward. No records of Fredericksburg Monthly Meeting are known to be in existence.

Bush River Monthly Meeting, in Newberry County, S. C., was established in 1770; Wrightsborough Monthly Meeting, in Georgia, 1773; Cane Creek Monthly Meeting, in Union County, S. C., 1799; Piney Grove Monthly Meeting, in Marlborough County, S. C., 1802.

Bush River Meeting was located in Newberry County, in the west-central part of South Carolina. Dr. Stephen B. Weeks in "Southern Quakers and Slavery", page 115, says: "The group of meetings clustering around Bush River was the most important in South Carolina. The origin of this meeting and the time it began cannot be discovered. William Coate was living near Bush River before 1762, and Samuel Kelly, a native of Kings's County, Ireland, removed to Newberry County, from Camden, in 1762. Other early Quaker settlers were John Furnas, David Jenkins, Benjamin and William Pearson. Robert Evans came from Camden, probably between 1762 and 1769."

In 1770 a committee appointed by Western Quarterly Meeting to visit Friends at Bush River Meeting in South Carolina recommended that a monthly meeting be settled there. This recommendation was approved by the Quarterly Meeting in 11th month, 1770, but the records seem to indicate that the new monthly meeting was not actually held until 4th month, 1772. Meetings for worship which are mentioned as reporting to Bush River Monthly Meeting include Bush River, Raburn's Creek, Tiger River, Padget's Creek, Mud Lick, Allwoods', White Lick, Edisto, Charleston and Rocky Springs.

Early members of Bush River Meeting (names taken from the first pages of the minutes), in addition to those mentioned by Dr. Weeks, included Jacob Chandler, Samuel Chapman, Eli Cook, Isaac Cook, William Cooper, Enos Elleman, Moses Embree, Robert Evans, Armil Fincher, Nathan Hawkins, James Haworth, Richard Henderson, Elias Hollingsworth, Isaac Hollingsworth, William Hollingsworth, John Jones, Robert Merrick, Henry Millhouse, David Mote, David Mote, Jr., William Neal, John Nelson, Samuel Nelson, Enoch Pearson, Samuel Pearson, William Pemberton, Peter Ruble, David Smith, Henry Stedham, Jonathan Taylor, William Wright.

About 1802, moved by a desire to live in a country where no slaves were held, Friends of Bush River began a migration to Ohio. Between 1802 and 1807 more than one hundred certificates of removal were issued, most of them being for families. This so depleted the membership that the monthly meeting seems to have been all but abandoned in 1808, though not formally laid down until 1822. A minute of Bush River Monthly Meeting, 1806,6,28, states that the Yearly Meeting "advises the Trustees, James Brooks, Samuel Brown, Isaac Kirk and John O'Neal, to sell or lease Bush River meeting house and lot, Rocky Spring meeting house and lot, and a meeting house lot at Camden."

In 1809 the few remaining members of Bush River and Cane Creek Monthly Meetings were joined to New Garden Monthly Meeting by order of New Garden Quarterly Meeting. The same procedure appears to have been followed as to Wrightsborough. The minutes of New Garden Monthly Meeting relating to the former members of Bush River, Cane Creek and Wrightsborough Monthly Meetings are quoted below because it has not been possible, in all cases, to separate them and assign each item to the proper meeting.

1809, 6,24. "Extracts from New Garden Quarterly Meeting, 1808,12,10 and 1809,3,10. Friends appointed to visit friends in South Carolina report about 130 members as follows. Cane Creek, Union District: Richard Cox and wife, Ann, and children, Rebeckah, David, Peter, John, Isaac, Richard and William; Isaac Hawkins and children, Jonathan and Phebe; Dinah, Isaac Enoch, Ann and Martha Hollingsworth. Bush River, Newberry District: Ann Herbert, Sr.; Isaac Kirk and wife, Rebekah, and children,

Ann Jenkins, Lydia Jenkins, Rebekah Jenkins, Isaac Jenkins and Phebe Kirk; James Brooks and children, David Singleterry, Daniel Offley and Martha; Phebe Pearson, widow; Rebekah Hawkins; Martha Knight; William Wright and wife, Mary, and children, Nathan, Sarah and Rachel; Hugh O'Neal and wife, Ann, and children, John Belton, Abigail, Rebekah, Hannah and Sarah; Rachel Coats; Sarah and Elizabeth Curl; Sarah Campbell; John O'Neal and wife, Hephziba, and children, Priscilla, Hannaueel, Mark. Achsah, Cary and Hiram; James Jay and wife, Jemimah, and children, Mills, Alexander, Mary, Rhoda, Layton, James, Ede (Edith), Dempsey, Isaac and Sarah; Lydia Herbert and children, Esther, Ann, Eleanor, Martha, Jobe and Lydia; William and David Miles; James Gilbreath (tanner) and wife, Charity, and daughter, Lydia; Hannah Pearson and children, Powel, Robert and Susanna; Ann Herbert and children, Hannah, Isaac, William and Peter; William, Rhoda and John Foster, children of Henry O'Neal; James, Jr. and John Gilbreath; Benjamin Weeks and wife, Abigail, and children, Susanna, Mary, Hannah, Clary, Abigail and Caron Happock; Robert Evans and wife, Caron Happock, and child, Abigail; Lydia Spears and children, Robert, Mary, Isaac and Moses Evans; Samuel Guant and wife, Susanna, and children, Samuel Kelly, Charles, Publias and Malichi; Hannah and John Kelly; Rebekah Elmore; Wm. Pugh and daughter, Hannah; Thomas O'Neal (now of Union Dist.) and wife, Sarah, and children, Mary, Rebekah and Robert; Sary Longshore and children, Sarah and Clyde. "Whose names we have taken and they request to be joined to New Garden Monthly Meeting and we think their situation will require some further care; with which this meeting unites. Extracted from minutes by Barnabas Coffin, Clerk."
"Some friends formerly belonging to Wrightsborough and Cane Creek Monthly Meetings request certificates to Miami Monthly Meeting and West Branch Monthly Meeting, Ohil. Friends appointed to produce them to next meeting."
1809, 7,29. Certificates signed for the following:
To Miami Monthly Meeting, Ohio: Richard Thompson; Thomas Hart; Elijah Mendenhall and wife; Martha, and daughter, Ann;

Isaac Thomson; Phinehas Hart; Mary Stubs; Esther Green and children, Jesse, Hannah and Amos.
To West Branch Monthly Meeting, Ohio: Bales Butler and wife and children, Samuel, Susanna, William and Mary; Susanna Butler.
1809. 8,26. Certificates signed for the following members of Wrightsborough and Bush River:
To Miami Monthly Meeting Ohio: William Hollingsworth; Richard Moore; David Jay; Joseph Hollingsworth; Exile Pearson; Dempsey Moore; Charity Killey; Susannah Henderson; Ann Williams; Elizabeth Brooks.

A few additional minutes, mostly disownments, relating to Bush River Friends between 1809 and 1818 will be found in the New Garden records. Fragmentary minutes in the Bush River book, covering the years 1819 and 1820, indicated an attempt to revive Bush River Monthly Meeting at that time. The attempt met with little success and the meeting was finally laid down about 1822 and the remaining members were attached to Springfield Monthly Meeting. The Springfield minutes recording this transfer are as follows:
1822, 5, 8. (Men's Minutes). The monthly meeting at Bush River being laid down, this meeting is informed that it is the request of the members of that preparative meeting to become members at Springfield M.M. which request this meeting grants and receives them accordingly; names are as follows: High O'Neal, Isaac Jenkins, James Galbreth, Isaac Evans, Isaac Harbert, William Harbert, Peter Herbert, William O'Neal, Samuel Speer, William Wright, Nathan Wright, John Mills Wright, James Anderson Wright, Timothy Pugh, Moses Evans, Cornealy M. Evans.
1822, 6, 5. (women's minutes). Bush River Monthly Meeting being laid down, the members requ4st to be joined to Springfield, viz: Sarah O'Neal, Lydia Gilbreath, Mary Evans, Rebekah Kirk, Phebe Kirk, Rebecca Jenkins, Margaret Dunken, Ann Herbert, Martha Wright, Rebekah Hawkins, Hannah Palmer, Elizabeth Carle, Rebecka Elmore, Martha Brooks, Lydia Speer, Hannah Hunt, Mary Wright, Sarah Wright, Rachel Wright, Sophia Wright, Sarah Pugh, Hannah Pugh, Catharine Pugh, Casander Pugh, Nancy Pugh, Ruth Pugh, Elizabeth Pugh, Keranhappuck Evans, Abigail K. Evans, Sophia M. Evans, Rebecca C. Evans.
The records books of Bush River Monthly Meeting, from which the following abstract has been compiled, consist of one volume of birth and death records, two volumes of marriage records; four volumes of

men's minutes (1772-1820), and one volume of women's minutes (1791-1801).

BIRTH AND DEATH RECORDS

Page 20.
John Addington
Mary Addington d. 4-25-1774.
Ch: William b. 4-14-1770.
    Alice " 3- 8-1773.
Elizabeth Addington, 2nd w. John
Ch: Joseph b. 7-21-1776.
    John   " 10-13-1777.
    Thomas " 12- 1-1778.
    Mary   " 11- 2-1780.
    Sarah   " 9-12-1783.

Page 48.
James Ballinger
Lydia Ballinger
Ch: Hannah   b. 11-29-1762.
    Isaac   "   4-14-1764.
    Jacob   " 12- 1-1765.
    Josiah   " 11-24-1767.
    Mary   "   5-21-1769.
    James   "   8-21-1771.
    Jonathan "   6- 7-1773.
    Lydia   "   2- 3-1775.
    Ann   "   2- 8-1777.
    Evan   " 11-23-1778.
    John   "   3-31-1781.
    Isaac & Sarah b. 3-27-1783.

Page 7.
Richard Battin
Catharine Battin
Ch: Ann   b. 12- 4-1776.
    James   " 12-19-1778.
    Richard   "   4-17-1781.
    John   "   8-28-1783.
    Catharine " 10- 2-1785.
    Jonathan " 12-25-1787.

Page 44.
Charles Bridges
Ede Bridges
Ch: John   b. 2-10-1779.
    William " 12- 1-1781.
    Mary   " 10-18-1783.
    Jesse   "   1- 6-1787.
    Charles d. 9-15-1796.

Page 28.
Samuel Brown
Ann Brown
Ch: Kameston b. 6-11-1772; d.
                 6-18-1774.
    Joshua   " 6-11-1774.
    Samuel   " 10-15-1777; d.
                 10-8-1778.
    Nancy   " 12-16-1779; d.
                 11-7-1781.
    Ann   " 1- 3-1782.

Page 21.
James Brooks
Sarah Brooks

James & Sarah Brooks cont'd.
Ch: Elizabeth   b. 6-24-1769.
    Susannah   " 7-17-1771.
    Joab   " 5-15-1773.
    Vashti   " 1-15-1776.
    Salla   " 3-17-1779.
    Nimrod   " 8- 9-1782.
    James   " 5- 6-1784.
    John   " 9- 1-1780.
    Mary   " 5-26-1788.
    David Singletary " 2- 9-1793.
    Daniel Ofley   " 8-15-1794.
(Last two ch. appear to be s. James
& 2nd w. Sarah, dt. David Singletary,
whom he m. 9-1-1791)
Page 4.
Sarah Brooks, w. James, d. 11-18-1789.

Page 23.
Ralph Cambbel b. 1-29-1770.
John Cambbel   " 6- 1-1772.

Page 40.
James Cammack
Joanna Cammack
Ch: Mary   b. 7-14-1775.
    Margaret " 11-16-1777.
    Ann   " 12-22-1781.
    John   " 7- 7-1789.
    James   " 4- 7-1793; d.
                    6-18-1793.
    Samuel   " 1-12-1796.
    William   " 4- 1-1797.
    Amos   " 12- 9-1798.
(Last three ch. appear to be s.
James & 2n w., Rachel Compton; their
m. rpd. 3-24-1795)

Page 5.
Joanna Carmmach d. 5-3-1793, in 35th
  yr.

Page 34.
Jacob Chandler
Alisabeth Chandler
Ch: David   b. 3-23-1759; d. at
                   about 4 weeks.
    Alisabeth " 9-19-1765.
    Jonathan " 2- 2-1768.
    Israel   " 3-25-1770.
    Gabriel   " 3-25-1772; d. 27th,
                   bur. at Bush River.
    Ann   " 12-14-1774; d. 28th.

Page 3.
Alibeth Clark, w. Henry, d. 3-30-1783.

Page 18.
John Clark
Mary Clark
Ch: Elizabeth b. 6-20-1767.
    Henry   " 3-28-1769.
    Rachel   " 9-10-1771.
    Hester   " 9- 6-1773.
    John   " 1-15-1776.
    Thomas   " 8- 1-1780.
    Mary   " 4-13-1783.
    Jonathan " 2-26-1785.

BUSH RIVER MONTHLY MEETING

Page 24.
Marmaduke Coate
Mary Coate
Ch: Esther   b. 9- 3-1766.
    Moses   "   9- 5-1768.
    Henry   "   8-18-1770.
    Samuel   "   8-28-1772.
    Sarah   " 12-11-1774.
    James   "   6-23-1777.
    William   "   1- 2-1779.
    John   "   7-19-1785.
    Jesse   "   1- 3-1788.

Page 27.
Samuel Compton
Elizabeth Compton
Ch: Rachel   b. 1-17-1764.
    William   "   5-15-1765.
    Samuel   " 12-26-1766.
    Sally   "   2-11-1769.
    Amos   "   7- 9-1770.
    John   " 12-29-1771.
    Stephen   "   8-29-1774.
    Matthew   " 12-17-1776.
    Joshua   "   5-30-1778.
    Elizabeth " 12-19-1779.
    Joseph   "   6- 8-1782.

Page 28.
Amos Cook
Elizabeth Cook
Ch: Levi   b. 11-16-1776.
    Mary   "   5-11-1779.
    John   "   7-28-1781.
    Dianah   "   2- 6-1783.
    Amos   " 10-13-1785.

Page 25.
Eli Cook
Martha Cook
Ch: Rachel   b. 10- 8-1772.
    Jonathan   "   4-17-1775.
    Eli   b.   6-21-1777;
              d.   9-28-1778.
    Mary   "   7-29-1779.
    Isaac   "   9-15-1781.

Page 14.
Isaac Cook
Charity Cook
Ch: Joseph   b. 12-23-1763.
    Sarah   "   8-22-1766.
    Rachel   "   2-29-1768.
    Thomas   "   1- 3-1770.
    Mary   "   1- 3-1772.
    Charity   "   2-24-1774.
    Ruth   "   8-25-1776.
    Wright   "   8-27-1778.
    Isaac   "   3-22-1781.
    Susannah   " 10-13-1783.

Page 24.
Isaac Cook, of neary Tygar River.
Sarah Cook (dt. William & Jean
  Smith, p. ?)
Ch: Isaac   b. 3-16-1771.
    Dinah   " 11-18-1772.
    William   " 11-20-1774.
    Rebeckah   "   2-27-1777.

Isaac & Sarah Cook cont'd.
    Olive   b. 5-28-1779.
    Ann   "   8-27-1782.
    Sarah   "   2- 9-1784.

Page 37.
Joseph Cook
Mary Cook
Ch: Ann   b. 10-13-1783.
    Isaac   "   4-24-1785; d.2-19-1803.
    Harbert"   2-11-1787; " 3-27-1807.
    Charity"   11-20-1788; " 1-21-1789.
    Rachel "   10-23-1790; "11-16-1795.
    Thomas "   9-10-1792; "11-30-1794.
    Jacob "   12-29-1794; "10-19-1795.
    John   "   2-20-1796.
    Joseph "   7-20-1799.
    Uriah "   5- 7-1800.
    Mary   "   6- 3-1803.
    Peter "   7- 1-1805.
Page 5.
Mary Cook, w. Joseph, d. 4-24-1807.

Page 47.
John Coppock
Abigail Coppock
Ch: Aaron   b. 9-20-1762.
    John   "   8-20-1766.
    Susannah   " 11-14-1769.
    Marget   " 12-20-1771.
    Abigail   "   2-28-1774.
    Mary   "   6-16-1776.
    Isaac   " 12- 2-1779.
    Ann   "   3-18-1781.
    Samuel   " 11- 1-1783.

Page 18.
Joseph Coppock
Jane Coppock
Ch: John   b. 2-14-1770.
    Thomas   "   2-20-1771.
    Benjamin   " 10-30-1772.
    Joseph   "   9-28-1774.
    Elizabeth " 11- 9-1776.
    William   "   3-29-1779; d.
                              10-26-1782.
    Margarett "   5-10-1781.
    Jane   "   2- 9-1784.

Page 35.
Richard Cox
Anna Cox
Ch: Thomas   b. 5-13-1775.
    Mary   "   2-14-1777.
    Rebeckah   "   1-18-1780.
    Tamer   "   5-15-1782.
Page 3.
Mary Cox, w. Thomas, d. 1-17-1784.

Page 39.
Samuel Duncan
Mary Duncan
Ch: Amelia   b. 2- 6-1777.
    Jesse   "   5-31-1778.
    Samuel   "   1- 6-1780.
    Enos   "   2-16-1782.
    Sary   "   4- 2-1784.
    Joshua   " 10-16-1785.

BUSH RIVER MONTHLY MEETING

Page 3.
Hester Edmundson, w. Caleb, d. 5-28-1783.

Page 10.
Enos Elliman
Catharine Elliman
Ch: Elizabeth b. 9-26-1758, Orange Co., N.C.
    Emme b. 5-15-1760, Orange Co., N.C.
    Hannah b. 2-8-1762, Orange Co., N.C.
    Mary b. 12-27-1763, Orange Co., N.C.
    John b. 4-17-1766, Orange Co., N.C.
    William b. 7-10-1769, Orange Co., N.C.

Page 4.
Enos Eleman d. 4-18-1787, in 55th yr., bur. Bush River.
Catharine Elleman, w. Enos, d. 11----1789, in 65th yr.)

Page 2.
John Elliman, Sr. d. 9-5-1775, aged 79 yrs., 3 mos.)

Page 4.
Mary Eleman d. 4-29-1787 in 80th yr., bur. 30th in Bush River Bur. Gr.

Page 31.
William Elmor
Abigail Elmor
Ch: Charity b. 12-14-1754; d. 3-6-1776.
    John " 3-8-1756.
    Sarah " 12-9-1757.
    Stephen " 5-31-1762.
    Mary " 7-15-1764.
    Rachel " 4-27-1766.
    Ridgeway " 3-5-1770.
    Joseph " 3-22-1772.
    David " 3-25-1774; d. & br. same day.

Page 17.
John Embree
Mary Embree
Ch: Sarah b. 12-27-1753.
    Rachel " 12-24-1756.
    Lydia " 2-10-1759.
    Jesse " 6-6-1761.
    Jonathan " 3-20-1764.
    Amos " 12-20-1766.
    Mary " 5-27-1769.
    John " 2-10-1772.

Page 6.
Moses Embree
Margaret Embree
Ch: Mary b. 5-15-1753.
    Thomas " 7-31-1755.
    John " 12-9-1757.
    Evan " 3-16-1760.
    Isaac " 6-24-1762.
    Sarah " 3-31-1767.
    Jacob " 10-17-1769.

Moses & Margaret Embree cont'd.
    Rebekah b. 1-13-1773.

Page 26.
Robert Evans
Rebeckah Evans
Ch: Ann b. 8-18-1763, about 6 AM
    Martha " 5-19-1766, " 11 PM
    Mary " 7-11-1768, " 5 AM
    Moses " 10-3-1770, " 6 AM
    Joseph " 1-11-1773, " 5 AM
    Margarett b. 5-13-1775. " 8 PM; d. 8-12-1777, bur. 13th,
    Sarah " 9-22-1777, about 4 PM
    Rebeckah " 7-2-1780, " 4 AM
    Robert "12-8-1783.

Page 3.
Robert Evans d. 3-4-1784, aged above 40 yrs., bur in Friends Bur. Gr. at Bush River.

Page 6.
Armel Fincher
Rebekah Fincher
Ch: Elizabeth b. 11-24-1759.
    Francis " 10-28-1765.
    Hester " 1-13-1772.
    Rebekah " 6-25-1774.

Page 12.
John Furnace b. 3-5-1736, Standing Stone, Old Ingland.
Mary Furnace, b. 9-19-1742, Nigton in Cumberland, Old England. married 3-24-1762, at Nigton Mtg.
Ch: Joseph b. 2-20-1763.
    Rebecah " 4-19-1764.
    John " 8-5-1765.
    Thomas " 3-23-1768.
    Esther " 7-4-1770.
    Robert " 6-27-1772.
    William " 5-29-1775.

Page 3.
Mary Gaunt, w. Zebulon, form. w. John Kelly, d. 5-9-1782, aged 47 yrs.

Page 11.
Jonathan Gilbert
Hanameel Gilbert
Ch: Cary b. 3-15-1766.
    Benjamin " 2-22-1769.
    Beulah " 9-8-1772.
    Hepsbah " 9-24-1774.
    Achsah " 2-21-1780.
    Jonathan " 2-21-1782; d. 1782.
    Mary Pearson " 2-4-1784; d. 8-5-1785.
    Thomas " 10-23-1785; " 10-27-1785.

Page 45.
Walter Harbert
Ann Harbert
Ch: Mary b. 1-15-1765.

Walter & Ann Harbert cont'd.
```
    Rebecah    b.  5-28-1767.
    John       "   3- 8-1769.
    Ann        "   4- 3-1771.
    Walter     "   6-13-1773.
    Alizabeth  "  11-18-1775.
    Rachel     "   2-13-1777.
    Charity    "   9-10-1781.
    Peter      "   4-14-1784.
    Thomas     "   8-10-1787; d.
                    5-13-1788.
```

Page 5.
Walter Harbert d. 10-26-1797.

Page 15.
Isaac Hasket
Lyddia Hasket
```
Ch: Jemima    b. 10-21-1765; d.
                  12-17-176-.
    Thomas    "  10-19-1766.
    Sarah     "   9-11-1768.
    Mary      "   9- 9-1770.
    Lyddia    "   5-29-1773.
    Rachel    "  12- 1-1775.
    Isaac     "  11-15-1777.
    Charity   "  10-27-1779.
    Hannah    "  12- 2-1781; d.
                  8-17-1782.
```

Page 2.
Isaac Hasket d. 5-2-1782.

Page 34.
Benjamin Hawkins
Martha Hawkins
```
Ch: Thomas    b.  9-20-1772.
    Isaac     "   3-2-1774; d.
                  8-13-1774.
    William   "   3-22-1775.
    Eli       "  11-18-1777.
    Joseph    "   7- 8-1780.
    Amos      "  10-26-1782.
```

Page 25.
Nathan Hawkins
Ann Hawkins
```
Ch: John      b.  6-15-1774.
    Rebeckah  "   1-12-1776.
    Isaac     "   1- 1-1778.
    Amos      "  12- 7-1779.
    Nathan    "   1-18-1782.
    Ann       "   6- 6-1784.
    James     "  12- 6-1786.
    Mary      "   1-25-1789.
```

Page 4.
Alisabeth Henderson, w. Richard,
  d. 4-26-1788.

Page 46.
Thaniel Henderson
Rebecah Henderson
```
Ch: Mary       b. 9----1762.
    William    "  2----1766.
    Richard    "  9----1772.
    Kesiah     "  9----1774.
    Daniel     "  9----1777.
    Thomas     "  8----1780;
```

Thaniel & Rebecah Henderson cont'd.
```
    Thomas    d.  8-8-1788.
    Martha    b. 12----1782.
    Eli       "   1- 2-1786.
    Nathaniel "   2- 8-1788.
```

Page 34.
Abraham Hollingsworth
Amey Hollingsworth
```
Ch: Levi      b.  3-14-1765.
    Thomas    "  11-30-1766.
    Martha    "  11-20-1768.
```

Page 3.
Abraham Hollingsworth d. 3-9-1771.

Page 14.
Isaac Hollingsworth
Susannah Hollingsworth
```
Ch: John      b. 11-21-1772; d.
                   9-9-1781.
    Rachel    "  12-19-1774.
    William   "  10-27-1776.
    Joel      "  12-29-1778.
    Ruth      "  10-10-1781.
    Cissiah   "   2-13-1784.
    Sarah     "   8-21-1786.
    Isaac     "  10-12-1790.
    John      "  10- 5-1792.
```

Page 5.
Jane Hollingsworth d. 6-7-1795,
  aged 65 yrs.

Page 5.
Joseph Hollingsworth d. 9-10-1792,
  aged about 54 yrs.

Page 4.
Mary Hollingsworth, w. Elias,
  4-15-1789, aged 39 yrs.

Page 30.
William Hollingsworth
Hannah Hollingsworth
```
Ch: Mary      b.  2-23-1764.
    Joseph    "   1-28-1866.
    Ann       "   5- 5-1768; d. at
                   about 15 mos.
    Rebeckah  "  12- 5-1771; d.
                   8-18-1773.
    Hanah     "   8-31-1773.
    William   "   6-23-1776.
    Petter    "   5-23-1779.
    John      "  11-10-1792.
```

Page 3.
Hannah Hollingsworth, w. William,
  d. 1-25-1783.

Page 35.
Ralph Hunt
Rachel Hunt
```
Ch: Mary      b.  1-11-1764.
    Samuel    "   6-19-1766.
    John      "   9-27-1768.
    Ralph     "   5-25-1772.
    Rachel    "   2-15-1775.
    Isaiah    "   7- 1-1777.
```

BUSH RIVER MONTHLY MEETING

Ralph & Rachel Hunt cont'd.
   Christianna b. 11- 6-1779.
   Edward " 4-13-1782.
   Abraham " 5-30-1784.
   Joanna " 1- 8-1786.

Page 4.
Rachel Hunt, w. Ralph, d. 3-18-1790.

Page 2.
Benjamin Inmon d. 7-2-1774, aged about 75 yrs.; bur. 3rd.

Page 19.
Joanna Insco b. 11-20-1707.
Abel Insco " 10-22-1760.
James Insco " 4-23-1765.

Page 39.
John Jay
Elizabeth Jay
Ch: Jessy b. 12- 8-1773.
   Thomas " 6-18-1775.
   Mary " 1-11-1777.
   Ann " 12-17-1778.
   John " 2-22-1782.
   Samuel " 1-12-1784.

Page 34.
William Jay
Mary Jay
Ch: John b. 10-26-1752.
   Mary " 9- 9-1755.
   Rachel " 8-16-1758.
   Lydia " 12- 3-1761.
   David " 5-28-1765.

Page 8.
David Jenkins
Elizabeth Jenkins
Ch: William b. 8-17-1755.
   Isaac " 9- 1-1757.
   David " 1-27-1760.
   Thomas " 5-23-1762.
   Mary " 8- 4-1764.
   Jesse " 10-17-1766.
   Amos " 3- 8-1769.
   Elizabeth " 10- 5-1772.
   Enoch " 7- 8-1776.

Page 5.
Elizabeth Jenkins, w. David, d. 10-15-1795.

Page 5.
Isaac Jenkins, d. 3-4-1798.

Page 30.
Samuel Kelly, Sr.
Hannah Kelly
Ch: John b. 4- 3-1758.
   Abigail " 10-22-1759.
   Samuel " 10-29-1761.
   Rebeckah " 12-18-1764.
   Ann " 8-12-1767.

Page 41.
Thomas Lamb
Sarah Lamb
Ch: Robert b. 5-23-1766.
   Elizabeth " 1-18-1768.
   William " 11-16-1769.
   Thomas " 11-16-1771.
   Joseph " 11-18-1773.
   Mary " 12-22-1775.
   David " 12-28-1777.
   John " 12-19-1779.
   Alce " 7- 8- 1782; d. 7-12-1782.
   Alce " 6-19-1783.
   James " 11-25-1785.

Page 44.
Gabriel McCool
Alisabeth McCool
Ch: Rachel b. 11-27-1774.
   Ann " 11-11-1776.
   James " 10-13-1777.
   John " 11-10-1780.
   Thomas " 3- 3-1782.
   Gabriel " 1-12-1784.

Page 36.
James McCool
Ann McCool
Ch: Mary b. 11-27-1743.
   John " 8-10-1745.
   James " 12-12-1747.
   Martha " 10-31-1749.
   Gabril " 8-17-1751.

Page 2.
James McCool, the elder, d. 2-9-1751, aged 42 yrs.

Page 7.
Samuel Miles
Mary Miles
Ch: Rhoda b. 1-30-1778.
   Lizabeth " 8-17-1780.
   Mary " 8-28-1782.

Page 1.
William Miles
Catharine Miles
S: Samuel b. 6-12-1750.

Page 12.
Henry Milhouse
Rebekah Milhouse
Ch: Robert b. 11-9-1761; Fredericksburg Tp., S.C.
   Mary " 6- 2-1763; same.
   Sarah " 3-24-1770. Bercley Co., S.C.
   Ann " 3- 4-1772, same.
   Henry " 8-14-1774; d. 4-19-1776; same.
   Dinnah " 8-29-1777, same.

Page 42.
Thomas Minton
Hannah Minton
Ch: Hannah b. 10-12-1762.

Thomas & Hannah Minton cont'd.
　Thomas　　b. 6-12-1763; d.
　　　　　　　　　3-4-1772.
　Richard　　" 4-23-1765.
　Lydia　　　" 4-26-1766.
　Mary　　　 " 5-26-1767.
　Joseph　　 " 7-14-1768.
　Hannah　　 " 2- 7-1770.
　Marget　　 " 12-28-1772.
　Rebeckah　 " 1-28-17--.
　Betty　　　" 10-13-1777.
　Parthenia " 1- 9-1780.
　Rachel　　 " 10- 6-1783.

Page 32.
Samuel Neilson
Catharine Neilson
Ch: Mary　　b. 12-26-1768.
　　Samuel　 " 8-12-1771.
　　Jesse　　" 12- 7-1773.

Page 2.
Mary Oglesby d. 10-30-1780.

Page 47.
Abijah O'Neall
Ann O'Neall
Ch: Maryann b. 10- 3-1785.
　　Sarah　　" 5- 3-1787.
　　John　　 " 3-23-1789.
　　William　" 3-10-1791.
　　Elisha　 " 5- 1-1793: d.
　　　　　　　　　9-4-1795.
　　Rebecah　" 9-23-1796.
　　Abijah　 " 12- 9-1798.

Page 42.
William O'Neal
Mary O'Neal
Ch: Abijah　 b. 1-22-1762.
　　Sarah　　" 7-18-1764.
　　Hugh　　 " 6- 9-1767.
　　William　" 2-14-1770.
　　John　　 " 3-16-1773.
　　Henry　　" 1-10-1776.
　　Thomas　 " 2- 2-1779.
　　Mary Ann " 12-14-1781; d.
　　　　　　　　　7-15-1782.

Page 3.
William O'Neal d. 11-5-1786,
　bur. at Bush River.

Page 36.
James Parnel
Esther Parnel
Ch: George　 b. 12-16-1776.
　　Elizabeth " 1-18-1779.
　　John　　 " 12-22-1781.

Page 7.
Sarah Patty, dt. Charles &
　Mary, b. 10-?-1774.

Page 11.
Enoch Pearson
Phebe Pearson
Ch: Martha　 b. 11-19-1775.

Enoch & Phebe Pearson cont'd.
　Samuel & Joanna b. 5- 1-1778.
　Rebekah　　 " 6- 1-1780.
　Mary　　　　" 7-18-1783.
　William　　 " 6-19-1787.
　Phebe　　　 " 8- 5-1789.

Page 4.
Enoch Pearson d. 3-23-1790.

Page 45.
Enoch Pearson, s. Thomas.
Ann Pearson
Ch: Robert　 b. 9-26-1785.
　　Rebecah　" 8-30-1789.
　　Ann　　　" 1-17-1793.
　　Thomas　 " 5- 8-1795.
　　Isaac　　" 5-19-1798.

Page 43.
Joseph Pearson
Melia Pearson
Ch: Ann　　　b. 12- 8-1785.
　　Sarah　　" 2-16-1787; d.
　　　　　　　　　12-11-1795.
　　Mary　　 " 4-13-1789.
　　Thomas　 " 5-31-1791.
　　Hannah　 " 8-19-1793.
　　James　　" 8-25-1795.
　　Melia　　" 3- 8-1798; d.
　　　　　　　　　5-29-1802.
　　Joseph　 " 4-23-1803.
　　Elizabeth " 11-16-1804.

Page 26.
Samuel Pearson d. 1-8-1790.

Ch: Mary　　 b. 2-26-1750.
　　Enoch　　" 1-14-1752.
　　William　" 4- 1-1754.
　　Martha　 " 1-15-1759.
　　Benjamin " 2-26-1763.
　　Hannah　 " 3-23-1765.
　　Samuel　 " 11- 3-1767.
　　Eunice　 " 3- 5-1770.
　　Sarah　　" 8-23-1773.

Page 29.
Thomas Pearson
Ann Pearson
Ch: Mary　　 b. 6-16-1753.
　　Joseph　 " 3-27-1755.
　　Ann　　　" 1-28-1759.
　　Enoch　　" 9-27-1761.
　　Benjamin " 10- 7-1766.
　　Thomas　 " 2-14-1769.
　　Samuel　 " 5- 5-1771.
　　Jonas　　" 9-14-1773.
Mary Pearson, 2nd w. Thomas.
Ch: Rebecakah b. 9-20-1776.
　　Mary　　 " 9-23-1778.

Page 2.
William Pearson, the elder, from
　Pa., d. 10-7-1782.

Page 38.
William Pearson
Ann Pearson

BUSH RIVER MONTHLY MEETING

William & Ann Pearson cont'd.
Ch: Mary   b. 8- 5-1776.
    Edna   " 12- 1-1778.
    Martha   "   2-14-1780.
    Sidney   " 11- 2-1783.
    Sarah   "   4-22-1786.
    Jesse   " 11-11-1788.
    Samuel   "   5-27-1791.
    Exile William "   3- 7-1793.
    Henry   " 10- 5-1796.
    Anne   " 12-19-1799.

Page 20.
Isiah Pemberton
Elizabeth Pemberton
Ch: George   b. 12-3-1753.
    William   "   2-29-1755;
                  d. 3-22-1777.
    Isiah   " 12-27-1756.
    Elizabeth   "   9-26-1758.
    Richard   "   6-22-1760.
    Hannah   "   3-18-1762.
    Ann   "   3-15-1764.
    Judeth   " 12-18-1765.
    Thomas   " 12-15-1766.
    John   "   2-22-1769.
    Sarah   "   9- 2-1772.
    Ruth   "   9- 3-1775.

Page 5.
Isiah Pemberton d. 7-13-1794.
Elizabeth Pemberton, w. Isiah.
  d. 12-28-1795.

Page 5.
Richard Pemberton d. 2-19-1805.

Page 1.
Azariah Pugh
Hannah Pugh
S: David b. 8-26-1758.

Page 39.
David Pugh
Rachel Pugh
Ch: Verhindo   b. 12-13-1782.
    Job   "   9- 5-1784.

Page 36.
Thomas Pugh
Ann Pugh
Ch: Alice   b. 7-10-1754.
    Bette   " 9- 6-1755.
    Sarah   " 3- 8-1758.
    Jane   " 3-21-1762.
    Ann   " 7-26-1764.
    Lydia   " 3-16-1767.
    Rachel   " 2-15-1770.

Page 32.
John Randel
Ann Randel
Ch: Sarah   b. 12-20-1763.
    Joseph   "   5-29-1765.
    Jonas   " 12- 4-1766.
    Isaac   " 12-12-1768.
    Thomas   "   1-12-1771.
    Ann   " 10- 9-1773.

John & Ann Randel cont'd.
Ch: Hannah   b. 2-12-1775.
    Moses   " 10-30-1776.
    John   " 11- 1-1779.
    Lydia   " 12- 4-1781.
    Rachel   " 12-27-1783.

Page 29.
Peter Ruble
Sarah Ruble
Ch: Susannah   b. 4-25-1761.
    Samuel   " 1- 5-1764.
    Jane   " 1- 9-1766.

Page 5.
Peter Ruble d. 1-29-1790.

Page 2.
Sarah Ruble d. 6-20-1769.

Page 4.
Samuel Russell d. 11-5-1782, bur.
  at Camden.

Page 10.
Daniel Smith
Elizabeth Smith
Ch: Hannah   b. 4-15-1765; d. ---
                 4-1781, A.M.
    Margarett"   9-26-1769; d.
                 9-2-1775.
    James   " 7- 8-1773.
    Elizabeth"   3-31-1777.
    Mary   " 11-18-1762; d.
                 12-1-1781, A.M.
    Daniel   " 9- 7-1802, P.M.

Page 9.
David Smith
Hannah Smith
Ch: Jeremiah b. 1-21-1762; d. 6-
                14-1762, Bucks Co.,
                Pa.
    Margaret " 9- 0-1763, d.same.
    March   " 8-30-1765, Bucks
                Co., Pa.
    Hannah   " 7-3-1767, same.
    Sarah   " 6- 5-1769.
    David   " 4-20-1771.
    Joseph   " 3-13-1773.
    George   " 1-21-1777.
    John   " 2-21-1775; d. 9-8-
                1778.
    William " 1-11-1779.
    Ruth   " 9-13-1781.

Page 23.
William Smith
Jean Smith
Ch: Mary   b. 6- 3-1748 O.S.
    John   " 1-31-1752 O.S.
    Sarah   " 3-12----- O.S., m.
        Isaac Cook; d. 4-20-1784, bur.
        at Friends Bur. Gr. at Tygar.
    Ann   b. 3-11-1754.
    Jean   " 1-23-1757.
    Olive   " 11-25-1758.
    Dinah   " 4- 1-1761.

William & Jean Smith cont'd.
Ch: William   b. 6- 3-1763; d.
                   4-20-1780.
    Joseph   " 6- 6-1766.
    Benjamin " 9-27-1770.

Page 17.
Samuel Spray
Mary Spray
Ch: Hannah   d. 8- 5-1784.
    Sarah   " 8- 8-1784.
    Dinah   b.10- 9-1784.
    Rebecah   " 10-20-1788.
    Rebecah   d. 2- 4-1788 (?).

Page 13.
Henry Stiddom
Martha Stiddom
Ch: Christian b. 5-13-1777.
    Eunice   " 9-13-1779.
    John   " 1-26-1782.
    Mary   " 9-12-1784.
    Anna   " 12-15-1788.
    Samuel   " 7- 8-1794.

Page 22.
John Steddom
Mary Steddom
Ch: Henry   b. 4-15-1754.
    Anna   " 8- 7-1756.

Page 16.
Jonathan Taylor, the elder, b.
  3-8-1718, Long Island, S^{o}hole,
  7th day of week.
Mary Taylor b. 7-29,1734, Balti-
  more Co., Md.
Ch: William   b. 3-16-1751.
    Elizabeth " 6-22-1752.
    Eleneor   " 5-12-1757.
    Richard   " 2-10-1755; d.
                   12-2-1780.
    Mary   " 6-22-1759.
    Jane   " 12- 4-1761.
    Rhoda   " 7- 2-1764.
    Jonathan " 9-26-1766; d.
                   6-26-1---.
  Above ch. b. near Opecan
  Creek, Frederick Co., Va.
    Martha   b. 9-21-1768.
    Jonathan " 11-12-1770.
    Isaac   " 11-17-1772.

Page 3.
William Taylor, s. Jonathan, d.
  10-12-17-1.

Page 8.
Richard Taylor

Ch: Ann   b. 11-13-1778.
    Mary   " 1- 1-1780.

Page 8.
William Taylor
Mary Taylor
Ch: Samuel   b. 2-10-1774.
    Martha   " 2-11-1776.

William & Mary Taylor cont'd.
Ch: Jonathan b. 3-15-1778.
    Prudence " 11-10-1780.

Page 1.
Elijah Teague
Alce Teague
S: Samuel b. 3-2-1759.

Page 19.
Isaac Thomas
Mary Thomas
Ch: Edward   b. 2-17-1761.
    Isaac   " 2- 1-1763.
    John   " 5-14-1766.
    Abel   " 11- 1-1768.
    Mary   " 3- 9-1771.
    Elizabeth   " 9-23-1773.
    Evan   " 3-18-1775.
    Nehemiah   " 3-17-1777.
    William   " 9-13-1779.
    Prudence & Sarah" 10-29-1781.

Page 40.
Richard Thompson
Susannah Thompson
Ch: Joseph   b. 12-16-1783.
    Hester   " 2- 9-1786.
    Isaac   " 1- 3-1788.
    Mary   " 12-25-1790.
    Richard   " 12- 8-1792.
    Nancy   " 2-16-1795.
    Samuel Brown   " 8- 7-1797.

Page 5.
Abraham Thorntown d. 6-2-1796.

Page 22.
John Wilson
Dinnah Wilson
Ch: Mary   b. 12-18-1760.
    Jehu   " 1- 1-1763.
    Seth   " 12- 7-1764.
    Phebe   " 2-18-1769.
    Esther   " 2- 9-1771.
    Sarah   " 5-19-1773.
    Christopher " 8-15-1775.
    Hannah   " 7-28-1778.
    John   " 2-28-1782; d.
      2-23-1784, bur. 25th at
      Friends Bur. Gr. at Tygar
      Ryver.

Page 2.
Rachel Wright, a friend of the
  Ministry, w. John, one of the
  first Beginers of a mtg at Bush
  River, d. 12-23-1771, aged
  about 52 yrs.

Page 33.
William Wright
Leah Wright
Ch: John   b. 3-7-1759.
    Rachel   " 11-16-1761.
    Leah   " 10-20-1764.
    Sophia   " 10-23-1767.
    Ruth   " 1-29-1770.
    William   " 3-20-1774.

BUSH RIVER MONTHLY MEETING

MINUTES AND MARRIAGE RECORDS

ADDINGTON.
1772, 9,24. Mary con her mou.
1773, 3,27. John recrq.
1775, 5, 3. John (Addenton), s Henry & Sarah, Dist. 96, S.C., m. Elizabeth Heaton.
1785, 3,26. James (Adenton) recrq.
1788, 8,30. Thomas & Henry, s James, recrq.

ALLISON.
1793, 9,22. Margaret (form Cox) dis mou.

ARNOLD.
1804, 8,--. Mary Jay & dt, Rachel Arnold, gc.

ATKINSON.
1807, 1,31. Samuel & fam, of Ga., gc.

BABB.
1792, 4,28. Mary dis.

BALLINGER.
1784, 10,7. Hannah, dt. James, Washington Co., Nolachucky, m. Isaac Embree.
1787, 8,25. Josiah dis.
1787, 9,29. Jacob dis.
1787, 10,27. Isaac dis mou.
1797, 10,28. James & fam gct New Hope MM.
1797, 11,24. James & fam gct Los Creek MM, Tenn.

BARNS.
1795, 3,24. Elizabeth & ch. gct Springfield MM.

BARRETT
1776, 2,24. Jacob (Barret) & ch. Joseph, Benjamin, Jemime, Arthur, Jacob & Lydia, rocf Hopewell MM. Va. dated 1774, 11,7.
1776, 10,25. Benjamin (Barret) dis.
1779, 3,27. Joseph (Barret) dis.
1784, 5,29. Jacob, Jr. dis mou.
1787. 12,29. James rocf Hopewell MM, Va., dated 1787, 10,1.
1789, 12,31. John, Dist. 96, S.C. s Benj., Va., dec, m. Rhoda Taylor.
1790, 11,27. John rocf Hopewell MM. dated 1790, 1,4.
1792, 11.24. James (Burrett) rst by rq.
1793, 4,27. John & w & ch gct Hopewell MM, Va.
1794, 12,27. _____ & w & ch, Jonathan & Benjamin, rocf Hopewell MM, Va.
1795, 10,31. James (Barrot) gct Holston MM. (Tenn.)

1796, 9,24. John (Barret) & w, Rhoda, & fam, of Rocky Spring, gct Hopewell MM, Va.

BATTEN.
1777, 8,30. Richard (Battin) & w & ch rocf Bradford MM, Chester Co., Pa., dated 1777, 5,16.
1792, 8,25. Richard & fam gct Wrightsboro MM, Ga.
1806, 12.27. Richard (Batton) rocf Salem MM, Ohio, to m.
1807, 1,1. Richard, Newberry Dist., S.C., Ann Cook.
1807, 4,25. Richard (Battin), Jr. & w gct Little Miami MM, Ohio.

BENBOW.
1798, 2.24. Edward rocf Cane Creek MM, N.C., dated 1797, 12,2.
1798. 5,26. Mary & ch, Berkly, Mary & Even, recrq.
1806, 4,26. Edward (Benbo) & fam gct Little Miami MM, Ohio.

BENSON.
1788, 4,26. James recrq.

BOWMAN.
1795, 3,24. Sarah dis mou.

BRAY.
1767, 6,--. Henry & s, John, Henry, & Edward, rocf Cane Creek MM, N.C., dated 1787, 2,3.

BRIDGES.
1781, 10,27. Charles recrq.
1800, 4,26. John dis.
1801, 9.26. William's death rpd.
1804, 3,31. Charles & w & two ch gct Miami MM. Ohio.

BROCK.
1789, 1,31. George, s Elias, recrq.
1792, 9,13. George, s Elias, dec, & Ann, Dist. 96, S.C., m. Charity Cook.
1804, 7,28. George dis.

BRODEY.
1801, 5,30. Mary (form Cook) rpd mou.

BROOKS.
1790, 3,4. Elizabeth, dt James, Newberry Co., S.C., m. Nebo Gaunt.
1791, 9,1. James, Newberry Co., S. C., m. Sarah Singletary.
1793, 12,28. Susannah Phillips (form Brooks) dis mou.
1794, 7,26. Hannah dis mou.
1796, 6,25. Sarah dis.
1797, 9,30. Joab dis.
1798, 4,5. Sarah. dt James, Newberry Co., S.C., m. Jessy Jay.
1800. 3,29. Hannah (form Wright) dis mou.

97

BROOKS cont'd.
1804, 3,31. Nimrod & Mary rqct
  Miami MM, Ohio.
1805, 11,30. John gct Miami MM,
  Ohio.
1820, 11,--. Daniel O. dis mou.

BROWN.
1775, 4,29. Samuel & w, Ann,
  rocf Nottingham MM, dated
  1774, 8,27.
1787, 6,--. Josiah & Uriah rocf
  Deep River MM, N.C., dated
  1787, 1,1.
1798, 5,--. Joshua, of Charleston, dis mou.
1806, 12,27. Samuel, Jr. rpd mou.
1807, 1,31. Samuel, Sr. & w rqct
  Little Miami MM, Ohio.
1807, 3,28. Samuel, Jr. & w gct
  Little Miami MM, Ohio.

BULL.
1774, 4,30. Robert dis.
1775, 1,27. Sarah & ch gc.

BYSHOP.
1788, 9,10. Elizabeth, dt Thomas,
  m Francis Fincher.

CAMMACK.
1780, 6,24. James (Cemmack) & ch,
  Mary & Margaret, recrq.
1793, 2,23. Mary (Camack) (form
  Hall) dis mou.
1795, 3,24. James (Commack) rmt
  Rachel Compton.
1805, 2,23. James & fam gct
  Miami MM, Ohio.
1805, 7,27. James (Cammac) dis.

CAMPBELL.
1775, 7,8. Mary (Cambell), widow,
  Dist. 96, S.C., m. Thomas
  Pearson.
1778, 4,25. Mtg appointed Thomas
  Pearson & John Clark guardians
  of Ralph & John Campbell, ch
  Samuel.
1793, 3,--. Ralph dis.
1794, 4,26. Sarah (form Hasket)
  dis mou.
1797, 2,25. John dis.

CARL.
1793, 6,24. Elizabeth rpd mou.

CHANDLER.
1783, 12,4. Elizabeth, dt Jacob
  & Ann, Dist. 96, S.C., m
  David Miles.
1790, 8,28. Jonathan dis mou.
1793, 6,29. Israel dis.
1794, 10,25. Jacob dis.

CHAPMAN.
1775, 2,25. Samuel, widower,
  dis mou.
1788, 6,27. Giles, Jr. dis mou.

CHAPMAN cont'd.
1778, 10,31. Samuel con his mou.
1780, 7,29. William, s Samuel dis.
1797, 9,30. Samuel dis mou. (rem)

CHEEK.
1781, 11,24. Ellis, s James, dis.

CLARK.
1774, 11,26. John rocf Warrington
  MM, Pa., dated 1774, 5,7.
1776, 12.28. William dis mou.
1778, 4,25. Mtg appointed Thomas
  Pearson & John Clark guardians
  of Ralph & John Campbell, ch
  Samuel.

COATE.
1780, 10,28. John (Coat) dis.
1790, 9,9. Mary (Coat), dt John,
  blacksmith, Dist. 96, S.C. m
  Samuel Pearson.
1792, 7,--. ____ recrq.
1793, 2.7. Henry (Coat), s Marmaduke, Newberry Co., S.C. m Mary
  Hasket.
1794, 6,28. Moses (Coat) rmt
  Elizabeth Coppock.
1795, 10,31. Sarah Hall (form
  Coate) dis mou.
1800, 4,26. John (Coat) dis.
1800, 5,8. Samuel (Coat), s Marmaduke, m Margaret Coppock.
1800, 10,29. James, s Marmaduke,
  Newberry Dist., S.C., m Mary
  Miles.
1803, 6,29. William, s Marmaduke,
  Newberry Dist., S.C., m Elizabeth
  Miles.
1804, 2,25. Moses & w & ch gct
  Miami MM, Ohio.
1804, 2,25. Samuel & w & ch gct
  Miami MM. Ohio.
1804, 7,28. Henry & fam gct Miami
  MM, Ohio.
1804, 8,25. Marmaduke & fam gct
  Miami MM, Ohio.
1805, 7,27. William (Coat) & fam
  gct Miami MM, Ohio.
1805, 8,31. Samuel gct Miami MM,
  Ohio.

COLE.
1776, 4,27. Hannah dis.

COMER.
1786, 7,29. Joseph rocf Cane Creek
  MM, dated 1785, 5,7.
1786, 7,29. Elizabeth & ch, Robert
  & Stephen, rocf Cane Creek MM,
  dated 1785, 5,7.

COMPTON.
1778, 6,27. Samuel & ch, Rachel,
  William, Samuel, Sarah, Amos,
  John, Stephen, Matthew & Joshua,
  recrq.

BUSH RIVER MONTHLY MEETING

COMPTON cont'd.
1792, 1,11. Sally Nelson, dt Samuel & Elizabeth, Newberry Co., S.C., m Robert Milhouse.
1792, 9,--. Amos gct Cane Creek MM, to m.
1793, 10,26. Amos (Cumpton) gct Cane Creek MM.
1795, 3,24. Rachel rmt James Commack.
1796,11,26. Samuel (Campton), Jr. rpd mou.
1798,11,24. Joshua gct Cane Creek MM, to m.
1798,11,24. Samuel, Jr. gct Cane Creek MM.
1800,5,30. Matthew gct _____ Creek MM.
1804,2,25. Samuel & w & ch gct Miami MM, Ohio.
1807,5,30. John gct Miami MM, Ohio.

CONNER.
1805,11,30. John & fam gct Miami MM, Ohio.

COOK.
1772,3,12. Eli, s Isaac & Mary, Craven Co., S.C., m Martha Hawkins.
1773,7,8. Ann, dt Isaac & Mary, dec, Craven Co., S.C., m Nathan Hawkins.
1775,4,6. Mary, Dist. 96, S.C., m James Townsand.
1775,4,12. Amos, s Isaac, m Elizabeth Townsend.
1782,11,30. Joseph dis mou.
1785,11,3. Sarah, dt Isaac & Charity, Newberry Co., S.C., m Zimri Gaunt.
1791,10,29. John recrq.
1792,4,28. Mary dis.
1792,9,5. Thomas, s Isaac & Charity, Dist. 96, S.C., m Kezia Henderson.
1792,9,13. Charity, dt Isaac & Charity, Dist. 96, S.C., m George Brock.
1793,2,28. (Rachel), dt Isaac & Charity, Newberry Co., S.C., m Thomas Lewis.
1795,3,29. Joseph dis.
1796,4,30. Joseph con his misconduct.
1798,3,1. Rut, dt Isaac, Newberry Co., S.C. m John Furnas.
1799,10,2. Wright, s Isaac & Charity, Laurence Co., S.C., m Rebeca Pearson.
1801,5,30. Mary Brodey (?) (form Cook) rpd mou.
1802,2,27. Isaac, Jr. rpd mou.
1802,4,29. Susannah, dt Isaac & Charity, Lawlaner Dist., S.C., m Caleb Lewis.
1805,2,23. Isaac, Jr. & fam gct Miami MM, Ohio.

COOK cont'd.
1805,8,31. Thomas & fam gct Miami MM, Ohio.
1805,10,26. John, of Mud Lick. dis.
1805,10,26. Isaac & w gct Miami MM, Ohio.
1806,1,25. Wright & fam gct Miami MM, Ohio.
1807,1,1. Ann, dt Joseph & Mary, Newberry Dist., S.C., m Richard Batten.
1807,5,30. Joseph & fam gct Little Miami MM, Ohio.

COOPER.
1773,5,29. William dis.
1778,6,27. Jacob, of Padget Creek, dis.
1779,4,11. William, Dist. 96, S.C., m Mary Hunter.
1781,1,27. Samuel, of Padget's Creek. dis.
1785,9,24. Nathan, of Padget's Creek, dis.
1787,1,27. Benjamin & w, Pharoba, & small ch, Isaac & Charity, rocf Wrightboro MM, Ga., dated 1786,12,2.
1787,4,28. Isaac & s, Isaac & Joseph. rocf Wrightsboro MM, Ga. dated 1787,4,-.
1797,10,28. Sarah rpd mou.

COPPOCK.
1771,12,30. Marther, dt Moses, dec, & Marther, Berkley Co., S.C., m William Tomlinson.
1774,4,30. Joseph & w rocf East Nottingham MM. Pa., dated 1772, 12,26.
1778,7,25. John rocf East Nottingham, Cicil Co., Md., dated 1777, 7,26.
1784,2,28. James dis mou.
1786,2,25. James rst by rq.
1787,8,2. Susannah, dt John & Abigail, Bush River, Dist. 96, S.C., m John Elleman.
1790,1,7. John, s John, Newberry Co., S.C., m Anne Jay.
1793,6,24. Mary Inman (form Coppock) dis mou.
1794,6,28. Elizabeth rmt Moses Coat.
1796,3,26. Abigail rmt Benjamin Weeks, of Deep River.
1796,6,25. Benjamin rmt Susannah Jay.
1796,10,29. Aaron gct New Hope MM, N.C. (Tenn.).
1796,12,31. Thomas dis mou.
1798,2,24. Isaac dis.
1798,7,28. Ann Haworth (form Coppock) dis mou.
1798,10,27. John, s Joseph, dis mou.
1799,9,28. John, Sr. dis.
1799,9,28. Joseph, Jr. dis mou.

COPPOCK cont'd.
1800,5,8. Margaret, dt Joseph, Newberry Co., S.C., m Samuel Coat.
1804,7,28. _____ & her tow ch gc.
1805,3,30. James & fam gct Miami MM, Ohio.
1805,4,27. Jane & two ch gc. (to Miami MM)
1806,8,30. James & fam gct Miami MM, Ohio.

COX.
1774,8,11. Ann, dt Thomas & Mary, Craven Co., S.C., m Isaac Hollingsworth.
1780,7,29. Richard & w, Ann, & ch, Thomas & Mary, rocf Wrightsboro MM, Ga., dated 1780,5,6.
1781,11,24. John dis. (rem)
1783,2,22. Thomas & fam gct Cane Creek MM, N.C.
1787,12,29. Thomas rocf Cane Creek MM, N.C., dated 1787,5,3.
1791,11,--. Jonathan & ch, Sarah, John, Mary & Elizabeth. recrq.
1793,9,22. Margaret Allison (form Cox) dis mou.
1794,11,29. Elizabeth (Cocks) (form Thomas) rpd mou.
1795,2,28. David & ch, Sarah & Elizabeth, recrq.
1795,3,24. Jane recrq.
1795,12,26. William & ch, Jemima, recrq.
1798,3,31. Sarah Hollingsworth (form Cox) dis mou.
1799,1,26. John, of Wrightsboro, Ga., rst by rq.
1799,2,23. John gct Wrightsboro MM.
1805,2,23. Jonathan & fam gct Miami MM, Ohio.
1806,3,29. William & fam gct Miami MM, Ohio.

DAVIS.
1803,10,8. Amos rocf Wrightsboro MM, Ga., dated 1803,10,1.
1805,3,30. Amos & fam gct Miami MM, Ohio.

DEMANS.
1775,11,10. Phebe, parents dec, Dist. 96, S.C., m Enoch Pearson.

DEMOSS.
1783,11.13. Joanna, Dist. 96, S.C., m Benja. Vanhorn.

DODD.
1783,1,25. William & John dis.

DOUGHERTY.
1800,3,29. Jane recrq.

DUNKIN.
1773,6,26. John recrq.
1775,3,25. Nelson & ch, Milcha, Richard & Elisha, recrq.
1776,11,30. John & Nelson dis.
1782,4,27. Samuel recrq.
1783,2,22. Rachel dis.
1787,6,--. Richard, s Nelson, dis mou.
1793,9,28. Elisha (Duncan) dis.
1801,2,28. Samuel & w, Mary, & ch gct New Hope MM.

EDMUNDSON.
1772,9,24. William & Joseph (Edmonson) roc, dated 1771,4,14.
1775,3,25. Isaac & Cabel J. rocf Warrington MM, Pa., dated 1774, 9,10.
1776,9,28. Isaac dis. (rem to MM at Warrington, Pa. without cert)
1778,2,28. Isaac, of Padget's Creek, dis.
1780,2,26. Caleb rocf Warrington MM, Pa., dated 1779,3,13.
1780,4,29. Joseph gct Warrington MM, Pa.
1784,11,--. Caleb, Sr. dis.
1785,7,30. Caleb, Jr. dis mou.

ELLEMAN.
1787,8,2. John, s Enos & Catharine, Bush River, Dist. 96, S.C., m Susannah Coppock.
1791,1,29. William dis mou.
1792,9.---. John (Elliman) rpd mou.
1796,1,30. Susannah (Elliman) gct New Hope MM.
1800,6,28. William (Elliman) con his mou.
1800,7,26. Jane (Eliman) & ch, Martha, Steedham & Esther Pearson, recrq.
1800,11,29. Jane (Eliman) & ch, David & Isaac, recrq.
1805,7,27. William & fam gct Miami MM, Ohio.
1805,7,27. Elizabeth & Hannah gc.

ELMORE.
1778,7.25. John dis.
1783,9,27. Stephen dis.
1794,4,26. Rebecca (form Kelly) rpd mou.
1796,4,30. Ridgeway dis.
1797,6,24. Rachel rmt William Miles.
1797,10,28. Joseph dis.
1798,2,24. Prudence (form O'Sayle) dis mou.

EMBREE.
1775,9,30. John & fam gct MM in Ga.
1784,10,7. Isaac, s Moses, Washington Co., Nolachucky, m Hannah Ballinger.
1784,10,30. John, s Moses & brother of Isaac, dis mou.

BUSH RIVER MONTHLY MEETING

ENGLISH.
1776,3,30. Mary (English), a girl of ten yrs, uc of Mary Kelly & fam, rocf Fredericks MM, near Camden, S.C., dated 1776,1,2.
1787,6,--. John, s Thomas, gct Deep River MM, N.C.
1787,12,29. Joshua, Edward & Thomas, s Thomas, dis.

EVANS.
1784,3,27. Robert's death rpd.
1784,12,21. Ann (Evins), dt Robert & Rebecca, Dist. 96, S.C., m Enoch Pearson.
1789,10,8. Martha, dt Robert, dec, & Rebecca, Dist. 96, S.C., m. David Jenkins.
1792,9,5. Mary, dt Robert & Rebecca, Newberry Co., S.C., m Seth Wilson.
1797,2,25. Moses rmt Lidia Hasket.
1799,1,3. Joseph, Newberry Co., S.C., m Rachel McCool.
1799,11,30. Benjamin recrq.
1800,1,1. Sarah, dt Robert, dec, Newberry Co., S.C., m Thomas O'Neall.
1800,5,31. Hannah rocf Cane Creek MM, dated 1799,11,19.
1803,4,30. Thomas, David & Elizabeth, recrq of father, Benjamin.
1803,11,2. Rebekah, dt Robert, dec, Newberry Dist., S.C., m Isaac Hasket.
1804,1,28. Benjamin & w & ch gct Miami MM, Ohio.
1805,2,28. Robert, s Robert, Newberry Dist., S.C., m Kerenhappock Gaunt.
1806,8,30. Joseph & fam gct Miami MM, Ohio.

FARMER.
1806,6,28. William & fam. of Ga., gct Miami MM, Ohio.

FINCHER.
1774,3,26. Jesse dis.
1780,3,25. John dis.
1788,9,10. Francis, s Armil, Union Co., S.C. m Elizabeth Byshop.

FLUKE (?).
1794,9,27. Elizabeth (form Kelly) rpd mou.

FRAZER.
1774,7,7. Isaac, s James, York Co., Pa., dec, m Mary Pearson.
1776,8,31. Isaac (Frasor) dis mou.

FURNAS.
1784,1,31. Mary's death rpd. (widow with ch)

FURNAS cont'd.
1790,4,29. Esther, dt John, Newberry Co., S.C., m Benjamin Pearson.
1790,9,25. John (Furness) gct Cane Creek MM, to m.
1790,9,30. Joseph, s John, dec, Newberry Co., S.C., m Sarah Pearson.
1792,2,25. Thomas Wilkinson (Furness) dis mou.
1797,3,25. Robert (Furnace) & w, Hannah, rocf Cane Creek MM, dated 1796,12,24.
1798,1,27. William dis mou.
1798,3,1. John, Newberry Co., S.C., m Ruth Cook.
1799,9,28. Robert (Furnace) & w & fam gct Cane Creek MM.
1799,9,28. Hannah & ch gct Cane Creek MM.
1804,8,25. John & fam gct Miami MM, Ohio.
1805,7,27. Joseph & fam gct Miami MM, Ohio.

GALBREATH.
1777,8,30. _____ (torn) & James, Jr. rocf Bradford MM, Chester Co., Pa., dated 1777,3,14.
1778,2,5. Mary (Gilbreath), dt James, Dist. 96, S.C., m Richard Taylor.
1794,12,27. James (Gilbreath) gct New Garden MM, N.C., to m.
1795,8,29. Susannah rocf New Garden MM, dated 1795,5,30.
1796,2,27. Ann rmt Walter Harbert.
1800,3,29. James & fam gct Deep River MM, N.C.
1800,3,29. Susanna (with h) gc.
1802,8,28. Nathan gct Wrightsboro MM, Ga., to m.
1804,7,28. _____ rmt Charity Starbert (?).
1804,12,6. Charity (Gilbreath), dt John, dec, Newberry Dist., S.C., m Robert Pearson.
1805,4,27. Nathan & fam gct Middleton MM, Ohio.
1805,4,27. William & fam gct Middleton MM, Ohio.

GANTER.
1783,2,22. Michael dis mou.

GAUNT.
1780,11,2. Zebulon, late of Camden Dist., m Mary Kelly.
1784,12,2. Maris, dt Zebulon & Ester, dec., Dist. 96, S.C., m Thomas Jenkins.
1785,4,30. Samuel, s Zebulon, Dist. 96, S.C., m Abigail Kelly.
1785,11,3. Zimri, s Zebulon, Newberry Co., S.C., m Sarah Cook.
1786,10,28. Zebulon dis mou.
1790,3,4. Nebo, Newberry Co., S.C., m. Elizabeth Brooks.

BUSH RIVER MONTHLY MEETING

GAUNT cont'd.
1794,7,26. Sarah rmt Henry Hollingsworth.
1802,4,29. Nebo, s Zebulon, dec, Newberry Dist., S.C., m Judith Wright.
1805,2,28. Kerenhappock, dt Samuel, Newberry Dist., S.C., m Robert Evans.
1805,3,30. Nebo & fam gct Miami MM, Ohio.
1807,7,11. Samuel, Newberry Dist, S.C., m Susanna Julien.

GILBERT.
1792,2,25. Beulah dis.
1792,11,29. Hepzibah, s Jonathan, Lexenton Co., S.C., m John O'Neall.
1793,11,30. Cary dis.
1797,8,26. Achsah Snelgrove (form Gilbert) dis mou.

GILCHRIST.
1792,5,28. Andrew dis. (rem to Phila. MM)

GRIFFIN.
1800,6,28. Lydia dis.
1802,11,27. Joshua, William & Isaac dis.
1804,3,31. Joel dis.

HACKNEY.
1797,11,24. Joseph & w, Mary (?) rocf Hopewell MM, dated 1797, 9,25.

HALL.
1793,2,23. Mary Camack (form Hall) dis mou.
1795,10,31. Sarah (form Coate) dis mou.

HAMMER.
1768,6,4. Margaret, dt John & Rachel Wright, Berkley Co., S.C., m Joseph Hollingsworth.
1789,1,31. David (Hamer) rpd mou.
1802,7,31. David dis.
1805,4,27. Charlotte & ch gc.

HANKS.
1787,3,--. William recrq.

HARBERT.
1776,3,30. Walter (Harbour) recrq.
1785,11,10. Rebecah (Herbart), dt Walter & Ann, Dist. 96, S. C., m Isaac Jenkins.
1789,2,--. John rpd mou.
1796,2,27. Walter rmt Ann Galbreath.
1796,4,30. John dis.
1798,2,24. Rachel (Harbour) dis.
1803,1,29. Walter dis.

HARRIS.
1785,8,27. David rocf Fairfax MM. (Va.), dated 1785,2,26.
1788,11,29. Hester Humphries (form Harris) dis mou.
1802,4,24. Elizabeth (form Rouston) rpd mou.

HASKET.
1773,1,31. Joseph rpd mou.
1773,5,29. Joseph (Haskett) rocf Simons Creek MM, N.C., dated 1771,3,20.
1775,11,25. Joseph gct Center MM. N.C.
1792,5,26. Thomas dis.
1793,2,7. Mary, dt Isaac, dec, Newberry Co., S.C., m Henry Coat.
1794,4,26. Sarah Campbell (form Hasket) dis mou.
1797,2,25. Lidia rmt Moses Evans.
1799,5,30. Ann & ch, Lyda & Mary, recrq.
1803,11,2. Isaac, s Isaac, dec, Newberry Dist., S.C., m Rebekah Evans.
1805,4,27. Thomas (Haskett) dis.
1806,4,26. Isaac & fam gct Little Miami MM, Ohio.

HAWKINS.
1771,10,10. Benjamin, s James & Marther, Craven Co., S.C., m Martha Hollingsworth.
1772,3,12. Martha, dt James & Marther, Craven Co., S.C., m Eli Cook.
1773,7,8. Nathan, s James & Marther, Craven Co., S.C., m Ann Cook.
1788,8,30. John, Isaac, Benjamin & James, s Isaac, recrq.
1789,2,--. Amos, s Isaac, recrq.

HAWORTH.
1768,10,10. Jemima, dt James, dec, & Sarah, Berkley Co., S.C., m John Wright.
1772,8,29. George & James dis.
1781,8,25. Absalom rocf Hopewell MM, dated 1780,12,7.
1784,4,24. Absolom dis mou.
1794,8,30. James rst on recommendation of New Hope Mtg.
1798,8,25. Ann dis.

HEATON.
1773,12,25. Joseph & w rocf Buckingham MM, Bucks Co., Pa., dated 1773,8,18.
1775,5,3. Elizabeth, dt Joseph, dec, & Leada, Dist. 96, S.C., m John Addenton.
1777,3,29. Benjamin rocf Wells MM. N.C., dated 1776,12,4.
1783,1,25. Benjamin gct New Garden MM, N.C.

BUSH RIVER MONTHLY MEETING

HEATON cont'd.
1785,3,26. John Weeks gct Deep River MM, N.C., at rq of grandfather, Benjamin Heaton.
1785,11,26. Benjamin & James Weeks, grandsons of Benjamin Heaton, gct Deep River MM,N.C.
1786,4,29. Benjamin gct New Garden MM, N.C.

HENDERSON.
1775,3,25. Shadrick dis mou.
1777,6,28. Thomas rocf Cane Creek MM, dated 1777,4,5.
1780,1,22. Nathaniel rocf Cane Creek MM. (N.C.), dated 1779, 11,12.
1781,6,30. Richard rpd mou.
1782,8,31. Richard dis.
1783,1,25. James dis mou.
1787,4,28. Nathan dis mou.
1787,4,28. William rocf Cane Creek MM, N.C., dated 1786, 12,2.
1790,9,25. William, Jr. dis mou.
1792,9,5. Kezia, dt Nathaniel & Rebecah, Dist. 96, S.C., m Thomas Cook.
1794,4,26. Richard, s Nathaniel & Rebecca, Dist. 96, S.C., rmt Rachel Hollingsworth. (Recorded in marriage book, but date torn off)
1800,8,1. Martha, dt Nathaniel & Rebekah, Edgesfield Dist., S.C., m Jacob Hollingsworth.
1805,8,31. Richard & fam gct Miami MM, Ohio.
1805,8,31. Thomas gct Miami MM, Ohio.
1806,9,27. Thomas, Jr. gct Miami MM, Ohio.

HODGE.
1775,1,27. Cert rec for Jacob, Phebe & William from Hopewell MM, Va., dated 1774,11,7; endorsed to Wrightsboro MM, Ga.

HOLLINGSWORTH.
1768,6,4. Joseph, s George & Hannah, Berkley Co., S.C., m Margaret Hammer.
1771,10,10. Marther, Craven Co., S.C., m Benjamin Hawkins.
1772,12,12. Isaac, s George, Berkley Co., S.C., m Susannah Wright.
1774,8,11. Isaac, s Joseph & Martha, Craven Co., S.C., m Ann Cox.
1775,10,28. Jonathan & David, ch Joseph. recrq.
1776,3,30. Elias, of Cane Creek, dis.
1776,7,27. Equille, of Cane Creek, dis.
1777,11,29. Abraham's death rpd. (leaving w, Amey, & ch)

HOLLINGSWORTH cont'd.
1778,7,25. Enoch rpd mou.
1780,2,26. Benjamin, s Elias, dis.
1783,10,25. Elias, s Elias, dis.
1786,3,25. John recrq.
1786,3,25. Jonathan dis mou.
1786,7,29. James & ch, Charity, Sarah & George, recrq.
1786,11,16. James, s George, dec, & Jane, Dist. 96, S.C., m Sarah Wright.
1786,11,25. David dis mou.
1787,8,25. Henry recrq.
1787,9,29. Nathan recrq.
1788,4,26. Levi dis mou.
1788,8,30. Abraham, Amos & Jacob, s Jacob, recrq.
1788,11,29. Thomas dis.
1789,3,12. John, s George, dec, & Jane, Lawrence Co., S.C., m Rachel Wright.
1790,4,24. Jonathan rst by rq. (had been dis mou.)
1790,5,29. Benjamin rst by rq.
1792,9,--. _____, of Cane Creek, recrq. (had been dis mou.)
1793,1,24. David con his mou.
1794,4,26. Rachel, dt Isaac & Susanna, Dist. 96, S.C., rmt Richard Henderson. (Recorded in marriage book, but date torn off)
1794,6,28. Susanna recrq.
1794,7,26. Henry rmt Sarah Gaunt.
1795,4,25. Elias dis. (rem)
1798,3,31. Catharine recrq.
1798,3,31. Sarah (form Cox) dis mou.
1798,5,26. Ann recrq.
1799,5,25. Isaac, s Margaret, rpd mou.
1799,9,12. Abraham, s Joseph, Lawrence Co., S.C., m Eunice Steddom.
1799,11,30. Dinah gct Cane Creek MM.
1799,11,30. Sarah rpd mou.
1800,1,25. Sarah & Charity dis mou.
1800,2.22. Elias dis.
1800,8,1. Jacob, s Joseph, dec, & Margaret, Lawrence Co., S.C., m Martha Henderson.
1800,9,27. George recrq.
1800,12,27. Isaac, Jr. gct Deep River MM, N.C.
1801,7,9. Ann, Newberry Dist., S.C., m James Nichols.
1801,8,29. Joel dis.
1802,8,28. William dis.
1803,10,--. Ezekiel dis.
1804,8,25. Abraham & fam gct Miami MM, Ohio.
1805,5,2. Sarah, dt Isaac & Susannah, Newberry Dist., S.C., m Samuel Stanton.
1805,8,31. George, Jr. gct Miami MM, Ohio.
1805,8,31. Henry & fam gct Miami MM, Ohio.
1805,8,31. Isaac & fam gct Miami MM, Ohio.

HOLLINGSWORTH cont'd.
1805,8,31. James & fam gct Miami
  MM, Ohio.
1805,8,31. Nathan gct Miami MM,
  Ohio.
1805,9,28. Joel con his misconduct & was rec in mbrp.
1806,2,22. Nathan gct Miami MM,
  Ohio.
1806,4,26. David & fam gct Little
  Miami MM, Ohio.
1806,5,31. Joel gct Little
  Miami MM, Ohio.
1806,7,28. John & fam gct Little
  Miami MM, Ohio.
1806,9,27. Jacob & fam gct
  Miami MM, Ohio.

HOOKER.
1776,9,28. Hannah & ch, Edward,
  Mary, William & John, rocf
  Gunpowder MM, Md.
1778,6,27. Edward dis mou.
1793,12,28. Judith rpd mou.

HOPKINS.
1799,11,30. John rocf MM in
  Phila., Pa., dated 1799,11,25.

HORNER.
1795,10,31. Ann rocf Hopewell
  MM, Va., dated 1795,9,28.
1802,9,25. Ann, w Thomas, gct
  Westland MM, Washington Co.,
  Pa. (rem near Miami River,
  Ohio)

HUMPHRIES.
1788,11,29. Hester (form Harris)
  dis mou.

HUNT.
1776,9,26. Ralph & small ch.,
  Mary, Samuel, John, Ralph &
  Rachel, recrq.
1764,8,28. Mary Pots (form Hunt),
  of Padget's Creek, dis mou.
1789,2,11. Samuel, s Ralph,
  Union Co., S.C., m Margaret
  Townsend.

HUNTER.
1779,4,11. Mary, Dist. 96, S.C.,
  m William Cooper.

HUTTON.
1798,4,28. Cert rec for John &
  s from Exeter MM, dated 1791,
  8,31; endorsed to Cane Creek
  MM.

INMAN.
1793,6,24. Mary (form Coppock)
  dis mou.

INSCO.
1783,12,11. Able, s John, dec,
  & Mary, now Pearson, Dist. 96,
  S.C., m Ann Pearson.

INSCO cont'd.
1788,8,30. James dis mou.
1806,5,31. Abel & fam gct Little
  Miami MM, Ohio.
1806,6,28. James & fam gct Little
  Miami MM, Ohio.

JACKSON.
1772,10,30. Walter rocf Cane
  Creek MM, N.C., dated 1772,10,3.

JAY.
1773,3,4. John, s William, dec, &
  Mary, Berkley Co., S.C., m
  Betty Pugh.
1773,3,11. Mary, dt William, dec,
  & Mary, Berkley Co., Dist. 96,
  S.C., m Charles Patty.
1788,8,30. William & James recrq.
1790,1,7. Anne, dt William, Newberry Co., S.C., m John Coppock.
1790,6,26. William, Jr. dis.
1791,4,7. James, Newberry Co.,
  S.C., m Jemima Mills.
1792,10,27. (Lay)ton recrq.
1793,5,30. Layton, s William, Newberry Co., S.C., m Elizabeth
  Mills.
1796,1,30. Susannah recrq.
1796,6,25. Susannah rmt Benjamin
  Coppock.
1798,4,5. Jessy, s John, Newberry
  Co., S.C. m Sarah Brooks.
1798,11,24. David recrq.
1799,3,7. Ann, dt John, Newberry
  Co., S.C., m Samuel Pearson.
1800,1,29. Thomas, s John, Newberry Co., S.C. m Mary Pearson.
1802,9,28. Layton & w, Elizabeth,
  & ch, Patience, Charlotte,
  William, John, James & Abigail,
  gct Westland MM, Washington Co.,
  Pa. (rem to northwest side of
  the Ohio.)
1803,12,31. Jesse & w, Sarah, &
  ch gct Miami MM, Ohio.
1803,12,31. John & w, Betty, & ch
  gct Miami MM, Ohio.
1804,8,--. Mary Jay & dt, Rachel
  Arnold, gc.
1805,8,31. David rqct Miami MM,
  Ohio.
1806,5,31. Thomas & fam gct Little
  Miami MM, Ohio.
1819,4,3. James & fam get Ohio.
1820,11,--. Mills dis mou.

JENKINS.
1781,11,24. William rpd mou.
1784,12,2. Thomas, s David &
  Elizabeth, Dist. 96, S.C., m
  Maris Gaunt.
1785,11,10. Isaac, s David &
  Elizabeth, Dist. 96, S.C., m
  Rebecah Herbart.
1786,6,24. Thomas rpd mou.
1789,10,8. David, s David & Elizabeth, Dist. 96, S.C., m Martha
  Evans.

BUSH RIVER MONTHLY MEETING

JENKINS cont'd.
1797,6,8. Jesse, s David, Newberry Co., S.C. m Hannah Russell.
1799,5,9. Elizabeth, dt David, Newberry Co., S.C., m Samuel Russell.
1799,11,14. Amos, s David, Newberry Co., S.C., m Elizabeth Russell.
1802,11,4. Rebekah (Jinkins), widow of Isaac, Newberry Dist., S.C., m Isaac Kirk.
1805,3,30. Amos & fam gct Miami MM, Ohio.
1805,8,31. David, Sr. & s Enoch, gct Miami MM, Ohio.
1806,4,26. David & fam gct Little Miami MM, Ohio.
1806,4,26. Eli gct Little Miami MM, Ohio.
1806,5,31. David, s Isaac, gct Little Miami MM, Ohio.
1806,7,26. William & fam gct Little Miami MM, Ohio.

JOHNSON.
1785,4,30. Lucy & ch, Charles, David, Collins, Sarah, James, Moorman & Judith, rocf South River MM, Campbell Co., Va., dated 1783,10,--.
1786,3,25. David dis mou.
1787,2,24. Charles dis mou.
1787,2,24. Collins dis.

JONES.
1773,1,30. Francis & w & ch, Rachel, Frances, Samuel, Henry, John, Hannah & Thomas, Jane, Elliman, Sarah, Joseph & Mary, rocf Cane Creek MM, N.C., dated 1772,10,3.
1773,1,30. Henry & w & ch. Elizabeth, George & William, rocf Cane Creek MM, N.C., dated 1772,10,3.
1773,1,30. James rocf New Garden MM, dated 1772,--,--.
1792,9,29. Joseph, s Francis & Sarah, Columbus Co., Ga., m Mary Taylor.
1793,1,26. Mary (with h) & dt gct Wrightsboro MM, Ga.
1794,11,29. Rachel (form Paty) dis mou.
1795,5,30. Margaret rocf Wrightsboro MM, Ga., dated 1793,7,6.
1802,7,31. Elisha recrq.
1805,12,28. Elisha gct Miami MM, Ohio.
1820,12,--. Robert rpd mou.

JULIAN.
1801,7,--. Charlotte rpd mou.
1807,6,11. Susanna (Julien), Newberry Dist., S.C., m Samuel Gaunt.

KELLY.
1776,3,30. Mary & ch, Isaac & Ann, & smaller ch not named, rocf Fredericks MM, near Camden, S.C., dated 1776,1,2.
1776,3.30. Mary English, a girl of 10 yrs., uc of Mary Kelly & fam, rocf Fredericks MM, near Camden, S.C., dated 1776,1,2.
1778,10,31. Isaac gct Fredericks MM, near Camden, S.C.
1780,11,2. Mary, widow of John, m Zebulon Gaunt.
1784,12,9. Ann, dt John & Mary, Bush River, Dist. 96, S.C., m Abijah O'Neall.
1785,4,30. Abigal, dt Samuel & Hannah, Dist. 96, S.C., m Samuel Gaunt.
1785,12,16. Samuel, s Samuel, Edgefield Co., S.C., m Elizabeth Milhouse.
1789,1,1. Samuel, Jr., Newberry Co., S.C., m Hannah Pearson.
1790,11,27. John, s John, dis mou.
1791,5,28. Samuel, Sr. dis.
1791,9,1. Robert, s John, dec, Newberry Co., S.C., m Sarah Paty.
1791,11,10. Ann, dt Samuel, Newberry Co., S.C., m Hugh O'Neall.
1794,4,26. Rebecca Elmore (form Kelly) rpd mou.
1794,9,27. Elizabeth Fluke (?) (form Kelly) rpd mou.
1800,9,17. Moses, Newberry Dist., S.C., m Mary Teague.
1802,9,25. Robert & w, Sarah, & ch gct Westland MM, Washington Co., Pa. (rem near Miami River, Ohio)
1802,9,25. Samuel & w, Hannah, & ch gct Westland MM, Washington Co., Pa. (rem near Miami River, Ohio)
1805,8,31. Moses & fam gct Miami MM, Ohio.

KIRK.
1794,4,26. John rocf MM in Phila., Pa., dated 1793,8,30.
1795,1,25. Isaac rocf Richland MM, dated 1794,9,10.
1802,11,4. Isaac, Newberry Dist., S.C., m Rebekah Jinkins.

KNIGHT.
1799,6,29. Martha rpd mou.

LAMB.
1775,3,25. William, of Padgit's Creek, dis.
1778,7,25. Thomas, Jr. rocf Fairfax MM, Va., dated 1775,3,25.
1779,10,30. Longshore, of Padget's Creek, dis mou.
1788,4,26. Robert, s Thomas, dis mou.
1789,4,25. William dis.

BUSH RIVER MONTHLY MEETING

LANCHESTER.
1799,5,25. Rachel rpd mou.

LAURANCE.
1790,11,11. Jane m Joseph Thompson.

LEWIS.
1792,1,28. Thomas, s Willia, recrq.
1792,1,28. Thomas, s Thomas, dec, recrq.
1793,2,28. Thomas, S.C., m (Rachel) Cook.
1797,9,30. Martha & ch, Caleb, Esther, Elizabeth & Mary, recrq.
1802,4,29. Caleb, s Thomas, dec, & Martha, Collaton Dist., S.C., m Susannah Cook.
1805,2,23. Thomas & fam gct Miami MM, Ohio.
1805,7,27. Thomas dis.
1806,7,26. Cabel & fam gct Little Miami MM, Ohio.
1806,7,26. Thomas, of Edisto, gct Little Miami MM, Ohio.

LONGSHORE.
1801,7,--. Sarah & ch. Sarah & Evelide, recrq.

McCLURE.
1800,8,30. Robert recrq.
1801,6,27. Margery & ch, John, Margaret, Mary, Margery, Robert & Jacob, recrq.
1806,7,26. Robert & fam gct Little Miami MM, Ohio.

McCOOL.
1773,4,24. Gabriel dis mou. (to first cousin)
1782,8,31. Gabriel con his misconduct.
1798,6,30. Gabriel McCool rq minute to travel in Va. with his mother, Ann Pugh.
1799,1,3. Rachel, Newberry Co., S.C., m Joseph Evans.
1799,10,26. James dis.
1801,1,31. Ann Wright (form McCool) dis mou.
1804,3,31. Thomas rpd mou.
1805,1,26. Gabriel, Jr. dis.
1806,8,30. Gabriel & fam gct Miami MM, Ohio.

McDANIEL.
1777,1,25. William recrq.

McDONALD.
1778,10,31. Joseph (McDonal) recrq.
1779,3,11. Joseph (McDonnald), s Mary, Dist. 96, S.C., m Elizabeth Parkins.
1780,11,9. William, s Thomas, dec. m Jemima Parkins.

McDONALD cont'd.
1801,2,5. Phebe, dt William, dec, m John Mills.
1805,2,23. Jemima & dt, Lydia, gc.
1805,4,27. John dis.

McNEAL.
1794,2,22. Mary Vernon (form McNeal) rpd mou.

MADDOX.
1806,10,25. Nathan, of Ga., gct Miami MM, Ohio.

MARSHALL.
1806,2,22. Elizabeth dis.

MENDENHALL.
1772,12,26. Phinehas & w & ch. Naomi, Grace, Abigail, Caleb & Joseph, roc.
1807,5,30. John, James & Marmaduke, s Marmaduke, gct Wainsville MM, Ohio. (pre---- at Miami MM)

MERRICK.
1774,11,26. Robert rocf Falls MM, Bucks Co., Pa., dated 1774,7,6.
1776,9,28. Robert & w & ch gct East Nottingham MM, Md.

MILES.
1771,1,1. Samuel, Lone Cane, Dist. 96, S.C., s William & Catharine, m Mary Taylor.
1776,4,27. William recrq.
1776,5,30. Samuel recrq.
1777,6,28. David & William recrq.
1778,12,3. William, s William & Catharine, Dist. 96, S.C., m Jane Taylor.
1783,12,4. David, s William & Catharine, Dist. 96, S.C., m Elizabeth Chandler.
1789,9,26. William, Sr., of Rocky Spring, dis.
1797,6,24. William rmt Rachel Elmore.
1797,12,6. Mary, dt Samuel, Newberry Co., S.C., m Henry O'Neall.
1800,10,29. Mary, dt William, Newberry Dist., S.C., m James Coate.
1801,7,2. Jonathan, s William, Newberry Dist., S.C., m Mary Pearson.
1802,4,24. David dis mou.
1803,6,29. Elizabeth, dt William, Newberry Dist., S.C., m William Coate.
1805,2,23. John, Sr. & fam gct Miami MM, Ohio.
1805,2,23. John, Jr. & fam gct Miami MM. Ohio.
1805,4,27. Samuel dis.
1806,7,26. Jonathan & fam gct Little Miami MM, Ohio.
1806,7,26. William & fam gct Little Miami MM, Ohio.

BUSH RIVER MONTHLY MEETING

MILLHOUSE.
1776,7,11. Jane (Millhouse), widow, m Benja. Vanhorn.
1785,12,16. Elizabeth (Milhouse), dt Samuel, dec, Craven Co., S.C., m Samuel Kelly.
1790,4,24. Samuel rpd mou.
1790,10,30. John, s Samuel, dis mou.
1791,5,28. John, Sr. dis.
1792,1,11. Robert (Milhouse), Union Co., S.C., s Henry & Rebecca, m Sally Nelson Compton.
1798,6,30. Charles dis mou.
1798,6,30. Daniel Henry dis.
1799,2,23. Robert gct Wrightsboro MM, Ga.

MILLS.
1782,7,27. John & ch, William, Marmaduke, Alexander, John, Jemima, Elizabeth & Mary, recrq.
1786,8,17. William, s John, Dist. 96, S.C., m Lydia Perkins.
1788,11,6. Alexander, s John, Newberry Co., S.C., m Eunice Pearson.
1789,12,31. Marmaduke, s John, Newberry Co, S.C., m Patience O'Neal.
1791,4,7. Jemima, Newberry Co., S.C., m James Jay.
1793,2,28. John, Newberry Co., S.C., m Mary Taylor.
1793,5,30. Elizabeth, dt John, Newberry Co., S.C., m Layton Jay.
1794,11,29. James & ch, William, John, Isaac, Jane, Sarah & David, recrq.
1800,10,30. Mary (Mill), dt John, Newberry Dist., S.C., m William Wright.
1801,2,5. John, s John, Newberry Dist., S.C., m Phebe McDonald.
1802,9,25. James & w, Lydia, & ch gct Westland MM, Washington Co., Pa. (rem near Miami River, Ohio)
1802,9,25. William, s James, rpd mou. (living at the Miami)
1804,7,28. William & fam gct Miami MM, Ohio.
1804,8,--. Marmaduke & fam gct Miami MM, Ohio.

MINTON.
1786,3,25. Richard, s Thomas, dis.

MOOR.
1782,5,25. Mordecai, s James, recrq.
1792,3,--. Mordecai dis.

MOTE.
1775,3,25. David & fam gct Wrightsboro MM. Ga.
1806,1,25. William gct Miami MM, Ohio.

NEEDERMAN.
1773,3,27. John recrq.

NELSON.
1773,6,26. Samuel & ch. Mary & Samuel, recrq.
1775,5,27. Jesse, s Samuel, recrq.
1777,7,26. Samuel & ch gct Cane Creek MM, N.C.

NICHOLS.
1794,5,31. James (Nicholas) recrq.
1801,7,9. James, Newberry Dist., S.C., m Ann Hollingsworth.
1805,5,25. James & fam gct Miami MM, Ohio.

O'NEAL.
1784,12,9. Abijah (O'Neall), s William & Mary, Bush River, Dist. 96, S.C., m Ann Kelly.
1789,12,31. Patience, dt Hugh, dec, Newberry Co., S.C., m Marmaduke Mills.
1791,11,10. Hugh (O'Neall), s William, dec, Newberry Co., S.C., m Ann Kelly.
1792,7,--. William dis.
1792,11,29. John (O'Neall), s William, dec, Newberry Co., S.C., m Hepzibah Gilbert.
1797,12,6. Henry (O'Neall), s William, dec, Newberry Co., S.C., m Mary Miles.
1800,1,1. Thomas (O'Neall), s William, dec, Newberry Co., S.C., m Sarah Evans.
1802,9,25. Abijah & w, Ann, & ch gct Westland MM. Washington Co., Pa., having rem near the Miami River, Ohio.
1803,5,--. Testification for Henry ordered.
1819,3,--. John & fam gct Ind.
1820,12,--. Hugh rpd mou.

O'SAYLE.
1798,2,24. Prudence Elmore (form O'Sayle) dis mou.

PARNEL.
1774,2,20. James recrq.
1784,5,18. James m Esther Towsent.

PATTY.
1773,3,11. Charles, Berkley Co., Dist. 96, S.C., m Mary Jay.
1783,1,25. Charles (Payty) dis.
1791,9,1. Sarah (Paty), dt Charles & Mary, Newberry Co., S.C., m Robert Kelly.
1794,11,29. Rachel Jones (form Paty) dis mou.

PATTY cont'd.
1801,7,--. Ann rpd mou.
1802,9,25. Mary (Peaty), w Charles, gct Westland MM, Washington Co., Pa. (rem near Miami River, Ohio)
1802,11,27. James (Peaty) recrq.
1806,8,30. James (Peaty) & fam gct Miami MM, Ohio.

PEARSON.
1772,10,1. Samuel, s Enoch, Berkley Co., S.C. m Mary Steddom.
1772,11,28. John & w & ch rocf Goshen MM, Chester Co., Pa., dated 1760,12,5.
1773,10,29. Mary, dt Samuel, Berkley Co., Dist. 96, S.C., m William Taylor.
1773,12,25. Thomas & ch. Joseph, Enoch, Benjamin, Thomas, Samuel, Jonas, Mary & Ann, recrq.
1774,1,20. Enoch rocf Buckingham MM, Bucks Co., Pa., dated 1773,8,18.
1774,1,20. Lawrance rocf Buckingham MM, Bucks Co., Pa., dated 1773,8,18.
1774,1,20. Elizabeth rocf Buckingham MM, Bucks Co., Pa., dated 1773,8,18.
1774,7,7. Mary, dt Thomas, Berkley Co., S.C., m Isaac Frazer.
1774,11,10. Enoch, s Samuel, Dist. 96, S.C., m Phebe Demans.
1775,7,8. Thomas, Dist. 96, S.C., m Mary Cambell.
1775,8,31. William, s Samuel, Dist. 96, S.C., m Ann Stidham.
1776,8,1. Martha m Henry Stiddom.
1778,3,23. William con his misconduct.
1778,4,25. Mtg appointed Thomas Pearson & John Clark guardians of Ralph & John Campbell, ch Samuel.
1778,6,27. Lawrence dis.
1778,10,31. Enoch, s John, of Padget Creek, dis.
1778,10,31. Enoch, s Joseph, (mentioned in minutes)
1779,3,27. John, s Joseph, rocf Middletown MM, Bucks Co., Pa., dated 1779,1,7.
1779,11,27. Mealin, s John, of Padget's Creek, dis.
1780,10,28. William d 7th day of the present, at his brother Thomas' & bur here.
1780,10,28. William rocf Uwchland MM, Chester Co., Pa., dated 1780,7,6.
1783,11,29. Joseph dis mou.
1783,12,11. Ann, dt Thomas & Ann, dec, Dist. 96, S.C., m Able Insco.
1784,9,25. Joseph rst by rq. (had been dis mou)

PEARSON cont'd.
1784,12,21. Enoch, s Thomas, Dist. 96, S.C., m Ann Evins.
1786,1,28. John, s Joseph, dis mou.
1788,11,6. Eunice, dt Samuel, Newberry Co., S.C., m Alexander Mills.
1789,1,1. Hannah, dt Samuel, Newberry Co., S.C., m Samuel Kelly, Jr.
1790,4,29. Benjamin, s Samuel, dec, Newberry Co., S.C., m Esther Furnas.
1790,9,9. Samuel, s Samuel, dec, Dist. 96, S.C., m Mary Coat.
1790,9,30. Sarah, dt Samuel, dec, Newberry Co., S.C., m Joseph Furnas.
1791,1,29. Benjamin rpd mou.
1791,9,24. William dis.
1792,5,28. Benjamin, s Thomas, dis mou.
1797,9,30. Benjamin rpd mou.
1797,9,30. Elizabeth & small ch, Joseph & Sally, recrq.
1798,3,31. Samuel, s Thomas, dis mou.
1799,1,31. Joanna, dt Enoch, dec, Newberry Co., S.C., m William Pugh.
1799,2,23. Mary & Martha dis.
1799,3,7. Samuel, s Enoch, dec, Newberry Co., S.C., m Ann Jay.
1799,10,2. Rebeca, dt Thomas & Mary, Newberry Co., S.C., m Wright Cook.
1800,1,29. Mary, dt Thomas, Newberry Co., S.C., m Thomas Jay.
1800,4,26. William's death rpd. Guardians appointed for his ch, Jesse, Samuel, William, Henry & Anne.
1800,5,30. Edna dis.
1800,9,27. Jonas dis.
1801,4,9. Thomas, s Thomas, Newberry Dist., S.C., m Olive Russell.
1801,7,2. Mary, dt Enoch, dec, Newberry Dist., S.C., m Jonathan Miles.
1801,7,--. Ruth rpd mou.
1803,12,31. Samuel & w & ch gct Miami MM, Ohio.
1804,12,6. Robert, s Enoch, Newberry Dist., S.C., m Charity Gilbreath.
1804,12,29. Ann, dt Joseph, dis.
1805,3,30. Samuel & fam gct Miami MM, Ohio.
1805,3,30. Thomas, Jr. & fam gct Miami MM.
1805,7,27. Benjamin & fam gct Miami MM, Ohio.
1805,7,27. Jesse & fam gct Miami MM, Ohio.
1805,7,27. Mary, Sr. gc.
1806,4,26. Benjamin & fam gct Little Miami MM, Ohio.

BUSH RIVER MONTHLY MEETING

PEARSON cont'd.
1806,4,26. Enoch & fam get Little Miami MM, Ohio.
1806,5,31. Thomas & fam get Little Miami MM, Ohio.
1806,8,30. Joseph & fam get Miami MM, Ohio.

PEMBERTON.
1774,3,26. Isaiah & ch, George, William, Isaiah, Richard, Thomas, John, Elizabeth, Hannah, Ann, Jude & Sarah, recrq.
1779,8,28. George, s Isaiah, dis mou.
1785,7,30. Richard dis mou.
1786,6,1. Ann, dt Isaah & Elizabeth, Dist. 96, S.C., m John Thomas.
1788,9,27. Isaiah, Jr. rpd mou.
1788,9,27. Thomas dis mou.
1793,1,24. John rpd mou.
1797,4,29. Ruth rmt Abel Thomas.
1799,6,29. Lidde recrq.
1800,10,25. Richard con his mou.
1800,11,29. Isaiah, William, Rachel, Elizabeth, Sarah & Anne, ch Richard, recrq.
1801,8,29. William dis mou.
1802,4,1. Sarah, dt Isiah & Elizabeth, both dec, Laurence Dist., S.C., m William Thomas.

PERKINS.
1779,3,11. Elizabeth (Parkins), dt Patience, Dist. 96, S.C. m Joseph McDonnald.
1780,9,30. Daniel dis.
1780,11,9. Jemima (Parkins), dt Charles, dec, Dist. 96, S.C., m William McDonald.
1781,5,26. Thomas dis.
1786,8,17. Lydia, dt Charles, dec, Dist. 96, S.C., m William Mills.
1793,3,--. Charles dis mou.

PHILIPS.
1793,12,28. Susannah (form Brooks) dis mou.

POTS.
1784,8,28. Mary (form Hunt), of Padget's Creek, dis mou.

PUGH.
1773,3,4. Betty, Berkley Co., S.C., m John Jay.
1775,9,30. Jesse dis mou.
1777,4,26. Thomas & fam get Hopewell MM, Va.
1782,1,26. David, s Azariah & Hannah, Dist. 96, S.C., m Rachel Wright.
1785,8,27. Ellis dis.
1790,12,2. Azariah, s Azariah & Hannah, Newberry Co., S.C., m Sophia Wright.

PUGH cont'd.
1797,6,24. David & w & ch get Cane Creek MM.
1797,6,24. Rachel (Pew) (with h) get Cane Creek MM.
1798,6,30. Gabriel McCool rq minute to travel in Va. with his mother, Ann Pugh.
1799,1,31. William, s Azariah, dec, Newberry Co., S.C., m Joanna Pearson.
1800,3,29. Thomas dis.
1801,1,31. Ellis con his misconduct.
1802,9,28. Ellis & w, Phebe, & fam get Westland MM, Washington Co., Pa. (removing to northwest side of the Ohio)
1804,8,25. Azariah & fam get Miami MM, Ohio.
1807,1,31. William rpd mou.

RAGAN.
1804,8,25. Mary gc (to Miami MM, Ohio)

RANDAL.
1775,10,28. Joseph & ch, Sarah, Joseph, James, Isaac, Thomas, Ann & Hannah, of Padjets Creek, recrq.
1785,7,30. Jonas dis mou.
1787,8,25. Joseph, Jr. dis mou.

RAVINCRAFT.
1774,8,27. William recrq.

REES.
1783,11,29. Solomon dis mou.
1785,2,26. Elizabeth dis.
1786,3,25. John dis mou.

RICKS.
1803,5,25. Robert rocf Deep River MM, N.C., dated 1803,5,2.
1803,9,--. Robert get MM in Va.

ROBERTS.
1780,9,6. Thomas (Robards), s Walter & Rebecah, dec, Dist. 96, S.C., m Ann Whitson.

RO-----.
1788,8,30. Thomas & John rocf Hopewell MM, Va., dated 1788,3,3.

RUBLE.
1788,8,30. Samuel dis mou.
1799,11,30. Samuel con his mou & presented recommendation from Lost Creek Mtg.
1800,12,27. Samuel get Lost Creek MM.

RUSSELL.
1797,6,8. Hannah, dt Samuel, dec, Newberry Co., S.C., m Jesse Jenkins.

BUSH RIVER MONTHLY MEETING

RUSSELL cont'd.
1799,5,9. Samuel, s Samuel, dec, Newberry Co., S.C., m Elizabeth Jenkins.
1799,11,14. Elizabeth, dt Samuel, dec, Newberry Co., S.C., m Amos Jenkins.
1801,4,9. Olive, dt Samuel, dec, Newberry Dist., S.C., m Thomas Pearson.
1805,3,30. Rosanna (Russel) & dt, Ann, gc.
1805,3,30. Samuel's death rpd. (father of infant boy, Isaac)

RUSTON.
1782,8,31. James recrq.
1802,4,24. Elizabeth Harris (form Ruston) rpd mou.
1805,9,28. John (Rustin) dis.

SANDEFER.
1796,2,27. Judah rocf Great Contentnea MM, N.C., dated 1795,1,10.

SANDERS.
1787,4,28. John & s, Benjamin, rocf Wrightsboro MM, Ga., dated 1787,4,--.

SIDEWELL.
1808,12,27. Nathan gct Concord MM, Ohio.

SINGLETARY.
1791,9,1. Sarah, dt David & Sarah, dec, m James Brooks.

SMITH.
1776,3,30. William, Aaron & Rachel, ch Ralph, Padget's Creek, dis.
1776,11,30. Zopher, s Ralph (above), of Padget's Creek, dis.
1778,9,26. William, of Cane Creek, dis.
1779,3,27. Daniel recrq.
1782,3,30. John dis mou.
1783,11,29. David, of Padget's Creek, dis.
1783,11,29. Joseph dis mou.
1784,4,24. David con his misconduct.
1789,8,29. Testification for Daniel, Jr. ordered.
1802,10,30. James dis.
1806,2,22. Daniel gct Deep Creek MM, N.C.

SNELGROVE.
1797,8,26. Achsah (form Gilbert) dis mou.

SPEERS.
1819,10,2. Samuel recrq.

SPENCER.
1820,1,--. (William) & w (Sarah) gct West Branch MM.

SPRAY.
1800,5,31. Naomi gc. (to Cane Creek MM, S.C.)

STANTON.
1805,4,27. Samuel pref Center MM. N.C., to m Sarah Hollingsworth.
1805,5,2. Samuel, s Samuel & Mary, Randolph Co., N.C., m Sarah Hollingsworth.

STARBERT (?).
1804,7,28. Charity m ____ Galbreath.

STEDDOM.
1772,10,1. Mary, widow, Berkley Co., S.C., m Samuel Pearson.
1775,8,31. Ann (Stidham), dt Mary, now w Samuel Pearson, Dist. 96, S.C., m William Pearson.
1776,8,1. Hanry (Stiddom), Dist. 96, S.C., s John, dec, & Mary, now Pearson, m Martha Pearson.
1799,9,12. Eunice, dt Henry, Newberry Co., S.C., m Abraham Hollingsworth.
1804,8,25. Henry & fam gct Miami MM, Ohio.

STEDMAN.
1775,1,27. James, mbr of East Nottingham MM, Pa., living here, dis by that mtg.
1782,7,27. Susannah (Stidman), dt Richard, dec, Pa., m Richard Thompson.

STEPHENS.
1790,10,30. Jonathan gct New Garden MM.

TAYLOR.
1771,1,1. Mary, dt Jonathan & Mary, Bush River Dist., m Samuel Miles.
1773,10,29. William, s Jonathan & Mary, Berkley Co., Dist. 96, S.C., m Mary Pearson.
1778,2,5. Richard, s Jonathan, Dist. 96, S.C., m Mary Gilbreath.
1778,12,3. Jane, dt Jonathan & Mary, Dist. 96, S.C., m William Miles.
1780,12,30. Mary, widow Richard, rq assistance in settling her affairs.
1789,12,31. Rhoda, dt Jonathan, Dist. 96, S.C., m John Barrett.
1791,5,28. Jonathan dis mou.
1792,2,25. Isaac dis mou.
1792,9,29. Mary, Newberry Co., S.C., m Joseph Jones.
1793,2,28. Mary, widow, Newberry Co., S.C., m John Mills.

BUSH RIVER MONTHLY MEETING

TAYLOR cont'd.
1793,7,27. Martha dis.
1797,1,--. Ann gct Wrightsboro MM. (Ga.)
1797,7,29. Jonathan dis.
1797,10,23. Samuel dis.

TEAGUE.
1800,9,17. Mary, Newberry Dist., S.C., m Moses Kelly.
1805,8,31. Samuel & fam gct Miami MM, Ohio.

THOMAS
1774,4,30. Edward, John, Isaac & Abel recrq. of father, Isaac, & mother.
1779,11,27. Abel rocf New Garden MM, N.C., dated 1779,9,25.
1783,6,12. Edward, s Isaac & Mary, Berkley Co., S.C., m. Mary Wright.
1786,6,1. John, s Isaac & Mary, Dist. 96, s.c., m Ann Pemberton.
1794,11,29. Elizabeth Cocks (form Thomas) rpd mou.
1797,4,29. Abel rmt Ruth Pemberton.
1801,11,28. Joseph rpd mou.
1802,4,1. William, s Isaac & Mary, Lawrence Dist., S.C., m Sarah Pumberton.
1805,3,30. Jesse & fam gct Miami MM, Ohio.
1806,2,22. William dis.
1806,3,29. John & fam gct Miami MM, Ohio.
1807,1,31. Edward & Mary gct Miami MM, Ohio.
1807,2,28. Joseph dis.
1819,6,5. Sarah gct Mill Creek MM, Ohio.

THOMPSON.
1773,12,25. Joseph & w, Ann, rocf Hopewell MM. N.C., dated 1773,9,6.
1773,12,25. Sarah, Richard, Mary, Jane & Joseph, ch Joseph & Ann, recrq.
1778,7,25. Joseph, Jr. recrq of father on recommendation from Hopewell MM, Va.
1778,7,25. Richard rec on recommendation from Hopewell MM, Va.
1782,7,27. Richard, s Joseph. Bush River, Dist. 96, S.C., m Susannah Stidman.
1790,4,24. Joseph, Jr. rpd mou.
1790,11,11. Joseph, Newberry Co., S.C., m Jane Laurance.
1795,6,27. Joseph, Jr's death rpd.
1798,3,31. Susan gc.
1798,4,28. Richard & fam gct Cane Creek MM.
1806,5,31. Joseph gct Little Miami MM, Ohio.

THORNTON.
1783,11,29. Eli rocf Deep River MM, N.C., dated 1783,9,1.
1797,2,25. Eli rpd mou. (second time)

TOMLINSON.
1771,12,30. William, s Jesiah, dec, Fredericksburg Tp., S.C., m Marther Coppock.

TOWNSEND.
1775,4,6. James (Townsend), s John & Elizabeth, Dist. 96, S.C., m Mary Cook.
1775,4,12. Elizabeth. dt John & Elizabeth, Dist. 96, S.C., m Amos Cook.
1781,1,27. James & William, s John, of Padget's Creek, dis.
1782,12,28. John, Jr., of Padget's Creek. dis.
1784,5,18. Esther (Townsent), dt John & Elizabeth, Dist. 96, S.C., m James Parnel.
1789,1,31. John, Jr. rst by rq.
1789,2,11. Margaret, dt John, m Samuel Hunt.

VANHORN.
1776,1,27. Cert rec for Benjamin from Pine Creek MM, Md., dated 1774,2,26; endorsed to New Garden, N.C.
1776,7,11. Benja., late of Pa., m Jane Milhouse.
1783,11,13. Benja., Dist. 96, S.C., m Joanna Demoss.
1785,2.26. Benjamin dis.
1798,10,27. Robert, Raburn's Creek, rpd mou.
1802,2,27. Benjamin's death rpd. (father of Jane & Rebecca)
1804,8,25. Roberts gc.

VERNON.
1772,9,24. James & Martha (Varman) roc (from Cane Creek MM, N.C.), dated 1772,5,2.
1794,2,22. Mary (form McNeal) rpd mou.
1794,4,26. Mary gct Wrightsboro MM, Ga.
1806,9,27. Nathaniel & fam gct Miami MM. Ohio.

WADSWORTH.
1799,11,30. Thomas' death rpd.

WALLES.
1796,1,30. Elizabeth gct Westfield MM.

WEEKS.
1779,8,28. William (Weeke), Jr. dis.
1785,3,26. John Weeks gct Deep River MM, N.C., at rq of grandfather, Benjamin Heaton.

BUSH RIVER MONTHLY MEETING

WEEKS cont'd.
1785,11,26. Benjamin & James Weeks, grandsons of Benjamin Heaton, gct Deep River MM, N.C.
1792,6,30. James rocf Deep River MM, N.C., dated 1792,--,5.
1794,2,22. Hannah gct Deep River MM. (N.C.)
1796,3,26. Benjamin, of Deep River, rmt Abigail Coppock.
1797,11,24. Benjamin (Weakes) rocf Deep River MM. N.C., dated 1796,4,--.
1798,1,27. James (Weaks) dis.

WEISNER.
1803,11,26. Jacob & ch, Elizabeth, Isaac & Mary (?), recrq.
1807,1,31. Jacob gct Miami MM, Ohio.

WHITSON.
1785,7,30. David, Willis, Jordan, Samuel & Solomon, ch Solomon, rocf Fairfax MM, (Va.), dated 1785,5,26.
1786,9,6. Ann, dt Solomon & Phebe, Dist. 96, S.C., m Thomas Robards.
1787,12,29. Solomon rocf Buckingham MM, Bucks Co., Pa., dated 1787,8,6.

WICKERSHAM.
1772,12,26. Jehu rocr New Garden MM, dated 1772,10,31.
1778,1,31. Jehu (Wilkersham) gct New Garden MM, N.C.

WILLIAM.
1800,10,25. Ann rpd mou.

WILSON.
1792,9,5. Seth, Union Co., S.C., s John & Dinah, m Mary Evans.
1793,4,27. Mary gct Cane Creek MM.

WRIGHT.
1768,10,10. John, s John & Rachel, Berkley Co., S.C., m Jemima Haworth.
1772,8,29. John, Jr. dis.
1772,12,12. Susannah, dt John & Rachel, Berkley Co., S.C., m Isaac Hollingsworth.
1774,7,30. Joseph dis.
1774,8,27. James rpd mou.
1777,11,29. William dis.
1778,5,30. John, Jr., s William, dis.
1778,7,25. Nathan rpd mou.
1782,1,26. Rachel, dt William & Leah, Dist. 96, S.C., m David Pugh.
1783,6,12. Mary, dt Joseph & Charity, Berkley Co., S.C., m Edward Thomas.

WRIGHT cont'd.
1786,11,16. Sarah, dt Joseph & Charity, Dist. 96, S.C., m James Hollingsworth.
1787,7,28. Thomas dis mou.
1789,3,12. Rachel, dt Joseph & Charity, Newberry Co., S.C., m John Hollingsworth.
1790,11,27. Nathan rocf Hopewell MM, dated 1790,2,1.
1790,12,2. Sophia, dt William & Leah, Lexonton Co., S.C., m Azariah Pugh.
1793,4,27. Nathan gct Hopewell MM, Va.
1794,8,30. James con his mou. (living at New Hope Mtg, N.C., Tenn.)
1795,4,25. Betty recrq.
1796,2,27. Jesse gct New Hope MM, N.C. (Tenn.)
1797,1,28. John dis.
1798,4,29. James & Joseph gct New Hope MM. (Tenn)
1798,10,27. William dis mou.
1800,3,29. Hannah Brooks (form Wright) dis mou.
1800,4,26. William, s Nathan, recrq.
1800,6,28. John, s Joseph, con his mou.
1800,9,27. Joseph, s William, dis mou.
1800,10,30. William, s Nathan, Newberry Dist., S.C., m Mary Mill.
1800,12,27. Isaac gct Lost Creek MM.
1801,1,31. Ann (form McCool) dis mou.
1801,3,28. Ann dis.
1802,4,29. Judith, dt John, dec, Newberry Dist., S.C., m Nebo Gaunt.
1803,4,30. Jemima & fam gct Westland MM, Washington Co., Pa.
1806,2.22. Jonah gct Miami MM, Ohio.
1806,3,29. John & w gct Maimi MM, Ohio.

WRIGHTSBOROUGH MONTHLY MEETING

Columbia (now McDuffie) County, Georgia

Wrightsborough Meeting was located in Columbia (now McDuffie) County, Georgia. In 1770 "the General Assembly of Georgia granted * * * a tract of 40,000 acres of land in St. Paul's Parish, * * * to be held in trust for the Quakers. Here they began the town of Wrightsborough, on Town Creek, sixteen miles from Appling, the county seat, and named it for Sir James Wright, Governor of the colony. The records date from 1773. In that year a preparative and a monthly meeting were organized in Wrightsborough township by representatives sent from New Garden. The certificates recorded show that the Quaker population was made up of settlers from South Carolina, North Carolina, Virginia, Pennsylvania, and Burlington in West New Jersey." ("Southern Quakers and Slavery," p. 118-119.)

Prior to the establishment of Wrightsborough Monthly Meeting, the meetings in Georgia had been attached to Bush River Monthly Meeting, in South Carolina. A list of the names of the members of the new meeting, compiled "by the order of Bush River Montly Meeting ye 4th of ye 10th month, 1774", and attested by William Wright and David Mote as Clerks, is recorded in the minutes of Wrightsborough Monthly Meeting under date of the 3rd of 12th month, 1774, as follows: "Benjamin Jackson and family; Richard Moor and family; John Jones and family; Jonathan Sell and family; John Stubbs and family; Catharine Sidwell and children; Benjamin Dunn and family; Isaac Cooper and family; Rachel Maddock and children, Samuel, Hannah and Benjamin; Margaret Day and son, John; Phineas Mendenhall and family; Joseph Mooney and family; Henry Jones and family; Sarah Curle; Peter Cox; Deborah Stubbs (now Cox) and family; James Vernon; Joseph Hollingsworth; Robert Hodgin and family; Walter Jackson and family; Martha Vernon; Rebecca Todd; Ruth Beedle; Hannah Hodgin; Francis Jones and family; John Hodgin and family."

John Stuggs, Henry Jones, John Hodgin, Joel Cloud, Thomas Sell, Nathan Stubbs and Francis Jones, Jr., were appointed as trustees, 3rd of 9th month, 1779, to receive a conveyance of land from the Governor for a meeting house.

The existing minutes of the monthly meeting end with the beginning of 1793. From other sources of information it is known that about 1800, just as in the case of the North and South Carolina meetings, there began a great migration to the territory north-west of the Ohio River. In "Southern Quakers and Slavery", page 124, Dr. Weeks says:-"In 1800 Joseph Cloud, a minister of North Carolina who had been among the meeting on 'the western waters', visited South Carolina and Georgia, no doubt in the interest of removal. Borden Stanton wrote them urging them to go west in 1802. A certificate from Wrightsborough Monthly Meeting to Cane Creek Monthly Meeting, N.C., dated June 4, 1803, is the last evidence we have of Georgia Friends. They had departed to the great West." Records now available show that Wrightsville Monthly Meeting was in existence at a later date than that mentioned by Dr. Weeks. Many certificates dated in 1804, and several as late as 4th month, 1805, were received by Miami Monthly Meeting, Ohio. The minutes of Lost Creek Monthly Meeting, Tennessee, also record the receipt of certificates from Wrightsborough bearing dates covering the same period. The latest date entered in Wrightsborough birth records is 7th of 5th month, 1805, the birth of Mary, daughter of John and Rachel Conner. On the 30th of 11th month, 1805, Bush River Monthly Meeting, S.C., issued a certificate, directed to Miami Monthly Meeting, Ohio, for this same John Conner and his family. The fact that the certificate was issued by Bush River seems to indicate that Wrightsborough M.M. had been laid down prior to that date. On the 28th of 6th month, 1808, Bush River issued a certificate to Miami for William Farmer and family, of Georgia, former members of Wrightsborough.

In 1809, certificates to Ohio were signed at New Garden Monthly Meeting, N.C., for former members of Bush River, Cane Creek (S.C.) and Wrightsborough Monthly Meetings. The minutes of this action (6th, 7th and 8th months, 1809), will be found in the introduction to Bush River records, page 1015.

The existing records of Wrightsborough Monthly Meeting, used in the proportion of the following abstract, consist of a book of birth and death records, and a book of minutes, 1772 to 1793. The minutes from 1793 to the closing of the meeting, about 1805, have been lost.

WRIGHTSBOROUGH MONTHLY MEETING

BIRTH AND DEATH RECORDS

Thomas Atkinson
Ruth Atjinson
Ch: William   b. 7-18-1782.
    Elizabeth   "   9-29-1784.
    Henry   "   2-21-1786; d.
                    10-30-1800.
    Martha   "   6-10-1787.
    Rachel   " 10-12-1788.
    Isaac   "   2- 7-1790; d.
                    6-27-1799.
    Ruth   "   5-25-1791.
    Edith   "   6-29-1793.
    Nathan   "   4-3-1795; d.
                    11-22-1800.
    David   "   8- 2-1797.

Mercer Brown
Sarah Brown
Ch: Betsy   b. 1- 8-1764; d.
                    9-6-1769.
    Mary   "   8-19-1765.
    Richard   " 10- 2-1767.
    Sarah   " 12-22-1769.
    Ann   "   3-13-1772; d.
                    3-23-178-(torn)
    Elizabeth   b. 5-15-1774; d.
                    4-17-1778.
    Margaret   " 11-16-1776.
    Phebe   "   3- 5-1778.
    Mercer   "   8-20-1781.

Richard Brown
Mary Brown b. 5-27-1769.
Ch: Sarah   b. 5-27-1769.
    Lydia   "   6-26-1790.
    Mercer   " 10-29-1792.
    John   "   3- 5-1794.
    William   "   1- 5-1796.
    Richard   "   5- 3-1798.
    Jonathan   " 12-28-1799.

Joel Cloud
Hannah Cloud
Ch: Mary   b. 5- 4-1779.
    Sarah   " 12-25-1780.
    Hannah   " 12-10-1782.
    Esther   " 12-25-1784.
    Lydea   " 10- 6-1786.
    Rebekah   "   8- 5-1789.
    Ann   " --- 6-1792.
    Joel, Jr.   " 10- 6-1793.

John Conner
Rachel Conner
Ch: William   b. 10-28-1795.
    John   "   4-27-1797;
                    d. same day.
    Catharine   "   4-29-1798.
    Jesse   "   8-10-1801.
    Thomas   "   1-29-1803.
    Mary   "   5- 7-1805.

Isaac Cooper
Prudence Cooper
Ch: Benjamin   b. 10-13-176-(torn)
    Isaac   "   9-15-1774.

Abiathar Davies
Lydia Davies
Ch: Amos   b. 11-17-1779.
    Rachel   "   6- 4-1781.
    Rhoda   "   3-17-1783.
    Samuel   "   2-20-1785.
    John   "   5- 2-1787.
    Mary   "   5- 9-1789.
    Sibilla   " 12- 7-1791.
    Benjamin   " 12- 3-1793.
    Sarah   "   6- 2-1796.
    Lydia   "   2-23-1798.
Above said Lydia Davies d. 2-27-
1802.

Amos Embree b. 12-20-1766.
Sarah Embree
Ch: Mary   b. 7-27-1788.
    Rebekah   " 12- 2-1789.
    John   "   3-27-1791.
    Sarah   "   5- 8-1794.
    Joseph   "   2-17-1796.
    Mercer   "   6- 6-1801.

William Farmer, s. John & Mary,
    b. 10-2-1800.

Thomas Gilbert, s. Joel & Eliza-
    beth. d. 4-11-1800).

Amos Green d. 2-23-1797.

Amos Green
Esther Green
Ch: Jesse   b. 12-13-1790.
    Hannah   " 12-14-1792.
    Amos   " 12-10-1794.

James Guest
Hannah Guest
Ch: Sarah   b. 5-16-1789.
    Mary   "   8-25-1790.
    James   "   2- 2-1793.
    Baker   "   3-11-1796.
    John   " 11-16-1797.

Elizabeth Jackson, widow Benjamin,
    d. 10-28-1782.

Francis Jones, Sr.
Sarah Jones d. 10-1-1801.
Ch: Rachel   b. 3-25-1801.
    Francis   " 10-20-1753.
    Samuel   "   3- 8-1755.
    Henry   " 10-22-1756.
    John   " 12-24-1758;
                    d. 7-10-----.
    Hannah   " 10- 9-1760.
    Thomas   "   3-16-1762;
                    c. 9-27-1785.
    Jane   "   6-24-1764.
    Elener   " 12-19-1766.
    Sarah   "   6-23-1767.
    Joseph   "   4-25-1769.
    Mary   "   2- 5-1771.
    Deborah   "   5- 7-1773.

WRIGHTSBOROUGH MONTHLY MEETING

Francis Jones, Jr.
Rachel Jones
Ch: Sarah   b. 2- 8-1776.
    Francis   " 2-18-1889; d.
                       3-17-1783.
    David   " 9-25-1780.

Henry Jones
Keziah Jones
Ch: Elizabeth   b. 9-26-1760.
    George   " 7-20-1770.
    William   " 8-10-1772.
    Sarah   " 2-19-1775.
    Kezia   " 11-20-17--(torn)
    Ann   " 3- 1-18--(torn)

John Jones d. 6- 9-1781.
Mary Jones " 10- 9-1802.

John Jones d. 1-20-1802.

Joseph Jones
Mary Jones
Ch: Rachel   b. 10- 6-1793.
    Rebekah   " 6-23-1796; d.
                    8-11-1796.

Samuel Jones
Mary Jones
Ch: John   b. 1-19-1781.
    Jonathan   " 1-23-1783.
    Samuel   " 9- 8-1786.
    Francis   " 3-31-1788.
    Dorcas   " 9-18-1789.
    Thomas   " 9-13-1790.
    Sarah   " 3- 9-1792.
    Jesse   " 4-15-1794.

Nathaniel Kellum
Elizabeth Kellum
Ch: William   b. 9- 1-1779.
    John   " 4-13-1784.
    Elizabeth " 8-24-1786.
    Sarah   " 9-22-1788.
    Nathaniel " 9-12-1791.
    Joseph   " 7-22-1794.
    Elijah   " 11-12-1797.
    Susanna   " 4-28-1799.

John McNeal, s. Mary Vernon by
   her first hl, b. 4-1-17--(torn)

Samuel Maddock
Rachel Maddock
Ch: Sarah   b. 6-24-1774.
    Joseph   " 11- 6-1775; d.
                    4-9-----(torn)
    Deborah   " 2-23-1777; d.
                    12-20-1777.
    Nathan   " 8-10-1777-(torn)
    Frances   " 12-19-1779.
    Hannah   " 9-19-1781; d.
                    3-26-1784.
    John   " 9-23-1783; d.
                    8-7-1794.
    Elener   " 3-10-1787.

James Mendenhall, 2nd s. Aaron &
   Prose, b. 9-26-1714.
Hannah Mendenhall, w. James, b.
   11-14-1716/7.

Joseph Mendenhall
Elizabeth Mendenhall
Ch: Phebe   b. 10- 7-1777.
    Robert   " 12-24-1779.
    Jonathan   " 5-6-179-(torn)

Marmaduke Mendenhall, s. James &
   Hannah, b. 11-23-1754; d. 2-23-
   1797.

Marmaduke Mendenhall
Alice Mendenhall
Ch: Son   b. 1-14-1779; d.
                       23rd.
    John   " 2- 8-1780; d.
                    9-12-1788.
    Elijah   " 7-28-1782.
    Mary   " 1-25-1785.
    Hannah   " 2-20-1788.
    John   " 5- 3-1790.
    James   " 12-21-----(torn)
    Marmaduke   " 8-17-179-(torn)
Alice Mendenhall d. 12-6-1797.

Daniel Milhouse, s. Robert &
   Sarah, b. 3-13-1800.

Joseph Mooney d. 10-2-1774.
Mary Mooney
Ch: Anne   b. 1-21-1747/8 O.S.
    John   " 12-10-1749 O.S.
    Prudence   " 6- 6-1752 N.S.
    Sarah   " 12-21-1754.
    Mary   " 4-18-1757.
    Joseph   " 7-28-1759.
    Deborah   " 4- 5-1762.
    Martha   " 7-27-1764; d.
                    8-9-1778.

James Moore
Alice Moore
Ch: Thomas   b. 4-15-1774.
    Auerila   " 12-31-1776.

Abraham Northdike (Nordyke)
Mary Northdike
Ch: Aden   b. 6-19-1762, 7:00 PM.
    Israel   " 2-17-1764, 3:00 PM.
    Benajah   " 1- 6-1766, 9:00 PM.
    Beulah   " 3- 8-1769, 6:00 PM.
    Micajah   " 3-26-1771, 5:00 PM.
    Daniel   " 4-27-1775, noon.
    Phebe   " 1- 9-1779.
    Hiram   " 2-23-1782.

Ephraim Owen
Sarah Owen
Ch: John   b. 8-24-1790.
    Benjamin   " 1-16-1792.
    Mary   " 2-25-1795; d.
                    9-22-1797.
Continued on next page.

WRIGHTSBOROUGH MONTHLY MEETING

Ephraim & Sarah Owen cont'd.
Ch: Ephraim   b. 5-11-1797.
    Elizabeth   " 7-30-1799.
    Sarah   " 4-27-1801.
    Ruth   " 1-27-1803.

Samuel Owen
Margery Owen
Ch: Sarah   b. 8-15-1796.
    Ephraim   " 12-23-1797.
    John   " 9-29-1800.
    Mary   " 6- 7-1802.

William Patton b. 7-29-1754
Rachel Patton " 1-30-1759.
Ch: Isaac   " 4-29-1778.
    Mary   " 2-27-1780.
    Ann   " 3- 9-1782.
    Grace   " 11- 9-1784.
    Mahlon   " 10-15-1787.
    William   " 5-28-1790.
    Rachel   " 6-23-1793.
    John   " 2-27-1796.
    Sarah   " 4-18-1799.

Thomas Phelan b. 10-28-1759.

Cn: Evane   b. 6-13-1775.
    Jeremiah   " 3- 2-1777.
    Elizabeth   " 6-14-1779.
    Mary   " 11-29-1787.
    Ann   " 5- 7-1789; d.
                    6-18-1789.

Joel Sanders   d. 2-2-1782.
Charity Sanders d. 1-27-1782.
Ch: Miriam   b. 11-28-1744 O.S.
    Benjamin   " 6-10-1746 O.S.
    John   " 2- 1-1748 O.S.
    Joel   " 6-19-1751 O.S.
    Dempsey &
      Lydia   " 3-19-1753.
    Hollorvel?   " 3-21-1755.
    Ferribe   " 9-15-1756.
    Thomas   " 4-18-1759.
    Josiah   " 3-13-1761.
    Abraham   " 8-13-1763.
    Mordecai   " 9-10-1764.
    Sarah   " 1-14-1767.

Joel Sanders, Jr.
Sarah Sanders
Ch: William   b. 6- 1-1778.
    Barbara   " 10-28-1780.

Mordecai Sanders
Margaret Sanders d. 7-28-1802.
Ch: Sarah   b. 5-24-1787.
    Charity   " 6- 8-1788.

Jonathan Sell
Sarah Sell
Ch: Thomas   b. 5-10-1756.
    Elizabeth   " 3-19-1758.
    Enos   " 8-21-1760.
    Deborah   " 10-22-1762.
    Patience   " 11-21-1767.
    Mary   " 10-13-1770.
    John   " 9-13-1773.

Jonathan & Sarah Sell cont'd.
Ch: Jonathan   b 3-10-1776.
    Sarah   "11-10-1778.

John Stubbs
Jane Stubbs
Ch: Esther   b. 8-28-1786.
    Sarah   " 6-15-1788.
    Margaret   " 6- 8-1790.
    Hannah   " 5-11-1792.
    Jane   " 2-19-1794.
    John   " 4-27-1796.
    Rachel   " 10-13-1789.
    Joseph   " 11- 6-1801.

Joseph Stubbs
Zilpha Stubbs
Ch: Mary   b. 6- 4-1784.
    Rachel   " 12-29-1785.
    Sarah   " 1- 7-1787.
    Jacob   " 11-17-1788.
    Isaac   " 3- 4-1790.
    Deborah   " 2-12-1792.
    Abraham   " 5-28-1793.
    Elizabeth   " 1-12-1795.
    Rebekah   " 5-18-1796.
    Iddo   " 1- 3-1798.
    Zilpha   " 11-18-1799; d.
                    4-5-1800.
    Eliza   " 3-15-1301.
    Rhoda   " 12- 5-1802.

Samuel Stubbs
Mary Stubbs
Ch: Rebekah   b. 3-10-1793.
    William   " 1-14-1795.
    Tabitha   " 12-23-1796.
    Newton   " 10-12-1798.
    Patcey   " 6-18-1800.
    Sarah   " 7- 7-1802.

Camm Thomas b. 8-8-1763.
Elizabeth Thomas b. 9-10-1771.
Ch: William   " 8-28-1791.
    Abijhai   " 5-25-1793.
    Asahel   " 9- 5-1795.
    Hezekiah   " 2-17-1798.
    Caty   " 4-19-1800.
    Priscilla   "12- 7-1803.

Rebeca Thomas, Sr. d. 10-27-1802.

Amos Vernon
Mary Vernon
Ch: James   b. 4-18-1800.
    Rachel   " 2-16-1802.

Content Vernon, dt. Robert & Ann,
  b. 4-30-1801.

Isaac Vernon
Mary Vernon
Ch: Amos   b. 1-21-1792.
    Mary   " 2-25-1794.
    Samuel   " 3-31-1797.
    Elizabeth   " 2- 7-1800.
John McNeal, s. Mary by her first
  h., b. 4-1-17--(torn).

WRIGHTSBOROUGH MONTHLY MEETING

James Vernon
Content Vernon
Ch: Amos   b. 12-27-1773.
    James   "   2- 7-1775.
    Robert   "   2- 2-1777.
    Solomon   "   7- 7-1779.
    Theodate "   3- 8-1781.

Nathaniel Vernon
Grace Vernon
Ch: Tamor   b. 1-15-1785.
    Margaret "   3-25-1787.
    Lydia   "   6-23-1789.
    William   "   6-12-1793; d.
                  9-2-1795.
    Thomas   "   8- 4-1796.
    Samuel   " 10-15-1799.

Nathaniel & Grace Vernon cont'd.
Ch: Ann   b. 3-22-1802.

Daniel Williams d. 2-7-1802.
Mary Williams
Ch: Sarah   b. 4- 9-1773.
    Edward   " 11- 7-1774.
    Sibbilla " 3-10-1776.
    Elizabeth " 3- 7-1778.
    Ruth   " 9-15-1780.
    Amy   " 7-30-1782.
    Rebecca   " 6-11-1785.
    Mary   " 12-23-1787.

Joseph Williams d. 4-20-1782.

117

MINUTES AND MARRIAGE RECORDS

ANGELY.
1782,9,7. Mary (form Dunn) dis mou.

ANGLIN.
1788,6,7. John & small ch. Susanna, Elijah, Nathan, Henry, John, Mary & Catharine, recrq.

ATKINSON.
1807,1,31. Samuel & fam, of Ga., gc. (cert issued by Bush River MM, S.C.)

BARNS.
1779,9,4. Jacob & w, Mary, & ch. Elizabeth, Mary, James, Olive, Abigail, Jacob, Jeremiah & Samuel, rocf Cane Creek MM, N.C., dated 1778,12,6.
1780,6,3. Mary David (form Barns) dis mou.
1780,10,7. James dis.
1783,2,1. Rache, Olive & Abigail (Barnes) dis.

BATTON.
1792,9,1. Richard & Cathren & ch, Ann, James, Richard, John, Cathren & Jonathan, rocf Bush River MM, S.C., dated 1792,8, 25.

BECK.
1782,11,2. John recrq.
1783,3,1. John gct Deep River, MM, N.C.

BENSON.
1776,2,3. Robert rocf Uwchland MM, Chester Co., Pa., dated 1774,11,10.
1776,2,3. William, Jr. rocf Uwchland MM, Chester Co., Pa., dated 1774,11,10.
1777,5,3. Alice rmt Marmaduke Mendenhall.
1780,10,7. William dis.
1783,9,6. Jane gct Hoepwell MM, Va.

BROOKS.
1784,8,7. Hannah (form Stuart) dis mou.

BROWN.
1773,11,4. Joseph & w & fam rocf Bush River MM; endorsed by New Garden MM, 1772,9,20.
1777,7,5. Joseph & w & fam gct New Garden MM, N.C. (some time rem)
1778,11,7. James recrq.
1783,2,1. James & w, Martha, & small ch, John, James, Rebecca, Polly & Phebe, rqct Deep River MM, N.C.

BROWN cont'd.
1783,3,1. Mary (form Hickson) dis.
1785,3,5. Mercer & Sarah rocf Fairfax MM, Va.; sent on by Bush River MM.
1787,9,11 Samuel rocf New Garden MM, N.C., dated 1787,6,30.
1790,1,2. Mary con her mou.
1790,4,3. Richard con his mou.

BUFFINGTON.
1777,2,1. Sarah con her mou.
1782.12,7. Sarah rqct Hopewell MM, Va.

BUNTING.
1790,5,1. Sarah's death rpd.

BUTLER.
1778,10,3. John (Buttler) rocf Uwchland MM, Chester Co., Pa., dated 1778,2,5.
1780,3,5. John (Buttler) rqct Uwchland MM, Chester Co., Pa., but decided not to rem because of the difficulty of traveling.
1781,10,6. John gct Uwchalnd MM, Pa.

CARL.
1784,4,3. Sarah gct Bush River MM, S.C.

CARSON.
1778,11,7. Thomas recrq.
1782,1,5. John, Jr. dis.

CLOUD.
1775,8,5. Joel rocf Kennett MM, Chester Co., Pa., dated 1775,1, 12.
1777,4,5. Joel gct Pa., to m.
1778,9,5. Joel & w, Hannah, rocf Bradford MM, Chester Co., Pa., dated 1778,4,23.
1793,1,5. Testimonial for Joel ordered.

CONNER.
1805,11,30. John & fam gct Miami MM, Ohio (certificate issued by Bush River MM, S.C.)

COOPER.
1783,3,1. Benjamin rmt Ferrebee Sanders.
1786,12,2. Benjamin & fam gct Bush River MM, S.C.
1787,4,7. Isaac & w & ch, Isaac & Joseph, gct Bush River MM, S.C.

COX.
1774,6,4. Richard rmt Ann Hodgin.
1780,5,6. Richard & w & small ch, Thomas & Mary, gct Bush River MM, S.C.
1791,9,3. Amey (form Sidwell) dis mou.

WRIGHTSBOROUGH MONTHLY MEETING

CREW.
1786,5,6. Littleberry (man) rocf Cedar Creek MM, Va., dated 1786,3,11.
1792,1,7. Letilberry (Crews) gct Springfield MM, N.C.

DAVIS.
1778,3,7. Abiather rocf Uwchland MM, Chester Co., Pa., dated 1777,10,9.
1778,12,5. Abiathar rmt Lydia Embree.
1780,6,3. Mary (form Barns) dis mou.

DAY.
1789,8,1. John con his mou.
1790,12,4. John dis.
1792,3,3. Margret dis.

DIXON.
1792,3,3. Eli rocf Goose Creek MM, Loudown Co., Va., dated 1791,10,24.
1792,3,3. John rocf Goose Creek MM, Loudown Co., Va., dated 1791,4,25.
1792,3,3. Solomon & w, Ann, & ch, Henry, Joseph, Solomon & Stephen, rocf Goose Creek MM, Loudown Co., Va., dated 1791, 10,24.

DUNN.
1775,5,6. Josiah dis mou.
1776,1,6. Sarah dis.
1776,6,1. Nehemieh dis.
1781,6,2. Elizabeth Stuart (form Dunn) dis mou.
1782,9,7. Mary Angely (form Dunn) dis mou.

EDWARDS
1790,4,3. Jane recrq.
1792,12,1. James rocf Goshen MM, Pa., dated 1791,11,11.

EMBREE.
1775,12,2. John & w & ch, Sarah, Rachel, Lydia, Jesse, Jonathan, Amos, John & Mary, rocf Bush River MM, S.C., dated 1775,9, 30.
1778,12,5. Lydia rmt Abiathar Davis.
1783,5,3. Jesse dis.
1788,12,6. Amos con his mou.
1789,3,7. Sarah con her mou.
1792,2,4. Jonathan (Embre) dis.

FARMER.
1788,5,3. William & w, Catharine, & ch, Joseph, Elizabeth, Benjamin, Mary, Catharine, Thomas & Hannah, rocf Cane Creek MM, N.C., dated 1788,2,2.

FARMER cont'd.
1788,5,7. Rachel & John, ch, William & Catherine, b since their rem from Cane Creek MM, rec as mbr also.
1789,8,1. Benjamin con his mou.
1789,8,1. Rebekah & small ch, John, William & Jesse recrq.
1789,12,5. William (Pharmer), Jr. rocf Cane Creek MM, N.C., dated 1789,10,3.
1789,12,5. William (Pharmer), Jr. con his mou.
1808,6,28. William & fam, of Ga., gct Miami MM, Ohio. (Cert issued by Bush River MM, S.C.)

GALBREATH.
1785,12,3. John (Galbreathe), of Bush River MM, rmt Sarah Sanders.
1786,6,3. John & Sarah gct Bush River MM, S.C.
1787,8,4. Alizabeth rmt Henry Jones.

GREEN.
1789,7,4. Amos rocf Concord MM, Chester Co., Pa., dated 1788. 11,5.
1790,1,2. Amos rmt Esther Hart.

GUEST.
1788,5,3. James recrq.
1788,9,6. James rmt Hannah Jones.

HAINES.
1777,4,5. Nathan rocf Goshen MM, Chester Co., Pa., dated 1775,7,7.
1777,4,5. Evan, Deborah, Jane & Ellis, ch Ellis, Sr., rocf Goshen MM. Pa., dated 1775,7,7.
1781,6,2. Evan (Hains) dis.
1785,9,3. Jane dis.
1786,12,2. Mary (Hanes) gct Deep River MM, N.C.

HALL.
1787,5,5. Phebe gct Bush River MM, S.C.

HART.
1788,8,2. Esther recrq.
1790,1,2. Esther rmt Amos Green.

HATHBORN.
1786,9,2. Hannah (form Sidwell) dis mou.

HICKSON.
1783,3,1. Mary Brown (form Hickson) dis.

HODGIN.
1774,6,4. Ann rmt Richard Cox.
1783,1,4. John (Hodgen) dis.
1788,12,6. William con his mou.
1789,6,6. Lydia dis.
1797,5,5. Agnes (Hodgen) & ch, Mary & John, recrq.

WRIGHTSBOROUGH MONTHLY MEETING

HOGE.
1775,4,1. Jacob, Phebe & William rocf Hopewell MM: endorsed by Bush River MM.
1789,3,7. Jacob dis.
1789,3,7. William dis.

HOLLIMAN.
1785,6,4. Elizabeth dis.

HOLLINGSWORTH.
1784,7,6. Joseph gct Cane Creek MM, N.C.

JACKSON.
1775,5,3. Thomas dis.
1777,6,7. Walter dis.
1779,9,4. Joseph & Deborah (now McGinty), ch Thomas, dec, rocf Cane Creek MM, N.C., dated 1778,12,6.
1780,4,1. Joseph dis mou.
1781,7,7. Absolam rocf Center MM, dated 1780,4,15.

JOHNSON.
1786,9,2. Susannah dis.

JONES.
1774,3,5. Rachel rmt Samuel Maddock.
1775,7,1. Francis, Jr. rmt Rachel Mote.
1775,7,1. John, Jr. con his mou.
1779,11,6. Samuel rmt Mary Mote.
1780,2,5. John rocf Cane Creek MM, N.C., dated 1779,2,6.
1782,4,6. John dis.
1782,4,6. Jonathan dis.
1782,7,6. Nathan dis.
1784,2,7. Henry & w, Keziah, & ch, Elizabeth, George, William, Sarah, Keziah, Ann & Henry, gct Cane Creek MM, N.C.
1785,5,7. Jane rmt John Stubbs.
1788,9,6. Hannah rmt James Guest.
1791,2,5. Mary rmt Samuel Stubbs.
1792,9,1. Joseph gct Bush River MM, S.C., to m.
1797,8,4. Henry rmt Alizabeth Galbreath.

KING.
1781,11,3. Mary (form Sidwell) dis mou.

LACY.
1792,8,4. Jane rocf Indian Spring MM, Md., dated 1792, 1,20.

LAY.
1781,10,6. William recrq.

McCOWEN.
1782,4,6. Bathsheba rocf Warrington MM, Pa., dated 1779, 5,12.

McGINTY.
1779,9,4. Joseph & Deborah Jackson (now McGinty), ch Thomas Jackson, dec, rocf Cane Creek MM, N.C., dated 1778,12,6.

McMUN.
1776,3,2. John rocf Cane Creek MM, N.C., dated 1775,5,6.
1776,6,1. John con his mou.

MADDOCK.
1773,11,4. Joseph rocf Cane Creek MM, dated 1773,8,7.
1773,11,4. Joseph appointed clerk.
1774,3,5. Samuel rmt Rachel Jones.
1783,10,4. Joseph dis war-like behavior.
1784,6,5. Joseph con his misconduct.

MENDENHALL.
1775,7,1. James & w & s, Marmaduke, rocf New Garden MM, N.C., dated 1775,4,29.
1775,8,5. Joseph rocf Concord MM, Chester Co., Pa., dated 1775,1,4.
1776,4,6. Joseph rmt Elizabeth Sell.
1777,5,3. Marmaduke rmt Alice Benson.
1779,2,6. Marmaduke & w gct Deep River MM, N.C.
1781,11,5. Hannah gct Deep River MM, N.C.
1783,5,3. Phinehas dis.
1783,10,4. Mary & Grace gct Deep River MM, N.C.
1783,12,6. Catharine (form Sidwell) dis mou.
1784,10,2. Marmaduke & w, Alice, & ch, John & Elijah, rocf Deep River MM, N.C., dated 1784,6,7.
1784,10,2. Mary rocf Deep River MM, N.C., dated 1784,6,7.
1784,11,6. Joseph & w, Elizabeth, & small ch, Phebe, Robert & Jonathan, gct Deep River MM, N.C.
1786,4,1. Mary dis.
1786,10,7. Catharine con her mou.
1791,5,7. Cabel & Joseph, s Phinehas, gct Deep River MM, N.C.
1792,11,3. Cathren con her mou.
1793,1,5. Cathren gct Deep River MM, N.C.

MIDDLETON.
1777,4,5. Joseph recrq.
1783,3,1. Joseph & small ch, Jehu & Hannah, gct Deep River MM, N.C.

MOONEY.
1781,8,4. Joseph (Moony) dis.
1791,1,1. John dis mou.

WRIGHTSBOROUGH MONTHLY MEETING

MOORE.
1778,1,3. John rocf Cane Creek MM, N.C., dated 1777,4,5.
1779,4,3. James (Moor), s John, recrq.
1781,8,4. James dis.
1785,4,2. John con his mou.
1789,4,4. Alexander (Moor) recrq.

MOORMAN.
1786,6,3. Lishy, Charles, Elizabeth & Milly, ch Benjamin, dec, rocf Cane Creek MM, N.C., dated 1786,3,4.

MORGAN.
1783,9,6. Deborah rocf Bush River MM, S.C.

MOTE.
1775,5,6. David & w & ch rocf Bush River MM, dated 1775,4,29.
1775,7,1. Rachel rmt Francis Jones, Jr.
1779,11,6. Mary rmt Samuel Jones.
1784,2,7. Jonathan con his mou.
1788,6,7. Ann & ch. Timothy, Ann & david, recrq.
1791,6,4. John con his mou.
1791,9,3. Jeremiah con his mou.

NIPPER.
1776,9,7. Ann dis.

NORDYKE.
1775,9,2. Abraham & w & ch rocf Burlington MM, West New Jersey, dated 1772,9,6.
1783,10,4. Abraham & w, Mary, & ch, Adan, Israel, Benajah. Beverley, Micajah, Daniel. Phebe & Hiram, gct Deep River MM. N.C.

PATTAN.
1790,4,3. William & Rachel & small ch, Isaac, Mary, Ann, Grace & Mahlon, recrq.

PHELAN.
1786,1,7. Thomas & ch. Evans, Jeremiah & Elizabeth, recrq. (rq made 1781,6,2 had been dropped)
1791,5,7. Mary (Phalan) & dt, Affinity, recrq.

PINSON.
1781,2,2. Rebecca dis.

PUGH.
1788,8,2. Elijah recrq.
1789,12,5. Jesse rocf Cane Creek MM, N.C., dated 1788, 11,1.
1791,9,3. Hannah con her mou.

RICKESON.
1785,12,3. Prudence dis.

SANDERS.
1775,5,6. Joel & w & ch rocf Cane Creek MM, dated 1773,1,7.
1776,1,6. John rmt Massey Sims.
1776,7,6. John, Jr. con his mou.
1777,2,1. Hollaway con his mou.
1781,2,2. Elizabeth dis.
1781,3,3. Hollowell's death rpd.
1782,10,5. John dis.
1782,10,5. Sarah, w Joel, recrq.
1782,12,7. John con his misconduct.
1783.3,1. Ferrebee rmt Benjamin Cooper.
1785,12,3. Sarah rmt John Galbreathe, of Bush River MM.
1786,8,5. Mordecai rmt Margaret Thomas.
1786,12,2. William & Barbara, small ch Joel, recrq of father.
1787,4,7. John & w, Mary, & ch, Margery, Charity, Benjamin & Prudence, gct Bush River MM, S.C.
1787,7,2. Thomas dis.
1790,10,2. Lydia Scot (form Sanders) dis mou.
1792,4,7. Abraham con his mou.

SCOFIELD.
1791,3,5. Joseph & w, Susannah, rocf Indian Spring MM. Md., dated 1790,5,21.

SCOT.
1784,9,4. Deborah (form Sell) dis mou.
1790,10,2. Lydia (form Sanders) dis mou.

SELL.
1776,4,6. Elizabeth rmt Joseph Mendenhall.
1781,6,2. Thomas (Sells) dis.
1784,9,4. Deborah Scot (form Sell) dis mou.
1785,2,5. Jonathan & w, Sarah, & ch, Patience, Mary, John, Jonathan, & Sarah, rqct Deep River MM, N.C.
1785,9,3. Sarah & ch gct Deep River MM, N.C.
1787,3,3. Jonathan gct Deep River MM, N.C.
1787,4,7. Enos gct Center MM, N.C.
1788,4,5. Thomas con his misconduct & presented recommendation from Muddy Creek Mtg., N.C.
1788,5,3. Thomas gct Deep River MM, N.C.

SIDWELL.
1773,12,4. John rocf Cane Creek MM, dated 1773,6,1.
1778,5,2. Ruth, w David, & ch, Mary, Elizabeth, Anne, David, Joseph & Ruth, recrq.
1781,11,3. Mary King (form Sidwell) dis mou.

SIDWELL cont'd.
1783,12,6. Catharine Mendehall (form Sidwell) dis mou.
1785,1,1. Mary & Elizabeth Waggoner (form Sidwell) both dis mou.
1786,9,2. Hannah Hathborn (form Sidwell) dis mou.
1786,12,2. Nathan con his mou.
1791,9,3. Amey Cox (form Sidwell) dis mou.

SIMS.
1776,1,6. Massey rmt John Sanders.

STANLEY.
1790,1,2. Thomas rocf Cedar Creek MM, Hanover Co., Va., dated 1787,1,13.
1791,6,4. Thomas gct Cedar Creek MM, Va.

STUART.
1773,12,4. Robert & w & ch, Gravener, Amos & Hannah, rocf New Garden MM, dated 1773,5,29.
1781,6,2. Elizabeth (form Dunn) dis mou.
1782,2,2. Amos dis.
1782,11,2. Gravener gct Center MM, N.C.
1784,8,7. Hannah Brooks (form Stuart) dis mou.
1788,5,3. Gravener (Stewart) returned cert granted to Center MM, N.C., in 1782, 11 mo., never having delivered it.
1788,5,3. Gravener (Stewart) con his mou.

STUBBS.
1779,7,3. Thomas dis.
1783,5,3. Nathan con his misconduct.
1783,8,2. Nathan gct Cane Creek MM, N.C.
1783,8,2. Isaac gct Cane Creek MM, N.C.
1785,3,5. Nathan rocf Cane Creek MM, N.C.
1785,5,7. John rmt Jane Jones.
1785,7,2. Nathan con his mou.
1785,10,1. Joseph con his mou.
1787,11,3. Nathan gct Cane Creek MM, N.C.
1790,11,6. Nathan & w, Elizabeth, & s, William, rocf Cane Creek MM, N.C., dated 1790,5,1.
1791,2,5. Samuel rmt Mary Jones.
1791,9,3. Isaac & w, Margaret, & ch, John & Samuel, rocf Deep River MM, N.C., dated 1791,6,6.

THOMAS.
1783,9,6. Rebecca & ch. Abishae, Margaret, Elizabeth. Camm, Sarah & Rebecca, rocf Goshen MM, Cester Co., Pa.
1786,8,5. Margaret rmt Mordecai Sanders.
1791,1,1. Camm con his mou.

TODD.
1792,8,4. Robert, Stephen, Theodate & William, small ch Rebecka recrq of mother.

VERNON.
1775,5,6. James con his mou.
1776,3,2. Isaac rocf Cane Creek MM, N.C., dated 1775,8,3.
1784,12,4. Content & ch, Amos, James, Robert, Solomon & Theodate, gct Cane Creek MM, N.C.
1786,7,1. Hannah gct Deep River MM, N.C.
1788,12,6. Grace rocf Deep River MM, N.C., dated 1788,9,1.
1791,2,5. Nathaniel (Varnon) rocf Deep River MM, N.C., dated 1791,1,3.
1791,10,1. Tamour, Margaret & Lydia (Varnon), ch Nathaniel, recrq of father.

WATSON.
1779,7,3. John recrq.

WEBB.
1774,12.3. Jesse rocf Hopewell MM, Va., dated 1774,7,4.
1787,12,1. Jesse rqct Center MM, N.C.

WILLIAMS.
1775,7,1. John rocf New Garden, Chester Co., Pa., dated 1775,5,6.
1775,7,1. Joseph & w & ch. Joseph, Elizabeth, Ennion & Mary, rocf New Garden MM. Chester Co., Pa., dated 1775,5,6.
1778,2.7. Daniel & w & small ch, Sarah & Sybbilla, rocf Uwchland MM, Pa., dated 1777,10,9.
1782,3,2. John dis.
1783,3,1. Ennion gct Deep River MM, N.C.
1783,5,3. Abigail, Grace & Mary rqct Bush River MM.
1783,7,5. Elizabeth dis. (rem)
1785,7,2. Grace & Mary gct Center MM, N.C.
1785,11,5. Abigail gct Center MM, N.C.
1786,11,4. Elizabeth con her misconduct & was gct Center MM, N.C.
1788,2,2. Henry rocf Hopewell MM, Va., dated 1787,12,5.
1791,5,7. Henry con his mou.

YORKE.
1792,8,4. William recrq.

CANE CREEK MONTHLY MEETING
Union County, South Carolina

Cane Creek Meeting was located on the Tiger River, in Union County, in the west-central part of South Carolina. A meeting for worship was authorized by Quarterly Meeting held at Cane Creek, North Carolina, in 11th month, 1775. A meeting had been established at Padgets Creek, in the same county, in 1774. These two meetings were attached to Bush River Monthly Meeting until 1789, when Cane Creek Monthly Meeting was established by action of New Garden Quarterly Meeting, with preparative meetings at Cane Creek and Padgets Creek. The first sitting of the Monthly Meeting was held the 21st of 11th month, 1789. The committee appointed by the Quarterly Meeting, to attend the opening, included John Sanders, William Stanley, Joseph Hiatt, Tristram Barnard, Barnabas Coffin and James Thornbrugh.

Some of the women Friends who were early members of Cane Creek Monthly Meeting, (names taken from the first pages of the women's minutes) included Keziah Bray, Elizabeth Comer, Elizabeth Cook, Martha Cook, Mary Cook, Prudence Cooper, Tamar Cox, Margaret Edmundson, Rebekah Fincher, Ann Hawkins, Edith Harlan, Lydia Highatt (Hiatt), Margaret Hunt, Sarah Lamb, Mary Marshall, Mary Milhous, Rebekah Milhous, Esther Parnell, Sarah Russell, Masse Sanders, Hannah Smith, Olive Smith, Mary Talbot, Phebe Whitson, Dinah Wilson.

Only a few certificates of removal were received and issued by the meeting between 1789 and 1803. In 1803 the migration to the north-west began with a few families, who received certificates to Westland Monthly Meeting, Pennsylvania. In 1804, a few more obtained certificates to Miami Monthly Meeting, Ohio. The migration became general in 1805, when more than twenty certificates, most of them for families, were issued to Miami. Four more were recorded in 1806. Three others, dated in 3rd month, 1807, but not recorded in the minute book, were received at Miami.

When the people of Cane Creek Monthly Meeting removed to Ohio they took the records with them. The book of records of births and deaths was continued in use by Caesars Creek Monthly Meeting, Ohio, and remains in the possession of that meeting to this day. Caesars Creek Monthly Meeting was largely made up of former members of Cane Creek Meeting, South Carolina. The books containing the marriage records and the minutes of the women's meeting were returned to North Carolina Yearly Meeting after more than one hundred years. The book of minutes of the men's meeting has not been found.

A copy of the Cane Creek-Caesars Creek birth records, containing also much collateral data, compiled by the late Kirk Brown, of Baltimore, is now in the care of North Carolina Yearly Meeting. From this book there is reproduced on the following pages all material which appears to have been in the original record book before it left South Carolina. Later births and other material, added in later years to complete these family records begun in the South, have also been included. To insure accuracy, all this has been checked with the original book, at Caesars Creek. Following these extracts from the birth records is an abstract of the women's minutes and the marriage records.

CANE CREEK MONTHLY MEETING, S.C.

BIRTH AND DEATH RECORDS

Page 19.
James Addington

Ch: Thomas   b. 2-12-1777.
    Mary   " 9-30-1778.
    Sarah   " 9- 6-1781.
    Henry   " 7- 2-1784.
    Rebecca   " 1-18-1787.
    Marthe   " 8-28-1789.
    James   " 1-15-1792.
    Karenhappuck " 3- 5-1795.
    John   " 5- 2-1797.

Page 3.
Henry Bray b. 8-29-1755. (s. Edward
Keziah Bray b. 3-19-1761. (dt. Richard Jones) (married 2-2-1778, New Garden MM records)
Ch: Jemima   b. 11-30-1778.
    John   " 5- 8-1780.
    Henry   " 2-18-1782.
    Sarah   " 1-26-1784.
    Edward   " 1-18-1786.
    Mary   " 5-25-1788.
    Richard   " 5-22-1790.
    Joseph   " 6-15-1792.

Page 36.
John Clerk, s. Henry & Elizabeth, d. 10-18-1796, bur. Pagets Creek.

Page 71.
Robert Comer (s. Joseph & Elizabeth)
Martha Comer (dt. John & Mary Hawkins)(married 11-9-1797)
Ch: Mary   b. 3-13-1799.
    Amos   " 11-28-1802.
    Ann   " 10- 5-1804.

Page 57.
Stephen Comer b. 12-14-1773. (s. Joseph & Elizabeth)
Mary Comer b. 11-15-1775. (dt. John & Mary Hawkins) (married 10-31-1799)
Ch: John   b. 7-1-1800.
    Joseph   " 4-17-1802.
    James   " 2- 5-1804.

Page 34.
Tamar Comer d. 10-27-1796.
Amos Compton (3rd s. Samuel & Elizabeth, b. 7-9-1770 (d. 9-14-1824, p. 16)
Rebecca Compton (dt. Henry & Rebecca Millhouse, b. 8-11-1767; d. 10-5-1844) (married 12-13-1792)
Ch: Betty b. 3-30-1794. (m. John Mills, 6-29-1820)
    Samuel b. 8-16-1796. (m. Alley ____; d. 3-12-1861)
    Mary b. 12-21-1798. (m. (1) ____ Sexton; (2) James

Amos & Rebecca Compton cont'd.
Ch: Mary cont'd. Moorman, 3-29-1843.)
    Rebecca b. 11-6-1800. (m. Elijah Ellis, 10-2-1823)
    Lydia b. 1-20-1803. (m. John Jay, 4-3-1823)
    Sally b. 2-13-1805. (d. 3-31-1823, p. 16)
    John b. 3-1-1807. (m. Rebecca Steddom, of Miami MM, 10-31-1833)
    Ann b. 1-13-1812.
Page 16.
Ann Compton d. 3-23-1827.

Page 53.
Joshua Compton (7th s. Samuel & Elizabeth, b. 5-30-1778 (d. 2-15-1802, p. 54)
Rebekah Compton (dt. Nathan & Ann Hawkins, b. 1-12-1776) (married 1-24-1799)
Ch: Nathan   b. 4-12-1800.
    Joshua   " 4-26-1802.

(Samuel Compton d. 2-6-1805)
Elizabeth Compton (widow Samuel, d. 5-17-1821; age about 83, bur. on Joseph Compton's land, p. 54)
Ch: Rachel   b. 1-17-1764.
    William   " 5-15-1764.
    Samuel   " 12-26-1766; d. 6-15-1850.
    Sally   " 2-11-1769.
    Amos   " 7- 9-1770; d. 9-14-1824.
    John   " 12-29-1771; d. 1-16-1860.
    Stephen   " 8-29-1774; d. 7-14-1862.
    Matthew   " 12-17-1776.
    Joshua   " 5-30-1778; d. 2-15-1802, in S.C.
    Elizabeth " 12-19-1779.
    Joseph   " 6- 8-1782; d. 7-27-1824)
(Samuel & Elizabeth Compton went from Bush River MM, S.C. to Miami MM, Ohio, where they were received 6-14-1804. Samuel d. soon after & was bur. on his farm.)

(Samuel Compton, 2nd s. Samuel & Elizabeth, b. 12-26-1766; d. 6-15-1850)
(Phebe Compton b. 1774; d. 10-----1839)
Ch:(John   b. 8-23-1797; m. Jane Engle, 10-6-1819.
    Elizabeth" 7-25-1800.
    Sarah   " 8-25-1803; m. Clayton Brown, 1-6-1831.
    Joshua   " 9-20-1807.
    Eli   " 10-20-1809; m. Eunice Walton, 10-30-1831

Samuel & Phebe Compton cont'd.
Ch: Rebecca b. 4-18-1812. (d.
              3-21-1820, p.93)
    (Seth   " 7-17-1814; m.
    (1) Mary ____, (2) Ruth
     Hawkins, 4-4-1867)

Page 51.
Stephen Compton (5th s. Sam'l &
  Elizabeth, b. 8-29-1774; d.
  7-14-1862)
Dinah Compton (dt. Henry &
  Rebecca Millhouse, b. 8-29-
  1777; d. 11-15-1853.)
  (married 1-25-1798)
Ch: Henry b. 10-21-1798.
    Sally b. 9-23-1800. (m. Wm.
      Horner, 4-3-1823.)
    (Amos
    Samuel b. 5-4-1805; m. Tamar
      Wilson, 11-16-1828.) (d.
      1-13-1835, p. 157)
    (William b. 4-11-1808.
    Nancy   " 11- 1-1810.
    Hannah   " 5-13-1813.
    John   " 8-10-1816; d.
              9-16-1843.
    Rebecca " 4-28-1822; m. Job
      Mills, 4-4-1840.)
(Tamar Owen, dt. Christopher &
  Mary (Cox) Wilson, & widow
  Samuel Compton, b. 6-26-1807;
  d. 3-5-1846, in Ind.)

Page 82.
John Conner
Rachel Conner d. 12-11-1814.
Ch: William   b. 10-28-1795.
    John   " 4-27-1797; d.
                  4-27-1797.
    Catharine " 4-29-1798.
    Jesse   " 2-12-1800.
    John   " 8-10-1801.
    Thomas   " 1-29-1803.
    Mary   " 5- 7-1805.
    Rachel   " 7-29-1807.
    Anna   " 7-27-1809.
    Rebecca   " 10- 4-1811.
    Isaac   " 9-25-1813.

Page 43.
Amos Cook
Elizabeth Cook
Ch: Levi b. 11-16-1776. (m. Ann
      Frazier, 12-27-1798.)
    Mary b. 5-11-1779. (m. Isaac
      Hawkins, 3-25-1802)
    John b. 1-28-1781. (m. Dinah
      Spray, 11-27-1805, at
      Miami; d. 9-22-1861)
    Dinah   b. 2- 6-1783.
    Amos   " 10-13-1785.
    Stephen " 11-14-1787.
    Abraham " 4-19-1792. (m.
      Ruth Hawkins, 9-10-1812.)
    Ruth b. 11-12-1794.
Ann Cook, w. Levi, b. 6-25-1775.

Page 11.
(Eli Cook, s. Isaac & Mary)
(Martha Cook, dt. James & Martha
  Hawkins)
  (married 3-12-1772, Bush River
  MM records)
Ch: James   b. 10- 3-1785.
    Martha   " 9-22-1787; d.
               7-24-1791.
    Phebe   " 12-17-1789.
    Nathan   " 5-28-1792.

Page 38.
Isaac Cook, Sr., s. Isaac & Mary,
  d. 4----1794, bur. Tyger River
  Bur. Ground.

Page 37.
Isaac Cook (s. Isaac & Sarah)
Sarah Cook (dt. Robert & Jean
              Millhouse)
  (married 10-7-1790)
Ch: Seth   b. 7-25-1794.
    Rebekah   " 4-25-1796.
    Robert   " 5-18-1799.
    Mary Wilkinson " 10-8-1801.

Page 32.
John Cook. s. Isaac & Mary, d. 11-
  15-1797, age 46.

Page 50.
Thomas Cox d. 5-14-1821, age 81.
Tamar Cox, w. Thomas. (b. 4-11-
  1749; d. 8-25-1829.

Page 47.
Francis Fincher
Elizabeth Fincher
Ch: Esther b. 12-23-1791.
    Arniel " 7-27-1796.
    Thomas " 9-11-1799.

Page 48.
Thomas Fincher, s. Francis &
  Elizabeth. d. 11-1-1800.

Page 47.
Rebeccah (Edmondson) Fincher b.
  4-23-1739.

Page 48.
Rebecca Fincher d. 10-31-1797.

(John Furnas b. 3-5-1736; d. 8-5-
  1777.)
(Mary (Wilkinson) Furnas b. 9-19-
  1742; d. 10-7-1782.)
  (married 3-24-1762, Nigton Meeting, Old England)
Ch:(Joseph b. 2-20-1863; d. 7-25-
    1812.
    Rebecca b. 4-19-1764; m. Sam'l
      League; d. 6-27-1842.
    John b. 8-5-1765; m. (1) Esther
      Wilson, 11-25-1790, (2) Ruth
      Cook, 3-1-1798, (3) Rebecca
      (Millhouse) Compton, 10-12-
      1826.

John & Mary Furnas cont'd.
Ch: Thos. Wilkinson b. 3-23-1768.
    Esther b. 7-4-1770; m. Benjamin Pearson, 4-29-1790; d. 5-14-1835.
    Robert b. 6-27-1772; m. Hannah Wilson, 2-11-1796; d. 2-16-1863.
    William b. 5-29-1775; m. Rachel Nesby, 1797; d. 12-21-1833.

Page 23.
Robert Furnas (s. John & Mary, b. 6-27-1772; d. 2-16-1863).
Hannah Furnas (dt. John & Dinah (Cook) Wilson, b. 7-28-1778; d. 2-17-1864.)
(married 2-11-1796)
Ch: Mary b. 11-25-1796. (m. John Cook, 9-11-1817; d. 10-20-1831)
    Esther b. 1-5-1799. (m. Daniel Mills)
    John   b. 3- 6-1801.
    Seth   " 3-26-1803.
    Joseph " 9- 9-1805. (m. Mary Easterling, 9-10-1829)
    Isaac b. 11-12-1807. (m. Matilda Compton, 10-31-1833; d. 9-16-1839.)
    Dinah b. 5-5-1810. (m. Robert Millhouse, 8-5-1830; d. 9-10-1841.)
    Robert b. 11-22-1812.
    (Rebecca b. 2-9-1815; m. Samuel Starbuck, 10-1-1832.
    Hannah b. 1-3-1818; m. Abner Mills, 2-27-1841.
    Sarah b. 5-29-1822; m. Clark Ferguson, 12-1-1842.)

Page 27.
Amos Hawkins (s. Isaac & Margaret, b. 1-7-1769) (d. 9-14-1833, age 64 yrs., p. 28)
Phebe Hawkins (dt. John & Dinah Wilson, b. 2-18-1769; d. 3-27-1857)
(married 12-6-1791)
Ch: Jonathan b. 9-24-1792.
    Mary   b. 9-24-1792. (m. Charles Mills, 3-5-1818; d. 12-30-1818)
    Margret b. 3-15-1797. (m. James Parnell, 12-12-1816.)
    Christopher b. 3-24-1801. (m. Mary Edwards, 10-6-1825; d. 8-5-1830).
    Ruth b. 11-28-1808.

Page 55.
Amos Hawkins (s. John & Mary, b. 3-11-1777; d. 10-13-1844)
Ann Hawkins (dt. Henry & Rebekah Millhouse, b. 1-24-1772; d. 4-2-1855)
(married 6-8-1797)

Amos & Ann Hawkins cont'd.
Ch: Henry b. 7-29-1798. (m. Anna Pearson, 11-29-1821; d. 8-15-1877)
    Mary b. 2-25-1800. (m. Elijah Mills, 3-1-1821)
    Rebecca b. 7-25-1802. (m. David Jay, 3-3-1825)
    Martha b. 4- 2-1806.
    John   " 10-21-1809.
    Amos   " 4- 6-1816. (m. Ruth Owen, 11-2-1842; d. 9-20-1852)

Page 67.
Isaac Hawkins (s. Nathan & Ann, b. 1-1-1779)
Martha Hawkins (dt. Joshua & Mary Kenworthy)
(married 1-27-1803)
Ch: Stephen b. 10-21-1804; d. 11-6-1804.
    Mary   " 7-15-1806.
    William " 9-22-1808.
    Rebecca " 4- 1-1812.
    Ann   " 7-13-1814.
    Sarah   " 6-29-1817.

Page 69.
James Hawkins (s. James & Martha, b. 1-25-1756, Loudon Co., Va.; d. 11-24-1840)
Sarah Hawkins (dt. John & Dinah (Cook) Wilson, b. 5-10-1773; d. 3-26-1871)
(married 6-7-1792)
Ch: Ruth b. 3-14-1793. (m. Abraham Cook, 9-12-1812)
    Dinah b. 11-22-1795. (m. Wm. Mills, 12-7-1815)
    Jehu b. 10-30-1796. (m. Susanna _____)
    (Benjamin b. 4-1-1808; m. Phamay Morgan, 4-3-1840; d. 10-7-1852.
    James, Jr. b. 6-1-1810; m. Patty Compton, 9-29-1836; d. 11-23-1839.
    Amos b. 5-23-1813; m. Massey Spray, 1-30-1840.)

Page 39.
John Hawkins (s. Nathan & Ann, b. 6-15-1774)
Sarah Hawkins (dt. Joshua & Mary Kenworthy, b. about 1760) (d. 3-28-1820, p. 40)
(married 7-28-1796)
Ch: Jesse   b. 7-12-1797.
    David   " 5-25-1799. (d. 3-27-1802, p.40)
    Dinah   " 3- 9-1802. (d. 4-18-1804, p.40)
    Jonathan " 10- 7-1805. (d. 1-7-1805, p. 40)
    Ann   " 10-31-1809.
    Hannah " 11-11-1811.

CANE CREEK MONTHLY MEETING, S.C.

Page 30.
Margret Hawkins, w. Isaac, Sr.,
d. 10-12-1796, age 49.
(Nathan Hawkins, s. James &
Martha)
(Ann Hawksin, dt. Isaac & Mary
Cook)
(married 7-8-1773, Bush River
MM records)
Ch: (John b. 6-15-1774; m.
Sarah Kenworthy, 7-28-
1796.
Rebecca b. 1-12-1776; m.
Joshua Compton, 1-24-1799.
Isaac b. 1-1-1779; m. Martha Kenworthy, 1-27-1803.
Amos   b. 12- 7-1779.
Nathan   "   4-18-1782.
Ann   "   6- 6-1786.
James   " 12- 6-1786.
Mary   "   1-25-1789.
Henry   " 12-10-1791.)

Page 65.
Levi Hollingsworth
Martha Hollingsworth
Ch: Mary   b. 1-22-1789.
    Amey   " 1-25-1791.
    Jesse   " 12-21-1792.
    Sarah   " 7-16-1795.
    Lydia   " 5-19-1798.
    Martha " 2-26-1802.

Page 42.
Anne Hussey d. 1-9-1801, age 82.

(John Kenworthy, s. Joshua &
Mary, b. 3-10-1774)
(Rebecca Kenworthy, dt. Isaac &
Sarah Cook, b. 2-27-1777)
(married 11-26-1801)
Ch: (Olive   b. 9-13-1802.
    William   " 10-23-1803,
             Cane Creek, S.C.
    Tamar   " 1- 1-1806; d.
             6-12-1812.
    John   " 3- 2-1808.
    Isaac   " 6- 1-1810.

Page 6.
Sarah Lamb, w. Thomas, d. 4-15-
1791, page 43.

Page 5.
Martha Lamb b. 8-20-1780.
Sarah Lamb b. 5-4-1791.

(Henry Millhouse b. 5-1-1736),
d. 5-22-1821, age 85, bur.
Cesars Creek, p. 60)
(Rebeckah Millhouse b. 8-11-
1739) (d. 8-11-1803, age 64,
bur. Tyger River, p. 60)
Ch:(Mary b. 5-2-1763; m. David
Whitson, 6-8-1797.
Rebecca b. 8-11-1767; m.
Amos Compton 12-13-1792;
d. 11-5-1844.

Henry & Rebeckah Millhouse cont'd.
Ch: Sarah b. 3-25-1770; m. Mordecai
Spray, 1793.
Ann b. 1-24-1772; m. Amos
Hawkins, 6-8-1797; d. 4-2-
1855.
Robert m. Sarah Compton 1791.
Dinah b. 8-29-1777; m. Stephen
Compton, 1-25-1798; d. 11-
15-1853.)
(According to records "Henry Millhouse was b. in Ireland, Parish of
Timahor, County of Kildare, and
was in the Station of a minister
near 50 years.")

Page 13.
Robert Milhous (s. Henry & Rebekah)
Sally Nelson Milhous (dt. Saml. &
Elizabeth Compton)
(married 1-11-1792, Bush River MM
records)
Ch: Henry   b. 5-19-1793.
    Samuel b. 1-23-1796. (m. Sarah
        (Sanders) Scott, 5-14-1829)
    John b. 5-22-1797. (m. Mary
        Mills, 6-10-1830)
    Rebeckah   b. 3-28-1799.
    Elizabeth b. 11-15-1802. (m.
        Wm. Mills (2nd w.), 6-4-1829)
    Ann   b. 1- 9-1804.
    Robert b. 4-7-1806. (m. Dinah
        Furnas, 8-5-1830)

Page 25
(Jonas Randel)

Ch: Rebekah   b. 6- 4-1785.
    John   " 11-16-1787.
    Jehu   " 7-27-1790.
    Jonathan " 2-27-1793.
    Walter(Robert) b. 6-20-1795.
    Elizabeth b. 10-11-1797.

Page 7.
(Thomas Roberds, s. Walter &
Rebecah)
(Ann Roberds, dt. Solomon & Phebe
Whitson)
(married 9-6-1786, Bush River MM
records)
Ch: Rebekah   b. 8- 8-1787.
    Walter   " 10- 2-1789.
    David   " 8-18-1792.

(James Spray)
(Sarah Spray)
(married about 1753, Chester Co.,
Pa.)
Ch:(Jesse   b. 12-23-1854.
    Samuel   " 3-23-1758; m.
        Mary Wilson, about 1788.
    Abner   b. 2-20-1761.
    Hannah   " 2-18-1763.
    James   " 1-14-1765.
    Mordecai " 2- 3-1767; m.
        Sarah Millhouse, about 1793.
    Thomas   b. 12-26-1768.
    William   " 12-17-1771.)

(Mordecai Spray, s. James & Sarah, b. 2-3-1767)
(Sarah Spray, dt. Henry & Rebekah Millhouse, b. 3-25-1770)
(married about 1793)
Ch:(Mary   b. 3- 1-1795.
    Henry   " 12-22-1797.
    William " 11- 6-1801.
    Jesse   " 11- 5-1803.
    John   " 5-17-1807.)

Page 1.
Samuel Spray (s. James & Sarah, b. 3-23-1758; d. 3-20-1838)
Mary Spray (dt. John & Dinah (Cook) Wilson, b. 12-18-1760; d. 18-1843)
(married about 1788)
Ch: John b. 2-15-1790. (m. Sarah Saunders, 9-30-1813; d. 6-6-1853)
    James b. 9-17-1793. (m. Charity Sanders)
    Dinah b. 10- 9-1794.
    Samuel " 4-30-1796. (m. (1) Esther Cook, (2) Keturah (Brock) Jay)
    Mary b. 6-30-1798. (m. Reason Regaen, 4-9-1818)
    (Jesse b. 2-5-1801; m. Mary Cook, 11-18-1819, at Silver Creek, Ind.)

Page 80.
Sarah Way, w. Joseph, b. 4-20-1784; d. 2-2-1812.

Page 59.
David Whitson b. 3-8-1769. (s. Solomon & Phebe)
Mary Whitson b. 5-2-1801. (dt. Henry & Rebeckah Millhouse)
(married 6-8-1797)
Ch: Phebe b. 6-25-1801.

Page 17.
Solomon Whitson (s. David) b. 4-2-1741. (d. 6-1-1798, p. 18)
Phebe Whitson b. 5-25-1745. (d. 6-13-1801, p. 18)
Ch: Ann   b. 12-27-1766.
    David   " 3- 8-1769.
    Silas Willis b. 2-26-1770. (d. 3-11-1771, p. 18)
    Mary b. 2-11-1772. (m. Jonathan Robards) (d. 12-30-1798, p. 18)
    Willis   b. 5-9-1774.
    Jordan b. 3-3-1777. (d. 4-1-1847, p. 18)
    Samuel b. 10-31-1779. (d. 9-18-1819)
    Phoebe b. 10-30-1781. (d. 5-6-1791, p. 18)
    Solomon b. 5- 7-1784.
    John   " 6-24-1787.
    Rowland " 8-13-1789. (d. 9-9-1789, p. 18)

(Christopher Wilson, s. John & Dinah, b. 8-15-1775; d. 4-3-1859)
(Mary Wilson, dt. Thomas & Tamar Cox, b. 4-9-1784; d. 9-12-1846)
(married 12-25-1800)
Ch: (John   b. 11-26-1801.
    Thomas   " 8- 2-1803.
    Hannah   " 7- 8-1805; m. David Barnet, 4-2-1829.
    Tamar b. 7-21-1807; m. Samuel Compton, 11-16-1828.
    Eli b. 10-6-1809.
    James b. 3-3-1811; m. Elizabeth Spray, 4-2-1835.
    Charles b. 2-4-1813.
    Dinah b. 9-20-1815; m. Joseph Spray, 4-4-1839.
    Martha   b. 1-27-1819.
    Jehu   " 6-11-1821.
    Seth   " 5-24-1823.)
    (d. 9-15-1833, p. 50)
    (Huldah b. 8-10-1825) (d. 7-13-1826, p. 50)

Page 9.
(Jehu Wilson, s. John & Dinah, b. 1-1-1763)
(Sarah Wilson, dt Isaac & Margaret Hawkins)
(married 12-2-1790)
Ch: Betty   b. 10-10-1791.
    Dinah   " 3-14-1794.
    John   " 12-17-1796.
    Isaac   " 7-26-1799. (m. Ann Easterling, 10-5-1820)
    Seth   b. 7-23-1801.
    Amos   " 1-10-1803.
    Ruth   " 9-17-1806.
    Gideon   " 3- 3-1812.

Page 45.
John Wilson (s. Christopher, Chester Co., Pa.)
Dinah Wilson (dt. Isaac Cook, of Pa.)
(married 1759, in Pa.)
Ch: Mary b. 12-18-1760. (m. Samuel Spray, about 1788; d. 6-8-1843)
    Jehu b. 1-1-1763. (m. Sarah Hawkins, 12-2-1790)
    Seth b. 12-7-1764.
    Phebe b. 2-18-1769. (m. Amos Hawkins, 12-6-1791; d. 3-27-1857)
    Esther b. 2-9-1881. (m. John Furnas, 11-25-1790; d. 9-13-1795)
    Sarah b. 5-19-1773. (m. James Hawkins, 6-7-1792; d. 3-26-1871)
    Christopher b. 8-15-1775. (m. Mary Cox, 12-25-1800)
    Hannah b. 7-28-1778. (m. Robert Furnas, 2-11-1796; d. 2-17-1864)
    John b. 2-28-1782. (d. 2-23-1784, p. 46)

CANE CREEK MONTHLY MEETING, S.C.

Page 46.
John Wilson, Sr. d. 5-12-1794, age 50 yrs. 1 mo. (John & Dinah Wilson moved from Pa. to Bush River MM, S.C. in 1770. John d. at Cane Creek, S.C. & Dinah went to Ohio.)

(Seth Wilson, s. John & Dinah, b. 12-7-1764)
(Mary Wilson, dt. Robert & Rebecca Evans, b. 7-11-1768) (d. 11-17-1793, p. 22)
(married 9-5-1792, Bush River MM records)

* *

MINUTES AND MARRIAGE RECORDS

ADDINGTON.
1790,5,22. Else Garrot (form Addington) dis mou.
1799,12,21. Rachel (form Randel) dis mou.
1802,9,18. Rebekah, widow James, relrq.
1802,10,23. Mary & Sarah, ch James & Rebekah, dis.
1803,5,21. Mary Roberds (form Addington) dis mou.
1803,8,20. Rebekah, Jr. dis.
1804,3,29. Elizabeth (form Randle) dis mou.

ARNOLD.
1797,3,18. Susannah & ch gct Springfield MM, N.C.

ASHFORD.
1798,4,21. Hannah (form Hollingsworth) dis mou.

BRAY.
1795,1,24. Keziah & dts gc.

BENSON.
1805,8,24. James & fam gct Miami MM, Ohio.

CAMPBELL.
1795,6,20. Elizabeth (form Parnel) dis mou.
1799,12,21. Rebekah (form Marshal) dis mou.
1803,4,23. Esther gct Westland MM, Pa.
1804,4,21. Rebekah (form Marshal) con her mou.
1804,5,19. Rebekah gct Westland MM, Pa.

CANNIDA.
1802,10,23. Rachel (form Minton) dis mou.

CLARK.
1799,5,18. Rachel Fincher (form Clark) dis mou.

Clark cont'd.
1801,4,18. Ester Pearson (form Clark) dis mou.
1805,2,16. Mary & some of her ch gct Miami MM, Ohio.

COMER.
1791,6,9. Anne, dt Joseph & Elizabeth, m Amos Hawkins.
1797,3,18. Rebekah dis.
1797,11,9. Robert, s Joseph & Elizabeth, Union Co., S.C., m Martha Hawkins.
1799,10,31. Stephen, Union Co., S.C., s Joseph & Elizabeth, m Mary Hawkins.
1799,11,31. Lydia, dt Joseph & Elizabeth, Union Co., S.C., m John Hawkins.
1804,9,27. Elizabeth, dt Joseph & Elizabeth, m Joseph Smith.
1805,2,16. Elizabeth gct Miami MM, Ohio.
1806,3,22. Robert & fam gct Miami MM, Ohio.

COMPTON.
1792,12,13. Amos, s Samuel & Elizabeth, Newberry Co., S.C., m Rebekah Milhous.
1798,1,25. Stephen, Union Co., S.C., s Daniel & Elizabeth, Newberry Co., S.C., m Dinah Milhous.
1799,1,24. Joshua, s Samuel & Elizabeth, Newberry Co., S.C., m Rebekah Hawkins.
1805,2,23. Amos & fam gct Miami MM, Ohio.
1805,3,23. Stephen and fam gct Miami MM, Ohio.
1805,8,24. Rebekah & two ch gct Miami MM, Ohio.

COOK.
1790,10,7. Isaac, s Isaac & Sarah, Union Co., S.C., m Sarah Milhous.
1792,11,1. Rachel, dt Eli & Martha m Jesse Kenworthy.

CANE CREEK MONTHLY MEETING, S.C.

COOK cont'd.
1793,1,3. Mary, dt Isaac & Mary, Union Co., S.C., m Ralph Hunt.
1793,8,1. John, s Isaac & Mary, dec, Union Co., S.C. m Olive Smith.
1795,3,12. Dinah, dt Isaac & Sarah, dec, m David Kenworthy.
1798,12,27. Levi, s Amos & Elizabeth, Union Co., S.C., m Ann Fraizer.
1799,9,26. Olive, dt William & Jean Smith, Union Co., S.C., m Benjamin Hawkins.
1800,2,15. Mary Paty (form Cook) dis mou.
1800,8,23. Lydea (form Cooper) dis mou.
1801,11,26. Rebekah, dt Isaac & Sarah, dec, m John Kenworthy.
1802,3,25. Mary, dt Amos & Elizabeth, Union Dist., S.C., m Isaac Hawkins.
1803,1,22. Amos & fam gct Westland MM, Pa.
1803,1,22. Levi & fam gct Westland MM, Pa.
1803,4,23. Ann Kenworthy (form Cook) rpd mou.
1805,3,23. Eli & fam gct Miami MM, Ohio.
1805,4,20. Isaac & fam gct Miami MM, Ohio.
1805,10,10. William, Union Dist., S.C., s Isaac & Sarah, m Sarah Hawkins.
1806,3,22. William & w gct Miami MM, Ohio.

COOPER.
1793,11,23. Prudence (with h) & dt, Phebe, gct Wrightsborough MM, Ga.
1799,10,19. Sarah rocf Bush River MM, dated 1799,9,28.
1800,2,15. Elizabeth (form Townsend) dis mou.
1800,8,23. Lydea Cook (form Cooper) dis mou.
1804,2,18. Joanna (form Hunt) dis mou.

COX.
1798,3,24. Sarah (form Townsend) dis mou.
1800,12,25. Mary, dt Thomas & Tamar, Union Dist., S.C., m Christopher Wilson.
1801,8,22. Mary Evans (form Cox) dis mou.
1803,5,21. Tomas & w & dt gct Westland MM, Pa.

DAVIS.
1794,2,15. Hannah (form Marshall) dis mou.

DODD.
1792,7,21. Sarah, Jr. dis.

DODD cont'd.
1792,9,26. Sarah, widow Thomas Dodd, Dist. 96, S.C., m John Nedarman.

DUCKET.
1790,1,23. Dinah (form Smith) rpd mou.

EDMUNDSON.
1796,12,24. Margret dis.

EVANS.
1790,10,23. Hannah (Evens) (form Smith) dis mou.
1799,4,30. Hannah con her mou.
1799,10,19. Hannah gct Bush River MM.
1801,8,22. Mary (form Cox) dis mou.

FINCHER.
1789,11,21. Rebekah appointed clerk.
1793,4,20. Rebekah Martengale (form Fincher) dis mou.
1797,8,19. Rachel rpd mou.
1799,5,18. Rachel (form Clark) dis mou.

FRAIZER.
1798,12,27. Ann, dt Isaac, Union Co., S.C., m Levi Cook.

FURNAS.
1790,11,25. John, s John, dec, Newberry Co., Dist. 96, S.C., m Esther Wilson.
1791,3,19. Esther gct Bush River MM, S.C.
1796,2,11. Robert, Union Co., S.C., s John & Mary, dec, Newberry Co., S.C., m Hannah Wilson.
1796,12,24. Hannah, w Robert, gc.
1803,4,23. Robert & w & ch gct Westland MM, Pa.

GARROT.
1790,5,22. Else (form Addington) dis mou.

GREGORY.
1801,9,19. Elizabeth (form Hawkins) dis mou.

HARRIS.
1790,1,23. Hannah Tolleson (form Harris) dis mou.

HAWKINS.
1790,12,2. Sarah, dt Isaac, Union Co., S.C., m Jehu Wilson.
1791,6,9. Amos, s James & Martha, Union Co., S.C., m Anne Comer.
1791,12,6. Amos, s Isaac & Margaret, Union Co., S.C., m Phebe Wilson.
1792,6,7. James, s James & Martha, Union Co., S.C., m Sarah Wilson.

CANE CREEK MONTHLY MEETING, S.C.

HAWKINS cont'd.
1793,3,23. Mary & ch, John, James, Sarah, Ann, Rebekah, Tamer, Lydia & William, recrq.
1793,3,23. Martha & Mary, dt John & Mary, recrq.
1795,6,20. Martha, dt Isaac, dis mou.
1796,7,28. John, Union Co., S.C., s Nathan & Ann, m Sarah Kenworthy.
1797,6,8. Amos, s John & Mary, Union Co., S.C., m Ann Milhous.
1797,11,9. Martha, dt John & Mary, Union Co., S.C., m Robert Comer.
1799,1,24. Rebekah, dt Nathan & Ann, Union Co., S.C., m Joshua Compton.
1799,9,26. Benjamin, Union Co., S.C., s James & Martha, m Olive Cook.
1799,10,31. Mary, dt John & Mary, Union Co., S.C., m Stephen Comer.
1799,11,31. John, Union Co., S.C., s John & Mary, m Lydia Comer.
1801,9,19. Elizabeth Gregory (form Hawkins) dis mou.
1802.3,25. Isaac, Union Dist., S.C., s Isaac & Margaret, m Mary Cook.
1803,1,27. Isaac, Union Dist., S.C., s Nathan & Ann, m Martha Kenworthy.
1805,1,19. Phebe, dt Isaac, dis.
1805,2,16. Benjamin & fam gct Miami MM, Ohio.
1805,2.16. Isaac, s Isaac, & fam gct Miami MM, Ohio.
1805,2,16. Isaac, s Nathan, & w gct Miami MM, Ohio.
1805,2,16. John & fam gct Miami MM, Ohio.
1805,8,24. Nathan & fam gct Miami MM, Ohio.
1805,10,10. Sarah, dt John & Mary, Union Dist., S.C., m William Cook.
1806,2,15. Sarah & ch gct Miami MM, Ohio.

HOLLINGSWORTH.
1790,1,23. Mary Johnson (form Hollingsworth) dis mou.
1792,5,19. Martha & Mary, dt Joseph, recrq.
1792,9,22. Martha, dt Emy, dis.
1793.3,23. Martha & ch. Mary, Eamy & Jesse, recrq.
1794,4,19. Mary Strawn (form Hollingsworth) dis mou.
1798,3,24. Mary, dt Isaac, dis mou.
1798,4,21. Hannah Ashford (form Hollingsworth) dis mou.
1799,1,19. Martha , dt Joseph, dis.

HOLLINGSWORTH cont'd.
1799,2,16. Ruth Young (form Hollingsworth) rpd mou.
1800,2,15. Dinah rocf Bush River MM, dated 1799,11,30.
1804,5,19. Ann, w Isaac, dis.
1805,1,19. Hannah, dt William, dis.

HUNT.
1793,1,3. Ralph, Union Co., S.C., m Mary Cook.
1799,3,23. Rachel Kelly (form Hunt) dis mou.
1801,6,20. Christen (woman) dis.
1804,2,18. Joanna Cooper (form Hunt) dis mou.
1805,2,16. Samuel & fam gct Miami MM, Ohio.
1805,5,22. Mary gct Miami MM, Ohio.

JOHNSON.
1790,1,23. Mary (form Hollingsworth) dis mou.

JONES.
1805,2,10. Rebekah (form Randle) dis mou.

KELLY.
1799,3,23. Rachel (form Hunt) dis mou.

KENWORTHY.
1792,2.18. Joshua & ch, Sarah, Martha, Mary & Tamer, rocf Cane Creek MM, N.C., dated 1791,12,3.
1792,11,1. Jesse, s David & Tamar, Union Co., S.C., m Rachel Cook.
1795,3,12. David, s Joshua & Mary, Union Co., S.C., m Dinah Cook.
1796,7,28. Sarah, dt Joshua, Union Co., S.C., m John Hawkins.
1801,1,24. Mary Massey (form Kenworthy) dis mou.
1801,11,26. John, Union Co., S.C., s Joshua & Mary, m Rebekah Cook.
1803,1,27. Martha, dt Joshua & Mary, Union Dist., S.C., m Isaac Hawkins.
1803,4,23. Ann (form Cook) rpd mou.
1804,4,21. Tamer dis.
1804,10.20. David & fam gct Miami MM, Ohio.
1804,10,20. Ann gct Miamme MM, Ohio.
1805,2,16. Jesse & fam gct Miami MM, Ohio.
1805,11,23. Ann gct Miami MM, Ohio.

LAMB.
1791,8,20. Sarah's death rpd.
1792,1,21. Phebe dis.
1794,4,19. Mary dis.
1801,1,24. Alce Ray (form Lamb) dis mou.

CANE CREEK MONTHLY MEETING, S.C.

MARSHALL.
1794,2,15. Hannah Davis (form Marshall) dis mou.
1799,12,21. Rebekah Campbell (form Marshal) dis mou.
1803,12,24. Mary (Marshal) & ch gct Westland MM, Pa.
1804,4,21. Rebekah Campbell (form Marshal) con her mou.

MARTENGALE.
1793,4,20. Rebekah (form Fincher) dis mou.

MASSEY.
1801,1,24. Mary (form Kenworthy) dis mou.

MILHOUS.
1790,10,7. Sarah, dt Robert & Jean, dec, m Isaac Cook.
1792,6,23. Sally Nelson (Milhouse) rocf Bush River MM, dated 1792,5,26.
1792,12,13. Rebekah, dt Henry & Rebekah, Union Co., S.C., m Amos Compton.
1794,2,15. Sarah Spray (form Millhous) dis mou.
1797,6,8. Ann, dt Henry & Rebekah, m Amos Hawkins.
1797,6,8. Mary, dt Henry & Rebekah, Union Co., S.C., m David Whitson.
1798,1,25. Dinah, dt Henry & Rebekah, Union Co., S.C., m Stephen Compton.
1805,3,23. Robert & fam gct Miami MM, Ohio.

MILLS.
1795,1,24. Jemima gc.

MINTON.
1792,2,18. Rebekah dis.
1794,11,22. Elizabeth Pearson (form Minton) dis mou.
1799,12,21. Parthenay dis.
1802,10,23. Rachel Cannida (form Minton) dis mou.

MORGAN.
1800,11,22. Asseneth (form Roberds) dis mou.

NEDARMAN.
1792,9,26. John, Dist. 96, S.C., m Sarah Dodd.

NORMAN.
1789,12,19. Margaret rocf Fairfax MM, Va., dated 1787,11,24.

PARNEL.
1795,6,20. Elizabeth Campbell (form Parnel) dis mou.

PATY.
1800,2,15. Mary (form Cook) dis mou.

PEARSON.
1794,11,22. Elizabeth (form Minton) dis mou.
1801,4,18. Ester (form Clark) dis mou.

PENNY.
1801,4,18. Esther (form Thompson) dis mou.

PUGH.
1804,3,24. David (Pew) & fam gct Miami MM, Ohio.

RANDLE.
1790,6,2. Hannah (Randel), dt Joseph, Union Co., S.C., m Thomas Roberds.
1791,11,19. Ann Roberts (form Randel) dis mou.
1799.12.21. Rachel Addington (form Randel) dis mou.
1802.10.27. Lydia (Randol), dt Joseph, Padgett's Creek, Union Dist., S.C., m Joseph Thompson.
1804,3,29. Elizabeth Addington (form Randle) dis mou.
1805,2,16. Rebekah Jones (form Randle) dis mou.
1805,3,23. Jonas & fam gct Miami MM, Ohio.
1805,8,24. Joseph & w gct Miami MM, Ohio.

RAY.
1801,1,24. Alce (form Lamb) dis mou.

ROBERTS.
1789,12,30. Jonathan (Roberds), s Walter & Rebekah, dec, Union Co., Dist. 96, S.C., m Mary Whitson.
1790,6,2. Thomas (Roberds), s John, Union Co., S.C., m Hannah Randel.
1791,11,19. Ann (form Randel) dis mou.
1792,4,21. Lydia, dt John, dis.
1792,5,26. Rebekah dis mou.
1798,7,21. Sarah (Roberds) rocf Hopewell MM, (directed to Bush River MM)
1798,8,18. Esther (Roberds) prcf Hopewell MM, Va., but, having been guilty of misconduct, she was dis.
1798,9,22. Ann & Sarah (Roberds) dis.
1800,11,22. Asseneth Morgan (form Roberds) dis mou.
1803.5,21. Mary (Roberds) (form Addington) dis mou.
1806,3,22. Thomas & fam gct Miami MM, Ohio.

SANDERS.
1795,1,24. Masce (with h) & dts gc.

CANE CREEK MONTHLY MEETING, S.C.

SINNERD.
1789,11,21. Margret, of Padget Creek, dis mou.

SMITH.
1790,1,23. Dinah Ducket (form Smith) rpd mou.
1790,10,23. Hannah Evans (form Smith) dis mou.
1791,8,20. Rebekah & ch, Buly, Leatitie & Mary, recrq.
1793,8,1. Olive, dt William & Jane, Union Co., S.C., m John Cook.
1798,10,20. Buly dis.
1801,11,21. Ruth dis.
1804,9,27. Joseph, s William & Jean, Union Dist., S.C., m Elizabeth Comer.
1805,2,16. Joseph & w gct Miami MM, Ohio.

SPRAY.
1794,2,15. Sarah (form Milhous) dis mou.
1797,5,20. Sarah con her mou.
1800,6,21. Naomi rocf Bush River MM, dated 1800,5,31.
1803,4,23. Samuel & w & ch gct Westland MM. Pa.
1803,4,23. Naomi gct Westland MM, Pa.
1805,3,23. Mordecai & fam gct Miami MM, Ohio.

STRAWN.
1794,4,19. Mary (form Hollingsworth) dis mou.
1799,2,16. Anne recrq.
1805,2,23. Anna gct Miami MM, Ohio.

THOMPSON.
1801,4,18. Esther Penny (form Thompson) dis mou.
1802,10,27. Joseph, s Richard, Padgetts Creek, Union Dist., S.C., m Lydia Randel.

TOLLESON.
1790,1,23. Hannah (form Harris) dis mou.

TOWNSEND.
1789,12,19. Elve & ch. Cole, James & Rachel, recrq.
1798,3,24. Sarah Cox (form Townsend) dis mou.
1799,10,19. Ruth Young (form Townsend) dis mou.
1800,2,15. Elizabeth Cooper (form Townsend) dis mou.
1803,3,19. John & w & ch gct Westland MM, Pa.
1804,10,20. Martha & ch gct Miami MM, Ohio.

WHITSON.
1789,12,30. Mary, dt Solomon & Phebe, Union Co., Dist. 96, S. C., m Jonathan Robards.

1797,6,8. David, s Solomon & Phebe, Union Co., S.C., m Mary Milhous.
1805,3,23. David & w & dt & brother gct Miami MM, Ohio.

WILSON.
1790,11,25. Esther, dt John, Union Co., Dist. 96, S.C., m John Furnas.
1790,12,2. Jehu, s John, Union Co., S.C., m Sarah Hawkins.
1791,12,6. Phebe, dt John & Dinah, Union Co., S.C., m m Amos Hawkins.
1792,6,7. Sarah, dt John & Dinah. m James Hawkins.
1793,5,18. Mary rocf Bush River MM, dated 1793,4,27.
1796,2,11. Hannah, dt John & Dinah, Union Co., S.C., m Robert Furnas.
1800,12,25. Christopher, Union Dist., S.C., s John & Dinah, m Mary Cox.
1803,5,21. Christopher & w & s gct Westland MM. Pa.
1803,5,21. Jehu & w & ch gct Westland MM, Pa.
1803,5,21. Dinah gct Westland MM, Pa.

YOUNG.
1799,2,16. Ruth (form Hollingsworth) rpd mou.
1799,10,19. Ruth (form Townsend) dis mou.

PINEY GROVE MONTHLY MEETING

Marlborough County, South Carolina

Piney Grove Meeting was located in Marlborough County in northeastern South Carolina, on the border of North Carolina. Meetings for worship appeared in Marlborough County about 1755. The first was Pee Dee, followed by Gum Swamp, Piney Grove and others. These meetings were under the jurisdiction of Cane Creek Monthly Meeting, North Carolina, during the earlier period but were later transferred to Deep River Monthly Meeting. In 9th month 1801, Deep River sent to New Garden Quarterly Meeting the request of Piney Grove Meeting for permission to hold a monthly meeting. This request was granted by the Quarterly Meeting in 12th month, 1801, and Piney Grove Monthly Meeting was opened on the 16th of first month, 1802.

Early members of Piney Grove Monthly Meeting, (names taken from the first pages of the minutes), included William Addams, Charles Baldwin, Solomon Barfield, William Beauchamp, Nicholas Clark, Thomas Cook. Armsberry Crew, Isom Haly, Josiah Lamb, Isaac Linnegar, John Marine, Jonathan Marine, Mary Marine, John Mendenhall, Stephen Mendenhall, Archelaus Moorman, Edward Moorman, John Moorman, Thomas Morris, Elisha Parker, Benjamin Pike, Thomas Ratliff, Abigail Robinson, Garris Stafford, Francis Thomas, Isaac Thomas, John Thomas, John Thomas, Sr., Lewis Thomas, Molly Thomas, Stephen Thomas, William Way, Lydia Weeks, Thomas Willcuts.

Meetings for worship and preparative meetings, mentioned as reporting to Piney Grove Monthly Meeting, include Piney Grove, Little Creek, Pee Dee, Rocky Fork and Gum Swamp.

The meeting was laid down the 18th of 2nd month, 1815, and the following minute entered in the records: "This meeting being reduced to a very small number, by Friends removing to the State of Ohio, to a situation not capable of holding a monthly meeting, to the reputation of truth, * * * unitedly agrees * * to discontinue our monthly and preparative meetings and send our records to the Quarterly Meeting."

By direction of New Garden Quarterly Meeting, the few members who remained at Piney Grove were transferred to Back Creek Monthly Meeting. Their names as given in Back Creek minutes under date of 27th of 1st month, 1816, were as follows: Samuel Chance, Armsley Crew, Littleton Digs and wife, Lydia, and children, Lucy and Caroline; William Digs and wife, Fany, and children, William Armsley, Margery, Mark. John, Benjamin, Hannah and Fanny; Isom Hailey and wife, Elizabeth; Mary Macy and children, Pheebe, William, Abigail and Henry; Arihelus Moreman; John Morman and wife, Rebecah, and children, Anna, Wilson, Judith, Rebecah, Julia and John; John Morman, 2nd, and wife, Sarah, and children, Hannah, Sampey, Mary, Anna, Ruth, Eliza, Sarah, Benjamin, Celia and John; Susanna Morman, widow, and children, Jesse, James, Tarlton and wife, Hannah. and children, Nancy, Henry and Thomas; Mathew, Jesse, Rachel, John and Benjamin Pike; Thomas Ratliff and wife, Sarah, and children, Thomas, Polly and Juliemma; Mary Roberts; Achsach Way; Anna, William, Caroline and Patience Way; William Way and wife, Abigail, and children, Henry, William, Abigail, Susannah and Moorman.

The records from which the following abstract has been prepared consist of one volume of birth, death and marriage records, and one volume of minutes, 1801 to 1815.

PINEY GROVE MONTHLY MEETING

BIRTH AND DEATH RECORDS

Page 15.
William Addams
Mary Addams
Ch: Jonathan b. 10- 3-1794.
    Hannah " 9- 4-1796.
    Beede " 12- 2-1798.
    John " 1-19-1801.
    William " 5-17-1804.

Page 21.
Matthew Almond
Rebeckah Almond
Ch: Matthew b. 6----1785.
    Rebeckah " 12-18-1784.
    Judith " 3-17-1806.
    Harris " 1- 5-1809.
    Elisabeth " 2-25-1811.

Page 26.
Solomon Barfield b. 3- 9-1766.
Miriam Barfield " 3-15-1771.
Ch: Demsey b. 9- 1-1795; d.
                    9-20-1799.
    Mary " 9-21-1796.
    Milicent " 10- 6-1797.
    Demaris " 10- 6-1797.
    William " 9-20-1799.
    Sarah " 9-20-1800.
    Ruth " 12-11-1801; d.
                    5-7-1802.
    Jonathan " 9-12-1803.
    Charity " 2-14-1805.

Page 17.
Abner Barker b. 8-11-1768.
Lydia Barker " 1-24-1767.
Ch: Nathan b. 4-29-1792.
    Mary " 11-24-1793.
    Hannah " 10-23-1795.
    Ruth " 11- 1-1797.
    Phebe " 4-24-1799.
    Nicholas " 1-24-1802.
    Allen " 3-10-1804.
    Matthew " 8- 1-1806.

Page 2.
William Beauchamp
Elizabeth Beauchamp
Ch: Henry b. --- 6-1776.
    John " ---13-1778.
    William " ---19-1780.
    Charles " 12-21-1781.
    Curtis " 12-21-1781.
    Levi " 10- 1-1785.
    Elleck " 11-12-1787.
    Matthew " 9- 1-1789.
    Russ " 9-1-1792.
    Milcar " 5- 5-1795.
    Caleb " 7-17-1797.

Page 13.
Daniel Dawson
Ann Dawson
Ch: Heneriter b. 3-30-1792.
    Lilley & Milley" 12-29-1793.
    Daniel " 11-12-1797.
    John " 9- 4-1800.

Daniel & Ann Dawson cont'd.
Ch: Noah b. 8-21-1806.

Page 14.
Obadiah Harris b. 8- 8-1774.
Mary Harris " 11- 3-1773.
Ch: Thomas b. 9-26-1796.
    David " 12-20-1798.
    Rachel " 8-14-1801.
    Betsy " 11- 8-1803.
    Susannah " 5-13-1805.
    Jonathan " 11-15-1806.
    John " 10-16-1808.
    Obadiah " 10-21-1810.

Page 19.
Thomas Knight
Christan Knight
Ch: John b. 4-10-1805.
    Benjamin " 7-19-1806.
    Solomon " 10-26-1807.

Page 22.
Anna Marine, dt. Jesse & Pheba, b.
3-22-1805.

Page 1.
Jonathan Marine b. 3----1752.
Mary Marine " 4- 4-1746.
Ch: Mary " 8-20-1776.
    Jonathan " 2-15-1780.
    John " 6-28-1782.
    Charles " 6-22-1784.
    Jesse " 5-18-1786.

Page 21.
Ziba Marine, dt. Charles & Abba,
b. 3-26-1805.

Page 3.
Thomas Moorman b. 1-23-1757; d.
11-27-1801.
Susannah Moorman b. 7-16-1754.
Ch: Tarlton b. 5-10-1783.
    Agnis " 3- 4-1785.
    Sarah " 1-15-1788; d.
                    9-15-1796.
    Thomas " 12-13-1789.
    Joseph " 3- 2-1793; d.
                    11-17-1809.
    Jesse & James " 6-27-1795.

Page 12.
Edward Moorman b. 3-19-1768; d.
3-4-1810.
(Charity Moorman, Deep River MM
records)
Ch: Benjamin b. 12-18-1792; d.
                      12-14-1807.
    Rebecca " 3-11-1796; d.
                    3-29-1804.
    Eli " 11- 7-1798.
Mary Moorman (2nd) w. Edward.
Ch: Agg-(torn) b. 3- 6-1801.
    Zachariah " 7-19-1803.
    Lewis " 1-29-1805.
    John " 4- 4-1807; d.
                  12-25-1810.
    Mary b. 1-29-1809; d. 5-25-1813.

Page 9.
John Moorman b. 12-9-1769.
Sarah Moorman b. 5-3-1773.
Ch: Hannah   b. 2-11-1794.
    Chuza   " 9-24-1795; d.
                  12-15-1798.
    Mary   " 9- 5-1797.
    Anna   " 8- 4-1799.
    Ruth   " 10-30-1801.
    Liza   " 10- 8-1803.
    Benjamin   " 12-12-1808.
    Selia   " 3-26-1810.
    John   " 11-12-1813.

Page 36.
Tarlton Moorman
Hannah Moorman
Ch: Harriett b. 1- 9-1810; d.
                 10-19-1814.
    Nancy   " 1-10-1812.
    Henry   " 7- 7-1813.
    Thomas   " 3-11-1814.

Page 32.
Uriah Moorman b. 8-6-1785.
Hannah Moorman b. 6-9-1782.
Ch: Maris   b. 9- 3-1807.
    John   " 12- 2-1808.

Page 8.
Thomas Morris b. 3-19-1769.
Sarah Morris " 1- 3-1770.
Ch: Elizabeth b. 9-17-1790.
    John   " 10-10-1792;d.
                  8-9-1793.
    Ann & Hannah " 8-26-1794.
    Aaron   " 1- 4-1797.
    Martha   " 1-15-1799;d.
                 12-10-1800.
    Caleb   " 3-17-1801.
    Jonathan   " 7-29-1803;d.
                  9-25-1803.
    Sarah   " 7-29-1804.
    Nathan   " 10- 8-1806.
    Thomas   " 4- 7-1809.
    Mary   " 7-12-1811.
    Selia   " 10-14-1814.

Page 16.
Thomas Parker
Anne Parker
Ch: Penninah b. 12-25-1803; d.
                 12-27-1805.
    Elizabeth " 3-11-1806; d.
                 11-23-1810.
    Jesse   " 8-13-1808.
    Selah   " 5-24-1811.
    Sarah   " 5- 3-1813.

Page 29.
Benjamin Thomas b. 1-9-1783.
Anna Thomas   " 2-26-1788.
Ch: Gulay   " 11-21-1807.
    Betty   " 12- 9-1809.

Page 7.
Isaac Thomas b. 11-16-1767.
Rachel Thomas " 10-19-1771.
Ch: Solomon   " 11-25-1792.

Isaac & Rachel Thomas cont'd.
Ch: Betty   b. 12-17-1794.
    Molley   " 12-14-1797.
    Achsa   " 6-16-1800.
    Rachel   " 8-15-1802.
    John   " 9-15-1806.
    Sarah   " 8-22-1809.

Page 1.
John Thomas, Sr. b. 6----1743.
Moley Thomas   " 11----1748.
Ch: Isaac   " 11-16-1767.
    John   " 3-28-1769.
    Betty   " 12-26-1770.
    ------   " 6----1773; d.
                    7-11-1775.
    Rebeckah   " 3-21-1775.
    Elijah   " 1-19-1777.
    Stephen   " 2-23-1779.
    Francis   " 2-19-1781.
    Benjamin   " 1- 9-1783.
    Christan   " 2-12-1785.
    Susannah   " 2-25-1787.
    Sarah   " 2-19-1790.

Page 5.
John Thomas
Lydda Thomas b. 5-13-1774.
Ch: Polly   " 12-19-1792.
    James   " 8-26-1794; d.
                4-21-1807.
    Jesse   " 9- 9-1796.
    Hannah   " 11- 4-1798.
    Nanney   " 10-27-1800.
    Lydia   " 3-19-1803.
    Ruth   " 4- 1-1805; d.
                4-23-1806.
    Huldah   " 4- 7-1809.
    Hendley " 5-22-1807.

Page 11.
Joseph Thomas
Hannah Thomas
Ch: Anna   b. 11-20-1802.
    Manlove " 10-22-1804.

Page 4.
Lewis Thomas, Sr. b. 5-10-1750.
Agnis Thomas, Sr. " 10- 6-1752.
Ch: Mary   " 11-21-1775.
    Anne   " 5-16-1777.
    Agnis   " 9-26-1778; d.
                10-27-1799.
    Joseph   " 1-20-1780.
    Susanna   " 9- 6-1781.
    Rebeckah " 5- 2-1783.
    Vildan   " 3- 6-1785.
    Lewis, Jr. " 11-11-1786.
    Elizabeth " 1-28-1789.
    Sarah   " 9- 5-1791.
    Stephen   " 5-29-1793.
    Ruth   " 2-19-1795.
    Rachil   " 6-19-1797.

Page 45.
Nancy Thomas, dt. Stephen & Lilly,
b. 11-2-1813.

PINEY GROVE MONTHLY MEETING

Page 22.
Stephen Thomas
Hannah Thomas
Ch: Mary   b. 12-20-1804.
    Sarah   "   1- 3-1807.
    Selah   " 11-21-1808.
    Charles " 10-15-1810.

Page 25.
Matthew Way b. 1-14-1784; d. 12-14-1811.
Agnis Way b. 3-4-1785; d. 3-15-1808.
Ch: Susannah b. 1- 4-1807.
    Moorman " 2- 9-1808.

Page 46.
William Way
Abigail Way
Ch: John   b. 2-27-1777; d. 6-11-1778, bur. Center on 12th.
    John   b. 12- 9-1778.
    Mary   "   3-23-1781.
    Matthew "   1-14-1784.

William & Abigail Way cont'd.
Ch: Paul   b. 2-24-1789.
    Hannah   " 11-14-1788.
    Lydia   " 1- 5-1791.
    Henry   " 3-13-1793.
    William " 6- 7-1795.
    Abigail " 11-27-1797.

Page 2.
Thomas Willcuts
Milley Willcuts
Ch: Benj. Thomas b. 12-29-1786.
    John Thomas "   8-19-1789.
    (or 1787) (sons of Milley Willcuts by former m.)
    Clark Willcuts b. 7- 8-1792.
    Christan Willcuts b.11-11-1793.
    Rachel   " b.12-14-1795.
    Hursley   " " 3- 4-1798.
    Joseph   " " 7-16-1799.
    Tabitha   " " 8- 7-1801:
                         d. 9-7-1801.
    Jonathan   " " 5- 8-1804.
    David   " " 8- 7-1805.

* *

MINUTES AND MARRIAGE RECORDS

ADAMS.
1802,10,16. Jonathan (Addams) recrq of father, William.
1810,8,18. William dis.

ALMOND.
1809,4,15. Matthew recrq.
1809,7,15. Harris recrq of father, Matthew.
1812,2,15. Matthew & fam gct MM beyond the Ohio.

BALDWIN.
1806,12,25. Charles, s Daniel & Mary, Guilford Co., N.C., m Sarah Thomas.
1807,4,18. Sarah gc.
1808,12,17. Charles & w, Sarah, & dt, Susanna, rocf New Garden MM, N.C., dated 1808,11,26.
1812,5,21. Daniel, s Daniel & Mary, Guilford Co., N.C., m Christian Wilcuts.
1813,9,18. Charles & fam gct White Water MM, Ind.

BARKER.
1805,11,16. Abner & s, Nathan, Nicholas & Allen, rocf Back Creek MM, N.C., dated 1805, 9,28.
1813,12,18. Abner & fam gct Cane Creek MM.

BEARFIELD.
1808,10,15. Solomon dis mou.
1809,2,18. Jonathan, Milly & Maries gc.

BEAUCHAMP.
1802,4,22. William, Jr., s William & Elizabeth, Richmond Co., N.C., m Milley Willis.
1804,11,17. Henry dis mou.
1808,6,18. Charles dis mou.
1809,10,21. John dis mou.
1811,2,16. Levi gct a MM in Ohio.
1811,2,16. William, Jr. & fam gct MM in Ohio.
1811,3,16. Mathew gct a MM in Ohio.
1811,3,21. Elick, s William & Elizabeth, Marlborough Dist., S.C., m Alice Mendenhall.
1811,4,20. William & fam gct MM in Ohio.
1812,11,21. Ellick & fam gct White Water MM, Ind.

BUNKER.
1803,1,13. Obed rocf New Garden MM, dated 1802,12,25.
1805,12,21. Obed dis.

CHARLES.
1804,2,18. Mary gc.

CLARK.
1802,3,25. Jonathan, s John & Margaret, dec, Guilford Co., N.C., m Ruth Moorman.
1802,6,19. Ruth gct New Garden MM, N.C.
1808,10,15. Nicholas, Jr. dis mou.

COOK.
1810,4,21. Thomas gct Deep River MM, N.C.

137

COX.
1804,3,17. Edmund rocf Contentnea MM, S.C., dated 1804,3,10.
1804,4,26. Abba, dt Josiah & Judeth, Richmond Co., N.C., m Charles Marine.
1804,5,24. Phebe, dt Joseph & Judah, Richmond Co., N.C., m Jesse Marine.
1807,3,2. Edmund gct Contentney MM, N.C.
1807,3,2. Judah gc.

DAWSON.
1802,4,17. Daniel & s, Daniel & John, recrq.
1813,1,21. Lilly, dt Daniel & Ann, Marlborough Dist., S.C., m Stephen Thomas.
1815,2,18. Daniel & fam gct Lick Creek MM, Washington Co., Ind.

DIGGS.
1803,12,17. John dis mou.
1811,3,21. Little Berry, s William & Fanny, Anson Co., N.C., m Lydia Way.

DILLON.
1808,6,18. Daniel, s Joshua, dis mou.
1808,9,17. Joshua, father of Daniel, dis.
1810,1,20. William dis.

HARRIS.
1803,1,20. Obadiah, s Obadiah & Mary, dec, Guilford Co., N.C., m Mary Moorman.
1807,6,20. Obadiah & s, Thomas, David & Jonathan, rocf Deep River MM, N.C., dated 1807, 4,6.
1811,4,20. Obadiah & fam gct a MM in Ohio.

HUCKEBY.
1806,9,20. Lewis Huckeby recrq of grandfather, Lewis Thomas.

KNIGHT.
1791,2,3. Rachel, dt Solomon & Elizabeth, Guilford Co., N.C., m Isaac Thomas.
1803,11,19. Thomas prcf New Garden MM, dated 1803,11,5, to m.
1804,1,26. Thomas, s Solomon & Elizabeth, dec, Richmond Co., N.C., m Christan Thomas.
1804,9,15. Sarah gc.
1810,8,18. Thomas dis.
1813,5,15. Thomas recrq.
1814,7,16. Thomas gct White Water MM.

LAM.
1804,7,21. Josiah & fam gct Lost Creek MM.

LINNEGAR.
1803,12,17. Isac gct Deep River MM.
1809,1,21. Isaac rocf Deep River MM, N.C., dated 1808,12,5.
1814,2,19. Isaac (Linegar) gct Deep River MM.

MACY.
1804,6,16. Joseph & ch, Mary, Phebe & William, rocf Deep Creek MM, N.C., dated 1804,2,4.

MARINE.
1804,1,21. John rpd mou.
1804,4,26. Charles, s Jonathan & Mary, Marlborough Co., S.C., m Abba Cox.
1804,5,24. Jesse, s Jonathan & Mary, Marlborough, S.C., m Pheba Cox.
1807,3,2. Jesse gct Contentny MM, N.C.
1807,3,2. Pheby gc.
1807,8,15. Jonathan dis.
1808,3,19. Charles dis.
1808,3,19. John dis.
1808,3,19. John & Asey recrq of father, Jonathan.
1811,2,16. Jonathan & sons gct a MM in Ohio.

MENDENHALL.
1806,6,21. Ely dis mou.
1806,11,20. Hannah, dt Stephen & Elizabeth, Richmond Co., N.C. m Uriah Moorman.
1807,12,19. Moses rocf Springfield MM, N.C., dated 1807,1,3.
1809,1,21. Mordicai dis mou.
1809,7,15. Stephen, Jr. gct New Garden MM, N.C.
1811,3,21. Alice, dt Moses & Betty dec, Marlborough Dist., S.C., m Elick Beauchamp.
1811,11,16. John gct Waynesville MM, Ohio.
1815,2,18. Stephen & fam gct Lick Creek MM, Washington Co., Ind.

MOORMAN.
1800,5,8. Edward (Morman), s Zachariah & Mary, Marlborough Co., S.C., m Mary Thomas.
1802,3,25. Ruth, dt Zachariah & Mary, Marlborough Co., S.C., m Jonathan Clark.
1803,1,20. Mary, dt Zachariah & Mary, Marlborough Co., S.C., m Obadiah Harris.
1806,1,1. Agness, dt Thomas, dec, & Susannah, Richmond Co., N.C. m Matthew Way.

PINEY GROVE MONTHLY MEETING

MOORMAN cont'd.
1806,10,22. Achsah, dt John & Rebeckah, Richmond Co., N.C., m Paul Way.
1806,10,23. Ann, dt Zachariah & Mary, Marlborough Dist., S.C., m Benjamin Thomas.
1806,11,20. Uriah, s Zachariah & Mary, Marlborough Dist., S.C., m Hannah Mendenhall.
1807,11,26. Tarlton, s Thomas & Susanah, Richmond Co., N.C., m Hannah Way.
1811,4,20. Uriah & fam gct a MM in Ohio.
1811,4,20. Zachariah & fam gct a MM in Ohio.
1815,2,18. Thomas gct White Water MM, Ind.

MORRIS.
1812,4,23. Anna, dt Thomas & Sarah, Marlborough Dist., S.C., m Solomon Thomas.
1815,2,18. Thomas & fam gct Lick Creek MM, Washington Co., Ind.

MUSGRAVE.
1789,11,19. Sarah, dt Caleb & Elizabeth, Wayne Co., N.C., m Morris Thomas, at Contentnea MH, N.C.
1808,3,19. Charity (Mustgrave) gc.

PARKER.
1802,2,20. Nathan rocf Deep River, N.C., dated 1801,10,10.
1803,3,3. Thomas, s Elisha & Elizabeth, Richmond Co., N.C., m Anne Peele.
1804,11,17. Elisha gct Contenty MM.
1804,11,17. Elizabeth gc.
1804,11,17. Nathan, s Elisha, gct Contentny MM.
1814,3,19. Thomas & fam gct White Water MM.

PEELE.
1803,3,3. Anne, dt Passco & Tabbitha, Richmond Co., N.C., m Thomas Parker.
1803,12,17. Pasco & s, John, recrq.
1804,11,17. William recrq.
1808,1,16. William dis mou.
1809,10,21. John dis.
1815,1,21. Tabitha (Peel) gc.

RATLIFF.
1811,12,21. Elijah dis mou.

STAFFORD.
1805,4,20. Garvis & fam gct Wainsville MM, Ohio.

THARP.
1804,8,18. Elizabeth gc.

THOMAS.
1791,2,3. Isaac, s John & Molley, Guilford Co., N.C., m Rachel Knight.
1789,11,19. Morris, s Zachariah & Ann, Wayne Co., N.C., m Sarah Musgrave, at Contentnea MH. N.C.
1800,5,8. Mary, dt Lewis & Agness, Richmond Co., N.C., m Edward Morman.
1802,9,18. James & Jesse recrq of father, John.
1804,1,21. Stephen gct Deep River MM, to m.
1804,1,26. Christan, dt John & Molley, Marlboro Co., S.C., m Thomas Knight.
1805,4,20. Daniel & Simeon recrq of father, Elijah.
1806,9,20. Lewis Huckeby recrq of grandfather, Lewis Thomas.
1806,10,23. Benjamin, s John & Molley, Marlborough Dist., S.C., m Anna Moorman.
1806,12,25. Sarah, dt John & Molley, Marlborough Dist., S.C., m Charles Baldwin.
1807,4,18. Francis gct Contentney MM, N.C., to m.
1807,7,18. Benjamin gct New Garden MM, N.C.
1807,7,18. Francis gct Contentoney MM, N.C.
1810,3,17. Joseph & s, Manlove & Stephen, gct Deep River MM, N.C.
1810,6,16. John, 3rd dis mou.
1810,6,16. Hannah gc.
1811,2,16. Benjamin & fam gct a MM in Ohio.
1811,2,16. John, 2nd & fam gct a MM in Ohio.
1811,6,15. Lewis, Jr. gct a MM in Ohio.
1812,4,23. Solomon, s Isaac & Rachel, Richmond Co., N.C. m Anna Morris.
1812,7,18. John, 3rd recrq.
1813,1,21. Stephen, s Lewis & Agnes Richmond Co., N.C., m Lilly Dawson.
1813,9,18. Isaac & fam gct White Water MM, Ind.
1813,9,18. John & fam gct White Water MM, Ind.
1813,9,18. Solomon & fam gct White Water MM, Ind.
1814,2,19. Elijah & fam gct White Water MM.
1814,2,19. John gct White Water MM.
1814,3,19. Stephen & fam gct White Water MM.
1815,2,18. Lewis & fam gct Lick Creek MM, Washington Co., Ind.
1815,2,18. Stephen & fam gct Lick Creek MM, Washington Co., Ind.

139

PINEY GROVE MONTHLY MEETING

THOMAS cont'd.
1815,2,18. Tilden & fam gct Lick Creek MM, Washington Co., Ind.

WAY.
1802,7,17. William & w, Abigail, & ch, Matthew, Paul, Hannah, Henry, William & Abigail, rocf Sentor MM, dated 1802,4,17.
1802,7,17. John & w, Patience, & ch, Mary, rocf Center MM, dated 1802,4,17.
1805,12,21. John dis.
1806,1,1. Matthew, s William & Abbigal, Marlborough. Co., S.C., m Agness Moorman.
1806,10,22. Paul, s William & Abigal, Marlborough Dist., S. C., m Achsah Moorman.
1807,11,26. Hannah, dt William & Abigail, Marlborough Dist., S.C., m Tarlton Moorman.
1811,3,21. Lydia, dt William & Abigail, Marlborough Dist., S.C., m Little Berry Diggs.

WILLCUTS.
1811,12,21. Clark dis mou.
1812,5,21. Christian, dt Thomas & Milly, Marlborough Dist., S. C., m Daniel Baldwin.
1814,4,16. Thomas & fam gct White Water MM.

WILLIS.
1802,4,22. Milley, dt Thomas & Lina, Marlborough Co., S.C., m William Beauchamp.

WILSON.
1804,1,21. Rebecca, of Little Creek, dis.

CHARLESTON MONTHLY MEETING
Charleston, South Carolina

The history of Charleston Meeting is given by Dr. Weeks in "Southern Quakers and Slavery", pages 93 and 94, as follows.

"The Charleston meeting dates from 1680. It was established by London Yearly Meeting and Charleston Friends considered themselves under the jurisdiction of no Yearly Meeting save London; they retained their connection with that and were bound by its principles and testimonies. They corresponded with London and Philadelphia, and many of the Friends there kept their membership in the old meetings. They were few in numbers, and for some twenty years prior to 1718 no settled meeting for business was held. In that year what was practically a monthly meeting was set up in Charleston. Its records continue, but with many breaks, until 1786. This may be taken as the probable limit of their ability to hold business meetings. Their first meetings were held in a private house, but they had a meeting-house as early as 1715. They did not come into the title to their property until 1731, when it was secured for them through English Friends. It was then conveyed to trustees, but the last survivor claimed the property as his own, locked up the meeting-house and would allow no meetings there. At this juncture Philadelphia Friends appeared on the scene, purchased all the claims of the heirs of this original trustee and then vested the property in others. Philadelphia Friends incurred much trouble and expense and got little return, for there did not appear to be more than fifteen members in the place in 1791; the property was going to decay and some of their agents were dishonest. In 1796 the property was transferred to Bush River Monthly Meeting, but there was little improvement, and as this meeting had become very weak in the meantime, trustees of North Carolina Yearly Meeting, appointed for the purpose, reconveyed the property to Philadelphia Yearly Meeting in 1812. Several unsuccessful efforts have been made by North Carolina Yearly Meeting since that date to again get possession of the property. The meeting for worship was finally laid down in 1837, when only three persons attended, two of whom were not Friends."

The records of Charleston Meeting consist of birth and death records, marriage records and minutes all entered in a single book. This book is in the care of Philadelphia Friends, at 302 Arch Street.

CHARLESTON MONTHLY MEETING

BIRTH AND DEATH RECORDS

Page 193.
John Allen, s. Nehemiah, Phila., Pa., d. 11-29-1720, bur. at Charlestowne.

Page 194.
Benjamin Austin d. 6-8-1735, bur. Friends' Bur. Gr. at Charlestown.

Page 195.
John Coming
Sarah Coming
Ch: Daniel d. 5-30-1730, bur. Friends' Bur. Gr.
    Sarah d. 6-8-1730, bur. Friends' Bur. Gr.
    Elizabeth d. 7-3-1735, bur. John's Island.
    Sarah d. 11-6-1735, bur. John's Island.
    Joan d. 5-5-1736, bur. John's Island.

Page 193.
John Cooper bur. 10 mo.-1815 at Charlestown Bur. Gr.

Page 194.
John Cox d. 3-19-1734, bur. Friends' Bur. Gr.

Page 194.
John Denton d. 4-15-1721, bur. at Charlestowne.

Page 196.
Capt. James Doughty d. 12-1-1749, bur. Friends' Bur. Gr.

Page 193.
Hephsibeth Elliott, w Thomas, d. 7-27-1719, bur. "on her h's plantation on Stone."

Page 170.
Thomas Fleming
Sarah Fleming
Ch: John   b. 2-17-1725.
    Daniel   " 1-21-1726.
    Sarah   " 6- 4-1729.
    Sarah   " 11-27-1730.
    Martha   " 4- 2-1732.
    Elizabeth " 9- 9-1733.
    Jean   " 8-31-1735.

Page 169.
Anna Goll, dt Christian & Isabella, b. 10-26-1708.

Page 194.
George Head bur. Friends' Bur. Gr.

Page 193.
Edward Holliday d. 1715, bur. Charlestown Bur. Gr.

Page 193.
John Jackson d. 6-27-1718, bur. Charlestown Bur. Gr.

Page 172.
Ruth Johnson, dt. Wm. & Ruth, b. 1769.

Page 197.
Wm. Johnson, school-master, d. 12-29-1768, bur. Friends' Bur. Gr.

Page 195.
Thomas Kemerly d. 9-30-1736, bur. Friends' Bur. Gr.

Page 195.
Iseabel Kimberly d. 11-10-1740, age 78 yrs. 10 das., bur Friends' Bur. Gr.

Page 194.
Joshuah Lanckaster d. 5-21-1734, bur. Friends' Bur. Gr.

Page 193.
George Meers d. 9-10-1717, bur. Charlestown Bur. Gr.

Page 197.
Asa Pancoast d. 1769, bur. Friends' Bur. Place.

Page 194.
Sarah Parsons d. 7-17-1734, bur. Friends' Bur. Gr.

Page 194.
Elizabeth Roberts d. 1-14-1722, bur. Friends' Bur. Gr., Charlestowne.

Page 196.
Thomas Shoemaker bur. Friends' Bur. Gr.

Page 171.
Joseph Shute
Anna Shute
Ch: Jesabel   b. 8-28-1732.
    Thomas   " 1-22-1733.
    Elizabeth " 9-12-1735.
    Thomas   " 7-21-1737.
    John   " 2-12-1739.
    Thomas   " 3-16-1741.
    Mary   " 5-27-1742.
    Mary   " 5-13-1743.

Page 195.
Thomas Shute, s. Joseph & Anna, d. 3-12-1735.
Thomas Shute, s. Joseph & Anna, d. 4-17-1738.
Both buried at Friend's Bur. Gr.

CHARLESTON MONTHLY MEETING

Page 196.
Thomas Shute, s. Joseph & Anna, d. 6 mo.-1741, bur. Friends' Bur. Gr.
Mary Shute, dt. Joseph & Anna, d. 8 mo.-1742, bur. Friends' Bur. Gr.
Anna Shute, w. Joseph, d. 4-26-1749, age 40 yrs. 6 mos. bur. Friends' Bur. Gr.

Page 196.
Mary Smith d. 10-15-1740, bur. Friends' Bur. Gr., Charleston, S.C.
Page 194.
Susannah Wigganton d. 7-29-1733, bur. Friends' Bur. Gr.

Page 194.
James Witter d. 7-9-1730, bur. on his plantation.

Page 169.
John Witter
Mary Witter
Ch: John   b. 10-24-1718.
    Mary   " 11-22-1720.
    James   " 9-23-1722.
    Elizabeth   " 8- 5-1724.
Ann Witter, 2nd w. John.
Ch: Norwood   b. 12-27-1728.
    Martha   " 10-24-1729.
    Samuel   " 11-10-1731.
    Thomas   " 10-27-1733.
    Jonathan   " 2-30-1736.

Page 194.
Mary Whitter, w. John, d. 11-11-1726, bur. at her h's plantation.

MINUTES AND MARRIAGE RECORDS

ARNOTT.
1731,8,7. Anna, Charleston, S.C., m Joseph P. Shute, at Charleston, MH.

CLIFFORD.
1721,3,6. Ann m Thomas Elliot, Sen., at Charleston MH.

ELLIOT.
1720,2,30. Thomas, Jr. m Bulah Law, at Charleston MH.
1721,3,6. Thomas, Sen., m Ann Clifford, at Charleston MH.

GOLL.
1716,4,24. Isabell m Thomas Kimberly, at Charleston MH.

KIMBERLY.
1716,4,24. Thomas m Isabell Goll, at Charleston MH.

LAW.
1720,2,30. Beulah m Thomas Elliot, Jr., at Charleston MH.

LINTON.
1769,12,4. Jacob rocf Bellehagen 6 weeks mtg, Ireland, dated 1769,10,9.

PENDARVIS(?).
1722,5,5. John dis.

SHUTE.
1731,8,7. Joseph P., s Thomas & Elizabeth, Phila., Pa., m Anna Arnott, at Charleston MH.
1750,12,12. Joseph & Mary W. m by a priest.

SIKES.
1751,8,18. Thomas & w, Isabella, & two ch came to this country from Ireland & settled in Charleston.
1765,6,30. Thomas & w, Isabella, & ch, George & Rachel, returned to Ireland; bur. 7 ch in Friends' Bur. Gr., Charleston, S.C.

145

--, B. D., 76; Samuel, 63; Bettie, 39; Jonathan, 68; Mary Jay, 104; Mills?, 104
ADAMS: Mrs., 18; Thomas, 18; William, 137
ADAMSON: Elizabeth, 24; James, 10, 12; James, Lt., 24, 25; John, 10, 12; Miss, 25
ADAMSONS: --, 39
ADDAMS: Beebe, 135; Hannah, 135; John, 135; Jonathan, 135, 137; Mary, 135; William, 134, 135, 137
ADDENTON: Elizabeth Heaton, 97, 102; Henry, 97; John, 97, 102; Sarah, 97
ADDINGTON: Alice, 89; Elizabeth Randle, 129; Elizabeth, 89, 132; Else, 129, 130; Henry, 97, 124; James, 97, 124, 129; John, 89, 97, 124; Joseph, 89; Karenhappuck, 124; Marthe, 124; Mary Roberds, 132; Mary, 89, 97, 124, 129; Rachel Randel, 129, 132; Rebecca, 124; Rebekah, 129; Rebekah, Jr., 129; Sarah, 89, 124, 129; Thomas, 89, 97, 124; William, 89
ADENTON: James, 97
ALEXANDER: David, 02; Elizabeth, 24
ALLEN: John, 142; Nehemiah, 142
ALLISON: Andrew, 26; Margaret Cox, 97, 100
ALMOND: Elisabeth, 135; Harris, 135, 137; Judith, 135; Matthew & Family, 137; Matthew, 135, 137; Rebeckah, 135
ANCRUM: --, 27, 36; W., 04; Wm., 04; William, 26
ANGELY: Mary Dunn, 118, 119
ANGLIN: Catharine, 118; Elijah, 118; Henry, 118; John, 118; Mary, 118; Nathan, 118; Susanna, 118
ARLEDGE: John, 07
ARNOLD: Mary Jay, 97; Rachel, 97, 104; Susannah & ch., 129
ARNOTT: Anna, 143
ASHFORD: Hannah Hollingsworth, 129; Hannah, 131
ATKINSON: David, 114; Edith, 114; Family, 97; Henry, 114; Isaac, 114; Martha, 114; Nathan, 114; Rachel, 114; Ruth, 114; Samuel & Family, 118; Samuel, 97; Thomas, 114; William, 114
AUSTIN: Benjamin, 142
B--, Jno. T., 84
B--, Rebecca O'Neall, 84
BABB: Mary, 97; Mercer, 46
BALDWIN: Charles & Family, 137; Charles, 134, 137, 139; Christian Wil(l)cuts, 137, 140; Daniel, 137, 140; Mary, 137; Sarah Thomas, 137, 139; Sarah, 137; Susanna, 137
BALLINGER: Ann, 89; Evan, 89; Family, 97; Hannah, 89, 97, 100; Isaac, 89, 97; Jacob, 89, 97; James, 89, 97; John, 89; Jonathan, 89; Josiah, 89, 97; Lydia, 89; Mary, 89; Sarah, 89
BARFIELD: Charity, 135; Demaris, 135; Demsey, 135; Jonathan, 135; Mary, 135; Millicent, 135; Miriam, 135; Ruth, 135; Sarah, 135; Solomon, 134, 135; William, 135
BARKER: Abner & Family, 137; Abner, 135, 137; Allen, 135, 137; Hannah, 135; Lydia, 135; Mary, 135; Matthew, 135; Nathan, 135, 137; Nicholas, 135, 137; Phebe, 135; Ruth, 135
BARNARD: Tristram, 123
BARNES: Abigail, 118; Olive, 118; Rache, 118
BARNET: David, 128; Hannah Wilson, 128
BARNS: Abigail, 118; Children, 97; Elizabeth, 97, 118; Jacob, 118; James, 118; Jeremiah, 118; Mary, 118, 119; Olive, 118; Samuel, 118
BARR: Mathis, 46
BARRET: Arthur, 97; Benjamin, 97; Family, 97; Jacob, 97; Jemime, 97; John, 97; Joseph, 97; Lydia, 97; Rhoda, 97
BARRETS: --, 81

BARRETT: Benj., 97; Benjamin, 97; Children, 97; Jacob, Jr., 97; James, 97; Jonathan, 97; John, 97, 110; Mrs., 97; Rhoda Taylor, 97, 110
BARRETTS: --, 56
BARROT: James, 97
BATTEN: Ann Cook, 97; Family, 97; Richard, 97, 99
BATTIN: Ann, 89; Catharine, 89; Children, 97; James, 89; John, 89; Jonathan, 89; Richard & Family, 97; Richard, 89, 97; Richard, Jr. & W., 97
BATTON: Ann, 118; Cathren, 118; James, 118; John, 118; Jonathan, 118; Richard, 97, 118
BAUM: -- 10
BAYS: Elizabeth O'Neall, 84; John, 84
BEARFIELD: Jonathan, 137; Maries, 137; Milly, 137; Solomon, 137
BEARFOOT: Geo., 04
BEAUCHAMP: Elick, 138; Alice Hendenhall, 137, 138; Caleb, 135; Charles, 135, 137; Curtis, 135; Elick, 137; Elizabeth, 135, 137; Elleck, 135; Ellick & Family, 137; Henry, 135, 137; John, 135, 137; Levi, 135, 137; Matthew, 135, 137; Milcar, 135; Milley Willis, 137, 140; Russ, 135; William Jr. & Family, 137; William & Family, 137; William, 134, 135, 137, 140; William, Jr., 137
BECK: John, 118
BEEDLE: Ruth, 113
BELTON: Abraham, 10, 12, 24; Ann, 24; Elizabeth Alexander, 24; Hannah, 10, 22, 48; Jno., 04; John, 12, 22, 24; Jonathan (or John), 10; Martha, 24; Mary, 24; Rebecca, 24; Robert, 36
BEMBO: Edward, 97; Family, 97
BENBOW: Berkly, 97; Edward, 97; Even, 97; Mary, 97
BENHAM: Barclay, 76
BENNET: John, 04, 05, 06
BENSON: Alice, 118, 120; James & Family, 129; James, 97; Jane, 118; Robert, 118; William, 118; William, Jr., 118
BISHOP: Georgil, 34
BLACK: John, 04, 05, 06, 14; [John], 11
BONAPARTE: Napoleon, 58, 72
BOONE: --, 56
BOWMAN: Sarah, 97
BOYKIN: Burwell, 24; Dr., 10; E.M., Dr., 24, 25; Lemuel, 25; William, 23
BRANHAM: Michael, 05, 06, 12
BRANNON: Michael, 07
BRAY: Edward, 97, 124; Henry, 97, 124; Jemima, 124; John, 97, 124; Joseph, 124; Keziah & dts., 129; Keziah Jones, 124; Keziah, 123; Mary, 124; Richard, 124; Sarah, 124
BREADY: D., 04; Daniel, 05, 06, 12; Samuel, 11; W., 04; William, 05, 06, 11
BRIDGES: Charles, 89, 97; Charles, & Family, 97; Ede, 89; Jesse, 89; John, 89, 97; Mary, 89; William, 89, 97
BRISBANE: Adam Fowler, 39
BROCK: Ann, 97; Charity Cook, 97; Elias, 97; George, 97, 99
BRODEY: Mary Cook, 97
BRODEY:(?) Mary Cook, 99
BROOKS: Children, 86; Daniel Offley, 88, 89; Daniel, 98; David Singletary, 89; David Singleterry, 88; Elizabeth, 88, 89, 97, 101; Hannah Stuart, 122; Hannah Wright, 97, 112; Hannah, 97, 118; James, 46, 48, 53, 60, 80, 87-89, 97; Joab, 89, 97; John, 60, 89, 98; Martha, 89; Mary, 89, 98; Nimrod, 60, 89, 98; Sall, 89; Sarah Singletary, 89, 97, 110; Sarah, 89, 97, 104; Susannah Phillips, 97; Susannah, 89, 109; Vashti, 89
BROWN: Ann, 89, 98, 114; Anna, 61,

69; Betsy, 114; Clayton, 124; Elizabeth, 114; Gen., 52; Jacob Roberts, 52; James, 39, 118; John, 114, 118; Jonathan, 114; Joseph & Family, 118; Joshua, 68, 89, 98; Josiah, 98; Kameston, 89; Kirk, 123; Lydia, 114; Margaret, 114; Martha, 118; Mary Hickson, 118; Mary, 114, 118, 119; Mercer, 114, 118; Nancy, 89; Phebe, 114, 118; Polly, 118; Rebecca, 118; Richard, 114, 118; Samuel, 46, 68, 69, 87, 89, 98, 118; Samuel, Jr. ? W., 98; Samuel, Sr. & W., 98; Sarah Compton, 124; Sarah, 114, 118; Thomas, 01; Uriah, 98; William, 114
BRYAN: Thomas, 05, 07
BUFFINGTON: Sarah, 118
BULL: Robert, 98; Sarah & Children, 98
BUNKER: Obed, 137
BUNTING: Sarah, 118
BURKE: --, 31
BURRETT: James, 97
BURTON: Robert, 48
BUTLER/BUTTLER: John, 118
BUTLER: Baal, 76; Bales, 88; Mary, 88; Mrs., 88; Samuel, 88; Susanna, 88; William, 88
BUXTON: Samuel, 05, 06, 10
BYSHOP: Elizabeth, 98, 101; Thomas, 98
CAIN: John, 11
CAMACK: Mary Hall, 98, 102
CAMBBEL: John, 89; Ralph, 89; Mary, 98
CAMDEN: Baron, 33; Lord, 30, 31; William, 33, 34
CAMMAC: James, 98
CAMMACK: Amos, 89; Ann, 89; James & Family, 98; James, 89, 98; Joanna, 89; John, 89; Margaret, 89; Mary, 89; Samuel, 89; William, 89
CAMPBELL: Elizabeth Parnel, 132; Elizabeth, 129; Esther, 129; John, 98, 108; Mary, 108; Ralph, 98, 108; Rebecah, 129, 132; Samuel, 98; Sarah Hasket, 98, 102; Sarah, 88
CAMPBELLS: --, 56, 81
CAMPTON: John, 71; Samuel, 99
CANNIDA: Rachel Minton, 132; Rachel, 129
CANTEY: James, 36; John, 23, 36, 39
CANTEYS: --, 13
CAREY: J., 04; James, 39
CARL: Elizabeth, 98; Sarah, 118
CARLE: Elizabeth, 88
CARNMACH: Joanna, 89
CARRISON: --, 13
CARSON: John, Jr., 118; Thomas, 118
CARTER: Robert, 36
CASTELO: --, 39
CASTON: Glass, 36
CATTERTON: Mark, 04-06, 12
CEMMACK: James, 98; Margaret, 98; Mary, 98
CHANCE: Samuel, 134
CHANDLER: Allsebeth, 89; Ann, 89, 98; David, 89; Elizabeth, 98, 106; Gabriel, 89; Israel, 89, 98; Jacob, 87, 89, 98; Jonathan, 89, 98
CHAPMAN: Giles, Jr., 98; Giles, Rev., 84; John A., 54; Lewis, 84; Rhoda O'Neall, 84; Samuel, 87, 98; William, 98
CHARLES XII: King of Sweden, 74
CHARLES: Mary, 137
CHARLTON: Thomas, 39
CHATHAM: --, 31
CHEEK: Ellis, 98; James, 98
CHESNUT: --, 97; James, 27, 39; John, 13, 27, 36, 39
CHOATE: Sen., 63
CHRISTMAS: Jonathan, 11
CLARK: Allbeth, 89; Elizabeth, 89; Ester, 129; Henry, 89; Hester, 89; John, 89, 98, 108, 137; Jonathan, 89, 137, 138; Margaret, 137; Mary & some of ch., 129; Mary, 89; Nicholas, 134; Nicholas, Jr., 137; Rachel, 89, 129, 130; Ruth Moorman, 137, 138; Ruth, 137;

Thomas, 89; William, 98
CLAY: Joseph, 39
CLEGG: Creese or Creesy, 82; Richard, 68, 69, 73, 81, 82
CLERK: Elizabeth, 124; Henry, 124; John, 124
CLIFFORD: Ann, 143
CLOUD: Ann, 114; Esther, 114; Hannah, 114, 118; Joel, 113, 114, 118; Joel, Jr., 114; Joseph, 113; Lydea, 114; Mary, 114; Rebekah, 114; Sarah, 114
COAT: Henry, 98, 102; John, 98; Maraduke, 98; Mary Hasket, 102; Mary, 98, 108; Moses, 98, 99; Samuel, 98, 100; William & family, 98; William, 98
COATE: Elizabeth Miles, 106; Esther, 90; Henry & family, 98; Henry, 63, 90, 98; James, 63, 90, 98, 106; Jesse, 63, 90; John, 46, 63, 90; Marmaduke & family, 98; Marmaduke, 63, 90, 98; Mary Haskett, 98; Mary Miles, 106; Mary, 90; Moses, 63, 90, 98; Moses & w., 98; Moses & Family, 98; Samuel, 63, 90, 98; Samuel & w., 98; Samuel & Family, 98; Sarah, 90, 98, 102; William, 87, 90, 98, 106; Wm., 46
COATS: Rachel, 88
COCKS: Elizabeth Thomas, 100, 111
COFFIN: Barnabas, 88, 123
COLE: Hannah, 98
COLLINS: John, 04-06, 13
COMER: Amos, 124; Ann, 124; Anne, 129, 131; Elizabeth, 98, 123, 124, 129, 133; Joseph, 98, 124, 129; Lydia, 13, 129; Martha Hawkins, 129, 131; Martha, 124; Mary Hawkins, 129, 131; Mary, 124; Rebekah, 129; Robert, 98, 124, 129, 131; Stephen, 98, 129, 131; Tamar, 124
COMING: Daniel, 142; Elizabeth, 142; Joan, 142; John, 142; Sarah, 142
COMMACK: James, 98, 99
COMPTON: Alley, 124; Amos & Family, 129; Amos, 90, 98, 99, 124, 125, 127, 129, 132; Ann, 124; Betty, 124; Daniel, 129; Dinah Milhous, 129, 132; Dinah Millhouse, 127; Dinah, 125; Eli, 124; Elizabeth, 90, 99, 124, 125, 127, 129; Eunice Walton, 124; Hannah, 125; Henry, 125; Jane Engle, 124; John, 90, 98, 99, 124, 125; Joseph, 90, 124; Joshua, 90, 98, 99, 124, 127, 129, 131; Mary, 124, 125; Matilda, 126; Matthew, 90, 98, 99, 124; Nancy, 125; Nathan, 124; Patty, 126; Phebe, 124, 125; Rachel, 69, 90, 98, 99, 124; Rebecca Hawkins, 127; Rebecca Millhouse, 124, 127; Rebecca Steddom, 124; Rebecca, 125; Rebekah & 2 ch., 129; Rebekah Hawkins, 124, 129, 131; Rebekah Milhous, 129, 132; Ruth Hawkins, 125; Sally Nelson, 99; Sally, 90, 124, 125, 127; Saml., 127; Samuel & Family, 99; Samuel, 90, 98, 99, 124, 125, 128, 129; Samuel, 2nd, 124, 125; Samuel, Jr., 99; Sarah, 98, 124, 127; Seth, 125; Stephen & Family, 129; Stephen, 90, 98, 124, 125, 127, 129, 132; Tamar Wilson, 125, 128; William, 90, 98, 124, 125
COMPTON/CUMPTON: Amos, 99
CONNER: Anna, 125; Catharine, 114, 125; Isaac, 125; Jesse, 114, 125; John & Family, 99, 113, 118; John 99, 113, 114, 125; Mary, 113, 114, 125; Rachel, 114, 125; Rebecca, 113, 125; Thomas, 114, 125; William, 114, 125
COOK: Abraham, 125, 126; Amos & Family, 130; Amos, 90, 99, 111, 125, 130; Ann Frazier, 125, 130; Ann, 90, 97, 99, 102, 125, 131; Charity, 23, 48, 49, 67, 80, 90, 97, 99; Dinah Spray, 126; Dinah, 90, 125, 126, 128, 130, 131; Eli & Family, 130; Eli, 87, 90, 99,

147

102, 125, 129; Elizabeth Townsend, 111; Elizabeth, 90, 123, 125, 130; Esther, 128; Herbert, 90; Isaac & Family, 130; Isaac, 46, 71, 87, 90, 95, 99, 125, 127-130, 132; Isaac, Jr. & Family, 99; Isaac, Jr., 99; Isaac, & Family, 99; Isaac, Sr. 125; Jacob, 90; James, 36, 125; John, 11, 39, 90, 99, 125, 126, 130, 133; Jonathan, 90; Joseph & Family, 99; Joseph, 90, 99; Kezia Henderson, 103; Levi & Family, 130; Levi, 90, 125, 130; Lydea Cooper, 130; Lydea, 130; Martha Hawkins, 102; Martha, 90, 123, 125, 129; Mary Furnas, 126; Mary Wilkinson, 125; Mary, 90, 99, 111, 123, 125, 127, 128, 130-132; Nathan, 125; Olive Smith, 130, 133; Olive, 90, 130, 131; Peter, 90; Phebe, 125; Rachel, 90, 99, 106, 129, 131; Rebeca Pearson, 108; Rebeckah, 90; Rebekah, 125, 130, 131; Robert, 125; Rut, 99; Ruth Hawkins, 125, 126; Ruth, 90, 101, 125; Sarah Hawkins, 130, 131; Sarah Milhous, 129, 132; Sarah, 90, 99, 101, 125, 127, 129; Seth, 125; Stephen, 125; Susannah, 90, 99, 106; Thomas & Family, 99; Thomas, 90, 99, 103, 134, 137; Uriah, 90; William & W., 130; William, 90, 131; Wright & Family, 99; Wright, 90, 99, 108
COOKS: --, 23
COOPER: Benjamin & Family, 118; Benjamin, 99, 114, 118, 121; Charity, 99; Elizabeth Townsend, 133; Elizabeth, 130; Ferrebee Sanders, 121; Ferree Sanders, 118; Isaac & W., 118; Isaac & Family, 113; Isaac, 99, 113, 114; Jacob, 99; Joanna Hunt, 131; Joanna, 130; John, 142; Joseph, 99, 118; Lydea, 130; Mary Hunter, 104; Nathan, 99; Pharoba, 99; Phebe, 130; Prudence (with H), 130; Prudence, 114, 123; Samuel, 99; Sarah, 99, 130; William, 87, 99, 104
COPPOCK: Aaron, 90, 99; Abigail, 90, 99, 112; Ann, 90, 99; Anne Jay, 104; Benjamin, 69, 90, 99, 100; Children, 100; Elizabeth, 90, 98, 99; Isaac, 90, 99; James & Family, 99; James, 46, 69, 99, 100; Jane & children, 100; Jane, 90, 100; John, 46, 69, 90, 99, 104; John, Sr., 99; Joseph, 90, 99, 100; Joseph, Jr., 99; Margaret, 98, 100; Margarett, 90; Marget, 90; Marther, 99, 111; Mary, 90, 99, 104; Moses, 69, 99; Samuel, 69, 90; Susannah, 90, 99, 100; Thomas, 90, 99; William, 90
COURSON: David, 11
COX: Abba, 138; Amey Sidwell, 118, 122; Ann Hodgin, 118, 119; Ann, 87, 100, 103; Anna, 90; David, 87, 100; Deborah Stubbs, 113; Edmund, 138; Elizabeth, 100; Isaac, 87; Jane, 100; Jemima, 100; John, 87, 100, 142; Jonathan & Family, 100; Jonathan, 100; Joseph, 138; Josiah, 138; Judah, 138; Judeth, 138; Margaret, 100; Mary, 90, 100, 118, 125, 128, 130, 133; Peter, 87, 113; Pheba, 138; Phebe, 138; Rebeckah, 87, 90; Richard & W., 118; Richard, 87, 90, 100, 119; Sarah Townsend, 133; Sarah, 100, 103, 130; Tamer, 123, 125, 128, 130; Tamer, 90; Thomas & Family, 100; Thomas, 90, 100, 118, 125, 128, 130; Tomas & W. & dt., 130; William & Family, 100; William, 87, 100
CREW: Armsberry, 134; Armsley, 134; Littleberry, 119
CREWS: Letilberry, 119
CROMWELL: --, 20
CRUMPTON: John, 46, 71
CUMPTON: Amos, 99
CURETON: Everard, 24; Family, 24; Rebecca Belton, 24
CURETONS: --, 12
CURL: Elizabeth, 88; Sarah, 88
CURLE: Sarah, 113
DARRINGTON: Nancy, 25
DAVID: Mary Barns, 118
DAVIES: Abiathar, 114; Amos, 114; Benjamin, 114; John, 114; Lydia, 114; Mary, 114; Rachel, 114; Rhoda, 114; Samuel, 114; Sarah, 114; Sibilla, 114
DAVIS: Abiathar, 119; Amos & Family, 100; Amos, 100; G., 07; Hannah Marshall, 130; Hannah, 132; Lydia Embree, 119; Mary Barns, 119
DAWSON: Ann, 135, 138; Daniel & Family, 138; Daniel, 135, 138; Henerlter, 135; John, 135, 138; Lilley, 135; Lilly, 138, 139; Milley, 135; Noah, 135
DAY: John, 113, 119; Margaret, 113; Margret, 119
DEKALB: --, 27, 37
DELOACH: Thomas, 25
DEMANS: Phebe, 100, 108
DEHOSS: Joanna, 100, 111
DENNYS: --, 56
DENTON: John, 142
DICKS: Zachary, 21, 53, 55, 56
DIGGS: Fanny, 138; John, 138; Little Berry, 138, 140; Lydia Way, 138, 140; William, 138
DIGS: Benjamin, 134; Caroline, 134; Fanny, 134; Fany, 134; Hannah, 134; John, 134; Littleton, 134; Lucy, 134; Lydia, 134; Margery, 134; Mark, 134; William Armsley, 134; William, 134
DILLON: Daniel, 138; Joshua, 138; William, 138
DIXON: Ann, 119; Eli, 11; Henry, 119; John, 119; Joseph, 119; Solomon, 119; Stephen, 119
DOBY: Ann Belton, 24; Family, 24; James C., 25; John, 24; Sarah English, 25
DODD: John, 100; Sarah, 130, 132; Sarah, Jr., 130; Thomas, 130; William, 100
DORVIS: Jess, 73
DOUGHTERY: Jane, 100
DOUGHTY: James, Capt., 142
DOWNING: Moses, 11
DRAKEFORD: John, 23
DRAYTON: Justice, 31
DUCKET: Dinah Smith, 130, 133
DUESTO: Anthony, 04-06, 12
DUNCAN: --, 76; Amelia, 90; Elisha, 100; Enos, 90; Jesse, 90; John, 47; Joshua, 90; Mary, 90; Samuel, 47, 90; Sarah, 47; Sary, 90
DUNKEN: Margaret, 88
DUNKIN: Elisha, 100; John, 100; Mary, 100; Milcha, 100; Nelson, 100; Rachel, 100; Richard, 100; Samuel & Family, 100; Samuel, 100
DUNLAPS: --, 12
DUNN: Benjamin & Family, 113; Elizabeth, 119, 122; Josiah, 119; Mary, 118, 119; Nehemiah, 119; Sarah, 119
DUNSWORTH: Ann, 11
DUYETT: Ann, 05, 07
EASTERLING: Ann, 128; Mary, 126
EDMONDSON: Joseph, 100; Rebeccah, 125; William, 100
EDMUNDSON: Cabel J., 100; Caleb, 91, 100; Caleb, Jr., 100; Caleb, Sr., 100; Hester, 91; Isaac, 100; Joseph, 100; Margaret, 123; Margret, 130
EDWARDS: James, 119; Jane, 119; Mary, 126; Sam, 78; Wm. Newitt, 04; William Newitt, 05, 06
ELEMAN: Catharine, 91; Enos, 91; Mary, 91
ELIMAN: Esther Pearson, 100; Jane, 100; Martha, 100; Steedman, 100
ELLEMAN: Catherine, 100; Elizabeth, 100; Enos, 87, 100; Hannah, 100; John, 99, 100; Susannah Coppock, 100; William & Family, 100; William, 100

ELLIMAN: Catharine, 91; Elizabeth, 91; Emme, 91; Enos, 91; Hannah, 91; John, 91, 100; John, Sr., 91; Mary, 91; Susannah, 100; William, 91, 100
ELLIOT: Thomas, 143; Thomas, Jr., 143; Thomas, Sr., 143
ELLIOTT: Hephsibeth, 142; Saml., 04; Thomas, 142
ELLIS: Elijah, 124; Rebecca Compton, 124
ELMOR: Abigail, 91; Charity, 91; David, 91; John, 91; Joseph, 91; Mary, 91; Rachel, 91; Ridgeway, 91; Sarah, 91; Stephen, 91; William, 91
ELMORE: John, 100; Joseph, 100; Prudence O'Sayle, 100, 107; Rachel, 100, 106; Rebecca Kelly, 100, 105; Rebecka, 88; Rebekah, 88; Ridgeway, 100; Stephen, 100
ELMORES: --, 56, 81
EMBRE: Jonathan, 119
EMBREE: Amos, 91, 114, 119; Evan, 91; Hannah Ballinger, 97, 100; Isaac, 91, 97, 100; Jacob, 91; Jesse, 91, 119; John & Family, 100; John, 91, 100, 114, 119; Jonathan, 91, 119; Joseph, 114; Lydia, 91, 119; Margaret, 91; Mary, 91, 114, 119; Mercer, 114; Moses, 87, 91, 100; Rachel, 91, 119; Rebekah, 91, 114; Sarah, 91, 114, 119; Thomas, 91
ENGLE: Jane, 124
ENGLISH: Beverly M., 25; Edward, 101; Elizabeth Adamson, 24; Elizabeth Tucker, 25; Elizabeth, 25; Family, 25; Harriet, 25; Harriet Fitzpatrick, 25; James, 25; John, 25, 101; Joseph, 25; Joshua, 10, 13, 24, 25, 36, 37, 101; Joshua, Sr., 25; Martha Allison, 25; Mary, 22, 24, 25, 101, 105; Nancy Darrington, 25; Robert, 10, 13, 22, 25; Sarah, 25; Thomas, 10, 13, 25, 101
EVANES: --, 13
EVANS: (4 daughters), 60; (son), 60; --, 60; Abigail K., 88; Abigail, 88; Ann, 91, 101; Benjamin & Family, 101; Benjamin, 101; Caron Happock, 88; Cornealy M., 88; David, 101; Elizabeth, 101; Hannah Smith, 130, 133; Hannah, 101, 130; Isaac, 88; Joseph & Family, 101; Joseph, 04, 10, 59, 91, 101, 106; Keranhappuck, 88; Kerenhappock Gaunt, 101, 102; Lidia Hasket, 101; Margarett, 91; Martha, 58, 91, 101, 104; Mary Cox, 130; Mary, 88, 91, 101, 112, 129, 130; Moses, 88, 91, 101, 102; Rachel McCool, 101, 106; Rebecca C., 88; Rebecca, 75, 101, 129; Rebeckah, 91; Rebekah, 101, 102; Robert, 10, 20, 22, 46, 50, 59, 87, 88, 91, 101, 102, 129; Sarah, 91, 101, 107; Sophia M., 88; Thomas, 101
EVENS: Hannah, 130
EVINS: Ann, 108
FAIN: Philip, 11
FARMER: Benjamin, 119; Catharine, 119; Elizabeth, 119; Hannah, 119; Jesse, 119; John, 114, 119; Joseph, 119; Mary, 114, 119; Rachel, 119; Rebekah, 119; Thomas, 119; William & Family, 101, 113, 119; William Pharmar, Jr., 119; William, 113, 114, 119
FERGUSON: Clark, 126; Sarah Furnas, 126
FINCHER: Armel, 91; Armil, 87, 101; Arniel, 125; Elizabeth Byshop, 98, 101; Elizabeth, 91, 125; Esther, 125; Francis, 91, 98, 101, 125; Hester, 91; Jesse, 101; John, 101; Rachel Clark, 130; Rachel, 129, 130; Rebecah Edmondson, 125; Rebecca, 125; Rebekah, 91, 123, 130, 132; Thomas, 125

FININ: Thomas, 11
FITZPATRICK: Harriet, 25
FLEMING: Daniel, 142; Elizabeth, 142; Jean, 142; John, 142; Martha, 142; Sarah, 142; Thomas, 142
FLOYD: Washington, 46
FLUKE: Elizabeth Kelly, 105
FLUKE:(?) Elizabeth Kelly, 101
FOSTER: Hal, 66
FOX: --, 31; George, 20, 49
FRAIZER: Ann, 130; Isaac, 130
FRASOR: Isaac, 101
FRAZER: Isaac, 101, 108; James, 101; Mary Pearson, 101 108
FRAZIER: Ann, 125, 130
FRIEND: W., 62
FROST: John, 46
FURNACE: Esther, 91; Hannah, 101; John, 91; Joseph, 91; Mary, 91; Rebekah, 91; Robert, 91, 101; Thomas, 91; William, 91
FURNAS: Dinah, 126, 127; Esther Whitson, 133; Esther Wilson, 130; Esther, 101, 108, 126, 128, 130; Hannah & Children, 101; Hannah Whitson, 133; Hannah Wilson, 126, 128, 130; Hannah, 126; Isaac, 126; John & Family, 101; John, 46, 80, 87, 99, 101, 125, 126, 128, 130, 133; Joseph & Family, 101; Joseph, 47, 79, 101, 108, 125, 126; Mary Easterling, 126; Mary Wilkinson, 125; Mary, 101, 125, 126, 130; Matilda Compton, 126; Rachel Nesby, 126; Rebecca, 125, 126; Robert & Family, 130; Robert, 79, 80, 126, 128, 130, 133; Ruth Cook, 101; Sarah Pearson, 101, 108; Sarah, 126; Thomas W., 79; Thos. Wilkinson, 126; William, 101, 125
FURNAS:? Sarah, 79
FURNASS: John, 10, 22
FURNESS: John, 101; Thomas Wilkinson, 101
GALBREATH:(see GILBREATH): --, 110; Alizabeth, 119, 120; Ann, 101, 102; Charity Starbert?, 110; James's Family, 101; James, 46, 101; James, Jr, 101; John, 46, 119; Nathan & Family, 101; Nathan, 101; Sarah Sanders, 119; Sarah, 119; Susanna, 101; Susannah, 101; William & Family, 101
GALBREATHE: John, 119, 121; Sarah Sanders, 121
GALBRETH: James, 88
GAMBLE: James, 07; John, 36
GANTER: Michael, 101
GARROT: Else Addington, 129, 130
GAUNT: Abigail Kelly, 101, 105; Charles, 88; Elizabeth Brooks, 97, 101; Ester, 101; Israel, 46; Judith Wright, 102, 112; Keren Happuch, 20, 50; Kerenhappock, 101, 102; Malichi, 88; Maris, 101, 104; Mary Kelly, 101, 105; Mary, 91; Nebo & Family, 102; Nebo, 01, 10, 13, 16, 97, 101, 102, 112; Publias, 88; Samuel Kelly, 88; Samuel, 48, 53, 88, 101, 102, 105; Sarah Cook, 101; Sarah, 102, 103; Susanna Julien, 102, 105; Susanna, 88; Zebulon, 10, 91, 101, 102, 105; Zimri, 10, 16, 99, 101; Zn, 16
GAUNTS: --, 13
GAUNTT: Samuel, 80
GEORGE II: King, 14
GIBSON: --, 08; Luke, 04, 07; Roger, 04, 07-09
GILBERT: Achsah, 91, 102; Benjamin, 91; Beulah, 91, 102; Caleb, 46; Cary, 91, 102; Elizabeth, 114; Hanamel, 91; Hepsbah, 91; Hepzibah, 102, 107; Joel, 114; Jonathan, 46, 91, 102; Mary Pearson, 91; Thomas, 91, 114
GILBREATH:(See GALBREATH): Charity Starbert?, 101; Charity, 88, 101, 108; James, 88, 101; James, Jr., 88; John, 88, 101; Lydia, 88; Mary, 101, 110
GILCHRIST: Andrew, 102

GLEN: Gov., 07-09
GOGGAN: --, 46
GOLL: Anna, 142; Christian, 142; Isabella, 142, 143
GORDON: Chief Justice, 36; Moses, 36
GRAY: John, 16; William, 05, 06; Wm., 04
GREEN: Amos, 88, 114, 119; Esther Hart, 119; Esther, 88, 114; Hannah, 88, 114; Jesse, 88, 114
GREENE: Nathaniel, Gen., 52
GREGORY: Elizabeth Hawkins, 130, 131; Richard, 07
GRIFFIN: Isaac, 102; Joel, 102; Joshua, 102; Lydia, 102; William, 102
GUESS: William, 05, 07
GUEST: Baker, 114; Hannah Jones, 120; Hannah, 114; James, 114, 119, 120; John, 114; Mary, 114; Sarah, 114
HACKNEY: Joseph, 102; Mary, 102
HAILE: Benjamin, 25
HAILEY: Elizabeth, 134; Isom, 134
HAINES: Deborah, 119; Ellis, 119; Ellis, Sr., 119; Evan, 119; Jane, 119; Nathan, 119
HAINS: Evan, 119
HALE: --, 62
HALEY: James, 11
HALL: James, 71; Mary, 102; Sarah Coate, 102; Sarah, 98
HALLS: --, 56, 81
HALY: Isom, 134
HAMER: David, 102
HAMMER: Charlotte & ch., 102; David, 102; John, 102; Margaret, 102, 103; Rachel Wright, 102
HANAHAM: Thos., 04; Thomas, 01
HANES: Mary, 119
HANKS: --, 80; James, 67; Kesiah, 80; Kirial, 67; Mary, 67, 80; William, 102
HARBERT: Alizabeth, 92; Ann Gilbreath, 101, 102; Ann, 91, 92; Charity, 92; Isaac, 88; John, 92, 102; Mary, 91; Peter, 92; Rachel, 92; Rebecah, 92; Thomas, 92; Walter, 91, 92, 101, 102; William, 88
HARBOUR: Rachel, 102; Walter, 102
HARE: Peter, 46
HARLAN: Edith, 123
HARLESTONE: Paul, 05
HARPER: Thomas, 05, 06
HARRIS: Betsy, 135; David, 102, 135, 138; Elizabeth Rouston, 102; Elizabeth Ruston, 110; Hannah, 130, 133; Hester, 102, 104; John, 135; Jonathan, 135, 138; Mary Moorman, 138; Mary, 135, 138; Michael, 02; Obadiah & Family, 138; Obadiah, 135, 138; Obediah, 138; Rachel, 135; Susannah, 135; Thomas, 135, 138
HARRISON: William, 07
HART: Amos, Esther, 119; Phinehas, 88; Thomas, 88
HASKET: Ann & ch., 102; Charity, 92; Hannah, 92; Isaac & Family, 102; Isaac, 46, 75, 76, 92, 101, 102; Jemima, 92; Joseph, 102; Lidia, 101, 102; Lyda, 102; Lyddia, 92; Mary, 92, 98, 102; Rachel, 92; Rebekah Evans, 101, 102; Sarah, 92, 98, 102; Thomas, 46, 75, 92, 102
HASKETT: Joseph, 102; Rebecca Evans, 75; Thomas, 102
HATHBORN: Hannah Sidwell, 119, 122
HAWKINS: Amos, 92, 102, 126-133; Ann Cook, 102; Ann Milhous, 131, 132; Ann Millhouse, 126, 127; Anna Pearson, 126; Anne Comer, 129, 130; Benjamin, 92, 102, 103, 126, 130, 131; Christopher, 126; David, 126; Dinah, 126; Elizabeth, 130, 131; Eli, 92; Hannah, 126; Henry, 126, 127; Isaac & Family, 102; Isaac & W., 131; Isaac, 87, 92, 125-128, 130, 131; Isaac, Sr., 127; James, 92, 102, 125-128, 130, 131, 133; James, Jr., 126; Jehu, 126; Jesse, 126; John & Family, 131; John, 92, 102, 124, 126, 127, 129, 131; Jonathan, 87, 126; Joseph, 92; Lydia Comer, 129; Lydia, 131; Margaret, 126, 128, 130, 131; Margret, 126, 127; Martha Hollingsworth, 102; Martha Kenworthy, 127, 131; Martha, 92, 99, 102, 124-127, 129-131; Marther Hollingsworth, 103; Marther, 102; Mary Cook, 125, 130, 131; Mary Edwards, 126; Mary, 92, 124, 126, 127, 129, 131; Massey Spray, 126; Mrs., 74; Nathan & Family, 131; Nathan, 87, 92, 99, 102, 124, 126, 127, 131; Olive Cook, 131; Olive Smith Cook, 130; Patty Compton, 126; Phamay Morgan, 126; Phebe Wilson, 128, 130, 133; Phebe, 87, 126, 131; Rebecah, 124; Rebecca, 126, 127; Rebeckah, 92; Rebekah, 88, 129, 131; Ruth, 125, 126; Sarah & Ch., 131; Sarah Kenworthy, 127, 131; Sarah Wilson, 128, 130, 133; Sarah, 126, 128, 130, 131, 133; Stephen, 126; Susanna, 126; Tamer, 131; Thomas, 92; William, 92, 126, 131
HAWORTH: Absalom, 102; Absolom, 102; Ann Coppock, 99; Ann, 102; George, 102; James, 87, 102; Jemima, 102, 112; Sarah, 102
HEAD: George, 142
HEARD: John, 28
HEATON: Benjamin, 102, 103, 111, 112; Elizabeth, 97, 102; Joseph, 102; Leada, 102
HENDERSON: Allsabeth, 92; Daniel, 92; Eli, 92; James, 103; Kesiah, 92; Kezia, 99, 103; Martha, 92, 103; Mary, 92; Nathan, 103; Nathaniel, 92, 103; Rachel Hollingsworth, 103; Rebecah, 92, 103; Richard & Family, 103; Richard, 87, 92, 103; Shadrick, 103; Susannah, 88; Thaniel, 92; Thomas, 92, 103; Thomas, Jr., 103; William, 92, 103; William, Jr., 103
HERBART: Ann, 102; Rebecah, 102, 104; Walter, 102
HERBERT: Ann, 88; Ann, Sr., 87; Eleanor, 88; Esther, 88; Hannah, 88; Isaac, 88; Jobe, 88; Lydia, 88; Martha, 88; Peter, 88; Walter, 53; Walter, Sr., 46; William, 88
HIATT/HIGHATT: Lydia, 123
HIATT: Joseph, 123
HICKSON: Mary, 118, 119
HILL: Nathaniel, 07
HODGE: Jacob, 103; Phebe, 103; William, 103
HODGIN/HODGEN: Agnes, 119; Ann, 119; John, 119; Lydia, 119; Mary, 119; William, 119
HODGIN: Ann, 118; Hannah, 113; John & Family, 113; John, 113; Robert & Family, 113; Robert, 113
HOGE: Jacob, 120; Phebe, 120; William, 120
HOLLAND: Philemon, 34
HOLLIDAY: Edward, 142
HOLLIMAN: Elizabeth, 120
HOLLINGSWORTH: --, 67; Abraham & Family, 103; Abraham, 92, 103, 110; Amey & ch., 103; Amey, 92, 127; Amos, 103; Ann Cox, 103; Ann, 87, 92, 103, 107, 131; Benjamin, 103; Catharine, 103; Cissiah, 103; David, 103, 104; Dinah, 87, 103, 131; Eamy, 131; Elias, 103; Eli, 103; Emy, 131; Enoch, 103; Esquille, 103; Eunice Steddom, 103, 110; Ezekiel, 103; George, 67, 103; George, Jr., 103; Hanah, 92; Hannah, 92, 103, 129, 131; Henry & Family, 103; Henry, 102, 103; Isaac & Family, 103; Isaac (Big), 46, 47; Isaac Enoch, 87; Isaac, 63-67, 80, 87, 92, 100, 103, 112, 131; Isaac, Jr., 103; Jacob & Family, 104; Jacob, 103, 104; James & Family, 104; James, 67,

81, 104, 112; Jane, 92, 103;
Jesse, 127, 131; Joel, 65-67,
92, 103, 104; John & Family, 104;
John, 65, 92, 103, 104, 112;
Jonathan, 103; Joseph, 88, 92,
102, 103, 113, 120, 131; Keziah,
65; Levi, 92, 103, 127; Lydia,
127; Margaret Hammer, 102, 103;
Margaret, 103; Martha Henderson,
103; Martha, 87, 92, 102, 103,
127, 131; Marther, 103; Mary
Johnson, 131; Mary, 92, 127, 131,
133; Nathan, 67, 103, 104; Petter,
92; Rachel Wright, 103, 112;
Rachel, 65, 92, 103; Rebeckah, 92;
Ruth, 65, 92, 131, 133; Sarah Cox,
100, 103; Sarah Gaunt, 102, 103;
Sarah Wright, 103, 112; Sarah,
50, 65, 92, 103, 110, 127; Susanna,
65, 66, 103; Susannah Wright, 103,
112; Susannah, 23, 48-50, 80, 92,
103; Susie, 64; Thomas, 92, 103;
William, 65, 87, 88, 92, 103, 131
HOOKER: Edward, 104; Hannah, 104;
John, 104; Judith, 104; Mary,
104; William, 104
HOPE: John, 05, 07
HOPES: Mr., 38
HOPKINS: Elizabeth English, 25;
John, 104; Miss, 25; Thomas, 25
HORNER: Ann, 104; Sally Compton,
125; Thomas, 104; Wm., 125
HOWARD: Edward, 07
HOWE: James, 81, 82, 83
HUCKEBY: Lewis, 138, 139
HUDSON: John, 04-06, 12
HUMPHRIES: Hester Harris, 102, 104
HUNT: Abraham, 93; Christen, 131;
Christianna, 93; Edward, 93;
Hannah, 88; Isaiah, 92; Joanna,
93, 130, 131; John, 92, 104;
Margaret Townsend, 104, 111;
Margaret, 123; Mary Cook, 130,
131; Mary, 92, 104, 109, 131;
Rachel, 92, 93, 104, 131; Ralph,
92, 93, 104, 130, 131; Samuel &
Family, 131; Samuel, 92, 104, 111
HUNTER: Mary, 99, 104
HUSSEY: Anne, 127
HUTTON: John & son, 104
INGLISH: Joshua, 37, 38
INMAN: Jehu, 46; Mary
Coppock, 99, 104
INMANS: --, 7;
INMON: Benjamin, 93
INSCO: Abel & Family, 104; Abel, 46,
69, 70, 93; Able, 104, 108; Ann
Pearson, 104, 108; James & Family,
104; James, 46, 69, 70, 93, 104;
Joanna, 93; John, 104; Mary, 104
JACKSON: Absolam, 120; Benjamin &
Family, 113; Benjamin, 114;
Deborah, 120; Elizabeth, 114;
John, 142; Joseph, 120; Thomas,
120; Walter & Family, 113; Walter,
104, 120
JAY: (3 daughters), 56; (7 sons),
56; Abigail, 104; Alexander, 88;
Ann, 93, 108; Anne, 99, 104; Betty
& Ch., 104; Betty Pugh, 104, 109;
Charlotte, 104; David, 88, 93,
104, 126; Dempsey, 88; Denny,
72-74; Ede(Edith), 88; Elizabeth
Mills, 104, 107; Elizabeth, 93;
Isaac, 68; James & Family, 104;
James, 72, 88, 104, 107; Jemima
Mills, 104; Jemimah, 88; Jesse,
72, 104; Jessy, 93; John, 46, 56,
72, 93, 104, 109, 124; Keturah
Brock, 128; Layton, 88, 104, 107;
Lydia Compton, 124; Lydia, 93;
Mary Pearson, 108; Mary, 88, 93,
104, 107; Mary?, 104; Memina
Mills, 107; Mills, 88; Patience,
104; Rachel, 93; Rebecca Hawkins,
126; Rhoda, 88; Sam, 73; Samuel,
72, 93; Sarah & ch., 104; Sarah
Brooks, 104; Sarah, 88; Susannah,
99, 104; Thomas & Family, 104;
Thomas, 72, 93, 104, 108; Walter
D., 72; Walter Denny, 75; William,
72, 93, 104; William, Jr., 104
JAYS: --, 57

JENKINS: (2 sons), 59; (4 Daughters),
59; Amos & Family, 105; Amos, 93,
105, 110; Ann, 88; David & Family,
105; David, 46, 47, 58, 59, 76,
77, 87, 93, 101, 104, 105; David,
Jr., 77; David, Sr., 105; Eli,
105; Elizabeth Russell, 105, 110;
Elizabeth, 93, 104, 105, 110;
Enoch, 93, 105; Hannah Russell,
105, 109; Isaac, 88, 93, 102, 104,
105; Jesse, 93, 105, 109; Lydia,
88; Maris Gaunt, 101, 104; Martha
Evans, 101, 104; Mary, 93; Rebecah
Herbart, 102, 104; Rebecah, 105;
Rebecca, 88; Rebekah, 88; Thomas,
93, 101, 104; William & Family,
105; William, 93, 104, 105
JENKINSES: --, 57
JINKINS: Rebecah, 105; Rebekah, 105
JOHNSON: Charles, 105; Collins,
105; David, 105; James, 105;
Judith, 105; Lucy, 105; Mary,
131; Moorman, 105; Ruth, 142;
Sarah, 105; Susannah, 120; Wm., 142
JOHNSTON: Chancellor, 46
JONES: Alizabeth Galbreath, 119,
120; Ann, 115, 120; David, 54,
75, 83, 115; Deborah, 114; Dorcas,
115; Elener, 114; Elijah, 65, 66;
Elisha, 65, 76, 77, 105;
Elizabeth, 105, 115, 120; Elliman,
105; F., 62; Frances, 105; Francis
& Family, 113; Francis, 105,
113-115; Francis, Jr., 113, 115,
120, 121; Francis, Sr., 114;
George, 105, 115, 120; Hannah,
105, 114, 119, 120; Henry & Family,
113; Henry, 105, 113-115, 119,
120; James, 105; Jane, 105, 114,
120, 122; Jesse, 115; John &
Family, 113; John, 78, 79, 87,
105, 113-115, 120; John, Jr.,
120; Jonathan, 115, 120; Joseph,
105, 110, 114, 115, 120; Kezia,
115; Keziah, 115, 120; L. J., 74,
75; Lambert J., 54; Margaret, 105;
Mary Mote, 121; Mary Taylor, 105,
110; Mary, 105, 114, 115, 120,
122; Nathan, 120; Rachel Mote,
120, 121; Rachel Paty, 105, 107;
Rachel, 105, 114, 115, 120;
Rebekah Randle, 132; Rebekah, 115,
131; Richard, 124; Robert, 105;
Samuel, 105, 114, 115, 120, 121;
Sarah, 105, 114, 115, 120; Susanna
Hollingsworth, 65; Thomas, 37, 39,
105, 114, 115; Wallace, 77;
Wallace, Jr., 77, 78; William,
105, 115, 120
JONES:? Philemon, 79
JULIAN: Charlotte, 105
JULIEN: Susanna, 102, 105
KELLEY: Timothy, 04; William, 05
KELLUM: Elijah, 115; Elizabeth, 115;
John, 115; Joseph, 115; Nathaniel,
115; Sarah, 115; Susana, 115;
William, 115
KELLY: Abigail, 93, 101, 105; Ann,
93, 105, 107; Anne, 22; Elizabeth
Milhouse, 105, 107; Elizabeth,
101, 105; Hannah Belton, 10, 22;
Hannah Pearson, 105, 108; Hannah,
48, 88, 93, 105; Isaac, 105;
John, 88, 91, 93, 105; John, Sr.,
47, 53; Mary & ch., 105; Mary &
Family, 101; Mary Teague, 105,
111; Mary, 101, 105; Moses &
Family, 105; Moses, 105, 111;
Rachel Hunt, 131; Rachel, 131;
Rebecca, 100, 105; Rebekah, 93;
Robert, 105, 107; Samuel, 10, 21,
22, 46, 51, 87, 93, 105, 107, 108;
Samuel, Jr., 52, 105; Samuel, Sr.,
52, 93, 105; Sarah Paty, 105, 107;
Sarah, 105; Timothy, 10, 14-16;
Walter, 10
KELLYS: --, 13, 80
KENERLY: Thomas, 142
KEMP: Sophia, 24
KENNEDY: John, 16
KENWORTHY: Ann Cook, 131; Ann, 130,
131; David & Family, 131; David,
130, 131; Dinah Cook, 130, 131;

151

Isaac, 127; Jesse & Family, 131; Jess, 129, 131; John, 127, 130, 131; Joshua, 126, 127, 131; Martha, 126, 127, 131; Mary, 126, 127, 131, 132; Olive, 127; Rachel Cook, 129, 131; Rebecca, 127; Rebekah Cook, 130, 131; Sarah, 127, 131; Tamar, 127; Tamer, 131; William, 127
KER: John Cessford, 42
KERSHAW: --, 27, 35, 37; Eli, 39; James, 25; John, 04, 18; Jos., 04; Joseph, 01, 11, 12, 25, 26, 28, 35, 37, 39, 40; Joseph, Col., 24; Sarah English, 25
KERSHAWS: --, 13; Mr., 38
KILLEY: Charity, 88
KIMBERLY: Iseabel, 142; Thomas, 143
KING: Mary Sidwell, 121; Mary, 120
KIRK: Children, 87; Isaac, 47, 63, 87, 105; John, 105; Phebe, 88; Rebekah Jinkins, 105; Rebekah, 87, 88
KIRKLAND: Joseph, 23, 36; Richard, 23
KIRKS: --, 60
KNIGHT: Benjamin, 135; Christian Thomas, 138, 139; Christian, 135; Elizabeth, 138; John, 135; Martha, 88, 105; Rachel, 138, 139; Sarah, 138; Solomon, 135, 138; Thomas, 135, 138, 139
LACY: Jane, 120
LAM: Alice, 93, 131, 132; David, 93; Elizabeth, 93; James, 93; John, 93; Joseph, 93; Josiah, 134; Josiah & Family 138; Longshore, 105; Martha, 127; Mary, 93, 131; Phebe, 131; Robert, 93, 105; Sarah, 93, 123, 127, 131; Thomas, 93, 105, 127; Thomas, Jr., 105; William, 93, 105
LANCE: Lambert, 04, 26, 27
LANCHESTER: Rachel, 106
LANCKASTER: Joshuah, 142
LANG: Family, 24; W. W., 12; William, 24, 39; Wm. Wiley, 18
LAURANCE: Jane, 106, 111
LAW: Beulah, 143; Bulah, 143
LAY: William, 120
LAYTONS: --, 56, 81
LEADOM: Thomas, 05; Thos., 04
LEADON: Thomas, 06
LEAGUE: Rebecca Furnas, 125; Sam'l, 125
LEE: Francis, 23
LENOIR: Family, 25; Isaac, 25
LEWIS: Caleb & Family, 106; Caleb, 99, 106; Elizabeth, 106; Esther, 106; Martha, 106; Mary, 106; Rachel Cook, 106; Susannah Cook, 106; Thomas & Family, 106; Thomas, 99, 106; Willia, 106
LINEGAR: Isaac, 138
LINNEGAR: Isaac, 134, 138; Isaac, 138
LINTON: Jacob, 143
LONGSHORE: Clyde, 88; Euclydus, 46, 47; Evelide, 106; Sarah, 88, 106; Sary, 88
LOOCOCK: --, 27, 36, 37; Aaron, 04, 26, 37, 38
LYLES: James, 24
MACY: Abigail, 134; Henry, 134; Joseph, 138; Mary, 134, 138; Phebe, 138; Pheebe, 134; William, 134, 138
MADDOCK: Benjamin, 113; Deborah, 115; Elener, 115; Frances, 115; Hannah, 113, 115; John, 115; Joseph, 115; Nathan, 115; Rachel, 113, 115; Samuel, 113, 115; Sarah, 115
MADDOX: John, 05; Joseph, 120; Nathan, 106; Rachel Jones, 120; Samuel, 120
MAHAFFEY: Oliver, 07
MALLOY: Ed, 04; Edward, 05, 06
MALONE: Cornelius, 04
MANSFIELD: --, 62
MARCHANT: Sampson, 46
MARINE: Abba Cox, 138; Abba, 135; Anna, 135; Asey, 138; Charles, 135, 138; Jesse, 135, 138; John, 134, 135, 138; Jonathan & sons, 138; Jonathan, 134, 135, 138; Mary, 134, 135, 138; Pheba Cox, 138; Pheba, 135; Phebe Cox, 138; Pheby, 138; Ziba, 135
MARION: Gen., 41
MARSHAL: Rebekah, 129
MARSHALL: Elizabeth, 106; Hannah, 130, 132; Mary & ch., 132; Mary, 129; Rebekah, 132
MARTENGALE: Rebekah Fincher, 130; Rebekah, 132
MARTIN: James, 04, 39
MASSEY: Mary, 131, 132
MATHIS: Daniel, 10, 11, 24, 39; Family, 26; Israel, 24, 39; Margaret C., 43; Mary, 24, 39; Mr. 42; S. 41; Samuel, 11, 24, 39-43; Sarah, 24, 40; Sophia Elizabeth, 43; Sophia, 10, 24, 39
MCCLURE: Jacob, 106; John, 106; Margaret, 106; Margery, 106; Mary, 106; Robert & Family, 106; Robert, 106
MCCONNAL: John, 04-06
MCCOOK: Elisha, 71
MCCOOL: Alisabeth, 93; Ann, 93, 106, 112; Gabriel & Family, 106; Gabriel, 93, 106; Gabriel, Jr., 106; Gabril, 93; James, 93, 106; John, 93; Martha, 93; Mary, 93; Rachel, 93, 101, 106; Thomas, 93, 106
MCCOOLE: Gabriel, 46, 61, 63; Squire, 62, 63; Thomas, 62
MCCORMICK: Patrick, 04-06; Thomas, 05, 06
MCCOWEN: Bathsheba, 120
MCCUTCHIN: Hugh, 02
MCDANIEL: Daniel, 05; William, 106
MCDONAL: Joseph, 106
MCDONALD: Jemima Parkins, 106, 109; Jemima, 106; John, 106; Joseph, 106; Lydia, 106; Mary, 106; Phebe, 106, 107; Thomas, 106; William, 106, 109
MCDONNALD: Elizabeth Parkins, 106, 109; Joseph, 106, 109
MCGINTY: Deborah Jackson, 120
MCGIRT: James, 04
MCGIRTT: James, 06, 13, 36
MCGOWAN: James, 02
MCGOWEN: James, 02
MCGRAW: Edward, 05
MCKENNIE: Benjamin, 07; Benjm., 04
MCKENZIE: John, 07
MCKINNIE: Benjamin, 05
MCLEOD: Elizabeth, 42
MCMUN: John, 120
MCNAIR: Elizabeth, 42
MCNEAL: John, 115, 116; Mary Vernon, 106; Mary, 111, 115, 116
MEERS: George, 142
MELONE: Cornelius, 11
MENDENHALL: Aaron, 115; Abigail, 106; Alice Benson, 118, 120; Alice, 115, 137, 138; Ann, 88; Betty, 138; Caleb, 106; Cabel 120; Catharine Sidwell, 120, 122; Catharine, 120; Cathren, 120; Elijah, 88, 115, 120; Elizabeth Sell, 120, 121; Elizabeth, 115, 138; Ely, 138; Grace, 106, 120; Hannah, 115, 120, 138, 139; James, 106, 115, 120; John, 106, 115, 120, 134, 138; Jonathan, 115, 120, 134; Joseph, 106, 115, 120, 121; Marmaduke, 106, 115, 118, 120; Martha, 88; Mary, 115, 120; Mordicai, 138; Moses, 138; Naomi, 106; Phebe, 115, 120; Phineas & Family, 113; Phineas, 106, 113, 120; Prose, 115; Robert, 115, 120; Son, 115; Stephen & Family, 138; Stephen, 138; Stephen, Jr., 138
HERRICK: Robert & w & ch., 106; Robert, 87
MICKLE: John, 24; Joseph, 23, 24; Joseph, Maj., 24; Martha Belton, 24; Robert, 24
MIDDLETON: Hannah, 120; Jehu, 120; Joseph, 120
MILES: Catharine, 93, 106; David, 46, 68, 88, 98, 106; Elizabeth

Chandler, 98, 106; Elizabeth, 98, 106; Jane Taylor, 106, 110; John, Jr. & Family, 106; John, Jr., 106; John, Sr. & Family, 106; John, Sr., 106; Jonathan & Family, 106; Jonathan, 106, 108; Lizabeth, 93; Mary Pearson, 106, 108; Mary Taylor, 106, 110; Mary, 93, 98, 106, 107; Rachel Elmore, 100, 106; Rhoda, 93; Samuel, 46, 68, 93, 106, 110; William & Family, 106; William, 46, 68, 88, 93, 100, 106, 110; William, Sr., 106; Wm., 46
MILHOUS: Ann, 127, 131, 132; Dinah Furnas, 127; Dinah, 129, 132; Elizabeth, 127; Henry, 132; Jean, 132; John, 14, 15, 16, 127; Mary Mills, 127; Mary, 123, 132, 133; Rebekah, 123, 129, 132; Robert & Family, 132; Robert, 127, 132; Sally Nelson, 127, 132; Samuel, 14, 15, 16, 127; Sarah Sanders Scott, 127; Sarah, 129, 132, 133
MILHOUSE: Abigail, 10; Ann, 93; Daniel, 115; Dinah, 10, 24; Dinnah, 93; Elizabeth, 105, 107; Henry, 10, 93, 107; Jane, 111; John, 10; Mary, 93; Rebecca, 107; Rebekah, 93; Robert, 09, 10, 13, 93, 99, 107, 115; Robt., 04; Sally Nelson, 107; Samuel, 10, 107; Sarah, 93, 115
MILHOUSES: --, 12, 13, 39
MILL: Mary, 107, 112
MILLER: Andrew, 42; Elizabeth, 42; John B., 43; Margaret C., 42; Thomas H., 43
MILLHOUSE: Ann, 126, 127; Charles, 107; Daniel Henry, 107; Dinah Furnas, 126; Dinah, 125, 127; Henry, 87, 124-128; Jane, 107; Jean, 125; John, 107; John, Sr., 107; Mary, 127, 128; Rebecca, 124, 125, 127; Rebekah, 126-128; Robert, 107, 125-127; Sarah Compton, 127; Sarah, 125, 127, 128
MILLS: --?, 104; Abner, 126; Alexander, 107; Betty Compton, 124; Charles, 69, 126; Daniel, 126; David, 107; Dinah Hawkins, 126; Elijah, 126; Elizabeth Milhous, 127; Elizabeth, 104, 107; Esther Furnas, 126; Eunice Pearson, 107, 108; Hannah Furnas, 126; Isaac, 107; James, 107; Jane, 107; Jemima, 104, 107, 132; Job, 125; John, 106, 107, 110, 124; Lydia Perkins, 107, 109; Lydia, 107; Marmaduke & Family, 107; Mary Hawkins, 107; Mary Taylor, 107, 110; Mary, 107, 127; Patience O'Neal, 107; Phebe McDonald, 106, 107; Rebecca Compton, 125; Sarah, 107; William & Family, 107; William, 46, 69, 107, 109; Wm., 126, 127
MINTON: Betty, 94; Elizabeth, 132; Hannah, 93, 94; Joseph, 94; Lydia, 94; Marget, 94; Mary, 94; Parthenay, 132; Parthenia, 94; Rachel, 94, 129, 132; Rebeckah, 94; Rebekah, 132; Richard, 94, 107; Thomas, 93, 94, 107
MITCHELL: John B., 69, 73, 81-84
MOON: Thomas, 11
MOONEY/MOONY: John, 120; Joseph, 120
MOONEY: Anne, 115; Deborah, 115; John, 115; Joseph & Family, 113; Joseph, 113, 115; Martha, 115; Mary, 115; Prudence, 115; Sarah, 115
MOOR: Alexander, 121; James, 107, 121; John, 121; Mordecai, 107; Richard & Family, 113
MOORE: Alice, 115; Auerilla, 115; Dempsey, 88; James, 115, 121; John, 121; Richard, 88; Thomas, 115
MOORMAN: Achsah, 140; Agg--, 135; Agness, 138, 140; Agnis, 135; Ann, 139; Anna, 136, 139; Archelaus, 134; Ashsah, 139; Benjamin, 121, 135, 136; Charity, 135; Charles, 121; Chuza, 136; Edward, 134, 135; Ely, 135; Elizabeth, 121; Hannah Mendenhall, 138, 139; Hannah Way, 139, 140; Hannah, 136; Harriett, 136; Henry, 136; James, 124, 135; Jesse, 135; John, 134-136, 139; Joseph, 135; Lewis, 135; Lishy, 121; Liza, 136; Maris, 136; Mary Compton, 124; Mary, 135, 136, 138, 139; Milly, 121; Nancy, 136; Rebecca, 135; Rebeckah, 139; Ruth, 136, 138; Sarah, 135, 136; Selia, 136; Susannah, 135, 138, 139; Tarlton, 135, 136, 139, 140; Thomas, 135, 136, 138, 139; Uriah & Family, 139; Uriah, 136, 138, 139; Zachariah & family, 139; Zachariah, 135, 138, 139
MOREMAN: Arihelus, 134
MORGAN: Asseneth, 132; Deborah, 121; Phamay, 126
MORGRIDGE: Timothy, 11
MORMAN: Anna, 134; Benjamin, 134; Celia, 134; Edward, 138, 139; Eliza, 134; Hannah, 134; Henry, 134; James, 134; Jesse, 134; John, 134; Judith, 134; Julia, 134; Mary Thomas, 138, 139; Mary, 134, 138; Nancy, 134; Rebecah, 134; Ruth, 134; Sampey, 134; Sarah, 134; Susanna, 134; Tarlton, 134; Thomas, 134; Wilson, 134; Zachariah, 138
MORONG: P., 39
MORRIS: Aaron, 136; Ann, 136; Anna, 139; Caleb, 136; Elizabeth, 136; Hannah, 136; John, 136; Jonathan, 136; Martha, 136; Mary, 136; Nathan, 136; Sarah, 136, 139; Selia, 136; Thomas & Family, 139; Thomas, 134, 136, 139
MOTE: Ann, 121; David & Family, 107; David, 87, 113, 121; David, Jr., 87; Jeremiah, 121; John, 121; Jonathan, 121; Mary, 120, 121; Rachel, 120, 121; Timothy, 121; William, 107
MOUZON: --, 25
MURCHISON: --, 39
MURRAY: Justice, 36
MURRELL: William, 39
MUSGRAVE: Caleb, 139; Elizabeth, 139; Sarah, 139
MUSTGRAVE: Charity, 139
NEAL: William, 87
NEALL: James, 68; Mahlon, 68; William, 68
NEDARMAN: John, 130, 132; Sarah Dodd, 132; Sarah, 130
NEEDERMAN: John, 107
NEGRO: Ben the Baker, 38; Jack, 53; Phillis, 38
NEILSON: Catharine, 94; Jesse, 94; Mary, 94; Samuel, 05, 94
NELSON: Jesse, 107; John, 87; Mary, 107; Sally, 107; Samuel, 87, 107
NESBY: Rachel, 126
NETTLES: William, 39; William, Capt., 24
NICHOLAS: James, 107
NICHOLS: Ann Hollingsworth, 103, 107; James & Family, 107; James, 103, 107
NIPPER: Ann, 121
NORDYKE: Abraham, 121; Adan, 121; Benajah, 121; Beverly, 121; Daniel, 121; Hiram, 121; Israel, 121; Mary, 121; Micajah, 121; Phebe, 121
NORMAN: Margaret, 132
NORTHDIKE/NORDYKE: Abraham, 115; Aden, 115; Benajah, 115; Beulah, 115; Daniel, 115; Hiram, 115; Israel, 115; Mary, 115; Micajah, 115; Phebe, 115
NORTON: Ioannis, 34
O'BRIEN: Patrick, 67
O'NEAL: Abigail, 88; Abijah & Family, 107; Abijah, 94, 107; Achsah, 88; Ann, 88, 107; Cary, 88; Hannah, 88; Hannauee1, 88; Henry, 88, 94, 107; Hephziba, 88;

High, 88; Hiram, 88; Hugh, 88, 94, 107; Jas., 04; John Belton, 88; John Foster, 88; John & Family, 107; John, 87, 88, 94, 107; Mark, 88; Mary Ann, 94; Mary, 88, 94, 107; Patience, 107; Priscilla, 88; Rebekah, 88; Rhoda, 88; Robert, 88; Sarah, 88, 94; Thomas, 88, 94; William, 88, 94, 107
O'NEALL: Abijah, 48, 52, 53, 94, 105, 107; Ann Kelly, 105, 107; Ann, 94; Anne Kelly, 22; Anne, 53; Elisha, 94; Elizabeth, 84; Family, 84; G. T., 84; Henry Miles, 84; Henry, 48, 53, 80, 84, 106, 107; Hepzibah Gilbert, 102, 107; Hugh, 22, 48, 53, 75, 105, 107; J. Belton, 01; John Belton, 22, 54; John Belton, Judge, 84; John H., Hon., 84; John, 48, 53, 80, 94, 102, 107; Judge, 20, 21, 46, 67, 73, 74, 78, 82; Mary Miles, 106, 107; Maryann, 94; Nancy, 74; Rebecah, 94; Rebecca, 84; Rhoda, 84; Sarah Evans, 101, 107; Sarah, 94; Thomas, 48, 80, 101, 107; Wm., 46; William, 48, 67, 68, 94, 107
O'SAYLE: Prudence, 100, 107
ODAM: Abraham, 25; Cibbie, 25
ODOM: Abraham, 04
OGLESBY: Mary, 94
OUSLEY: James, 01; Jas., 04
OWEN: Benjamin, 115; Elizabeth, 116; Ephraim, 115, 116; John, 115, 116; Margery, 116; Mary, 116; Ruth, 116, 126; Samuel, 116; Sarah, 115, 116; Tamar, 125
PAGET: Roger, 04-06, 11; Thomas, 07
PAINE: William, 07
PALMER: Hannah, 88
PANCOAST: Asa, 142
PARKER: Anna Peele, 139; Anne, 136; Elisha, 134, 139; Elizabeth, 136, 139; Jesse, 136; Nathan, 139; Penninah, 136; Sarah, 136; Selah, 136; Thomas & Family, 139; Thomas, 136, 139
PARKINS: Charles, 109; Daniel, 46; Elizabeth, 109; Jemima, 106, 109; Patience, 109
PARNEL: Elizabeth, 94, 129, 132; Esther Townsent, 111; Esther Towsent, 107; Esther, 94; George, 94; James, 94, 107, 111; John, 94
PARNELL: Esther, 123; James, 126; Margret Hawkins, 126
PARSONS: Sarah, 142
PATTAN/PATTON: Ann, 116, 121; Grace, 116, 121; Isaac, 116, 121; Mahlon, 116, 121; Mary, 116, 121; Rachel, 116, 121; William, 116, 121
PATTON: John, 116; Sarah, 116
PATTY: Anna Brown, 61; Charles, 60, 94, 104, 107; David, 60; James, 46, 60, 61, 69, 78; "Jimps", 61; Mary Jay, 104, 107; Mary, 94; Sarah, 94
PATY: Charles, 107; Mary Cook, 130, 132; Mary, 107; Rachel, 105, 107; Sarah, 105, 107
PAYNE: John, 04; Wm., 04
PAYTY: Charles, 107
PEARSON: Ann Evins, 101, 108; Ann Jay, 104, 108; Ann Stidham, 108, 110; Ann, 94, 95, 104, 108; Anna, 126; Anne, 95, 108; Benjamin & Family, 108; Benjamin, 46, 59, 83, 87, 94, 101, 108; Black smith Enoch, 76; Charity Gilbreath, 101, 108; Edna, 95, 108; Elizabeth Minton, 132; Elizabeth, 94, 108; Enoch & Family, 109; Enoch, 46, 76, 87, 94, 100, 101, 108, 109; Ester, 129; Esther Furnas, 101, 108, 126; Eunice, 94, 107, 108; Exile William, 95; Exile, 88; Hannah, 88, 94, 105, 108; Henry, 95, 108; Isaac, 76, 79, 94; James, 94; Jesse & Family, 108; Jesse, 95, 108; Joanna, 94, 108, 109; John & Family, 108; John, 108; Jonas, 94, 108; Joseph & Family, 109; Joseph, 94, 108, 109;

Lame Enoch, 76; Lawrance, 108; Martha, 94, 95, 108, 110; Mary Cambell, 98; Mary Campbell, 108; Mary Coat, 108; Mary Insco, 104; Mary Steddom, 108, 110; Mary, 94, 95, 101, 104, 106, 108, 110; Mary, Sr., 108; Mealin, 108; Mella, 94; Muck Enoch, 76; Olive Russell, 108, 110; Phebe Demans, 108; Phebe, 88, 94; Pony Enoch, 76; Powel, 88; Preacher Enoch, 76; Rachel Reagan, 79; Rebecah, 94; Rebecakah, 94; Rebecca, 99, 108; Rebekah, 94; Robert, 76, 88, 94, 101, 108; Ruth, 108; Sally, 108; Samuel & w. & ch., 108; Samuel, 46, 87, 94, 95, 98, 104, 108, 110; Sarah, 94, 95, 101, 108; Sidney, 95; Susanna, 88; Tennt Enoch, 76; Thomas Jr. & Family, 108; Thomas & Family, 109; Thomas, 57-59, 69, 76, 80, 94, 98, 108-110; Thomas, Jr., 108; Thos., 46; William, 59, 87, 94, 95, 108, 110; Wm., 46
PEARSON? Esther, 100
PEATY: Charles, 108; James & Family, 108; James, 108; Mary, 108
PEAY: Austin F., 25; Mary English, 25
PEEL: Tabitha, 139
PEELE: Anna, 139; Anne, 139; John, 139; Pasco, 139; Passco, 139; Tabbitha, 139; William, 139
PEMBERTON: Ann, 95, 109, 111; Anne, 109; Elizabeth, 95, 109; George, 46, 71, 95, 109; Hannah, 95, 109; Isaah, 109; Isaiah, 71, 109; Isaiah, Jr., 109; Isiah, 95, 109; John, 71, 95, 109; Jude, 109; Judeth, 95; Laurence, 109; Lidde, 109; Rachel, 109; Richard, 95, 109; Robert, 71; Ruth, 95, 109, 111; Sarah, 95, 109; Thomas, 95, 109; William, 87, 95, 109
PENDARVIS:(?) John, 143
PENNY: Esther Thompson, 133; Esther, 132
PENNYS: --, 81
PERKINS: Charles, 109; Daniel, 109; Lydia, 107, 109; Thomas, 109
PHALAN: Affinity, 121; Mary, 121
PHELAN: Ann, 116; Elizabeth, 116, 121; Evane, 116; Evans, 121; Jeremiah, 116, 121; Mary, 116; Thomas, 116, 121
PHILIPS: Susannah Brooks, 109
PHILLIPS: Susannah, 97
PIKE: Benjamin, 134; Jesse, 134; John, 134; Mathew, 134; Rachel, 134
PINSON: Rebecca, 121
PITT: --, 31, 32
PLUNKETT: Timothy, 11
POSTELLS: --, 39
POTS: Mary Hunt, 104, 109
POWERS: Mr., 38
PRATT: Charles, 31, 33; Family, 33; John, Sir, 31
PROMETHEUS: --, 58
PUGH(PEW): David, 132; Rachel, 109
PUGH: Alice, 95; Ann, 95, 106, 109; Azariah & Family, 109; Azariah, 46, 96, 109, 112; Bette, 95; Betty, 104, 109; Casander, 88; Catharine, 88; David & Family, 109; David, 95, 109, 112; Elijah, 121; Elizabeth, 88; Ellis & Family, 109; Gabriel McCool(?) 109; Hannah, 88, 95, 109, 121; Jane, 95; Jesse, 109, 121; Joanna Pearson, 108, 109; Job, 95; Lydia, 95; Mrs., 74; Nancy, 88; Phebe, 109; Rachel Wright, 109, 112; Rachel, 95; Ruth, 88; Sarah, 88, 95; Sen., 46; Sophia Wright, 109, 112; Thomas & Family, 109; Thomas, 95, 109; Timothy, 88; Verhindo, 95; William, 53, 108, 109; Wm., 88
PUMBERTON: Sarah, 111
RAGAN: Mary, 109
RAGLAND: John, 04, 07
RANDAL: Ann, 109; Hannah, 109; Isaac, 109; James, 109; Jonas, 109; Joseph, 109; Joseph, Jr., 109; Sarah, 109; Thomas, 109

RANDEL: Ann, 95; Elizabeth, 127; Hannah, 95; Isaac, 95; Jehu, 127; John, 95, 127; Jonas, 95, 127; Jonathan, 127; Joseph, 95; Lydia, 95, 133; Moses, 95; Rachel, 95, 129; Rebekah, 127; Sarah, 95; Thomas, 95; Walter (Robert), 127
RANDLE/RANDEL: Ann, 132; Elizabeth, 132; Hannah, 132; Jonas & Family, 132; Joseph, 132; Joseph, Mrs., 132; Lydia (Randol), 132; Rachel, 132; Rebekah, 132
RANDLE: Elizabeth, 129; Rebekah, 131
RATCLIFF: Charles, 05, 07; Chas., 04
RATLIFF: Elijah, 139; Juliemma, 134; Polly, 134; Sarah, 134; Thomas, 134
RATTRAY: --, 08; Alexander, 05, 07
RAVINCRAFT: William, 109
RAWDON: Lord, 13
RAY: Alce Lamb, 131, 132
REAGAN: Children, 79; Rachel, 79; Reason, 46; Samuel, 79
REAGIN: John, 46; Joseph, 46
REES: Elizabeth, 109; John, 109; Mrs., 38; Roger, 38; Solomon, 109
REGAEN: Mary Spray, 128; Reason, 128
REYNOLDS: Joshua, Dr., 24, 43; Sophia Elizabeth Mathis, 43
RICKESON: Prudence, 121
RICKS: Robert, 109
RO-----: John, 109; Thomas, 109
ROBARDS: Ann Whitson, 112; Jonathan, 128, 133; Mary Whitson, 128, 133; Thomas, 112
ROBERDS: Ann Whitson, 127; Ann, 132; Asseneth, 132; David, 127; Esther, 132; Hannah Randel, 132; John, 132; Jonathan, 132; Mary Addington, 129; Mary Whitson, 132; Mary, 132; Rebekah, 127, 132; Sarah, 132; Thomas, 127, 132; Walter, 127, 132
ROBERTS/ROBARDS: Ann Whitson, 109; Rebecah, 109; Thomas, 109; Walter, 109
ROBERTS: Ann Randel, 132; Elizabeth, 142; John, 132; Lydia, 132; Mary, 134; Rebekah, 132; Roger, 07; Thomas & Family, 132
ROBINSON: Abigail, 134
RORK: Bryan, 04-06, 11
ROUSTON: Elizabeth, 102
RUBLE: Jane, 95; Peter, 87, 95; Samuel, 95, 109; Sarah, 95; Susannah, 95
RUSSELL: Ann, 110; Charles, 04, 07; Elizabeth Jenkins, 105, 110; Elizabeth, 105; Hannah, 105, 109; Isaac, 110; Olive, 108, 110; Rosanna, 110; Samuel, 10, 16, 95, 105, 109, 110; Sarah, 123
RUSTIN: John, 110
RUSTON: Elizabeth, 110; James, 110
SANDEFER: Judah, 110
SANDERS: Abraham, 116, 121; Barbara, 116, 121; Benjamin, 110, 116, 121; Charity, 116, 121, 128; Dempsey, 116; Elizabeth, 121; Ferrebee, 121; Ferree, 116; Ferribe, 116; George, 36; Hollaway, 121; Hollorvel?, 116; Hollowell, 121; Joel, 116, 121; Joel, Jr., 116; John, 110, 116, 121-123; John, Jr., 121; Josiah, 116; Lydia, 116, 121; Margaret Thomas, 121, 122; Margaret, 116; Margery, 121; Mary, 121; Masce (with h) & dts., 132; Masse, 123; Massey Sims, 122; Miriam, 116; Mordecai, 116, 121, 122; Prudence, 121; Sarah, 116, 119, 121; Thomas, 116, 121; William, 116, 121
SAUNDERS: Sarah, 128
SAVAGE: Henry, 01
SCOFIELD: Joseph, 121; Susannah, 121
SCOT: Deborah Sell, 121; Deborah, 121; Lydia Sanders, 121; Lydia, 121
SCOTT: John, 04; Sarah, 127; William, 07; Wm., 04
SEAWRIGHT: Robert, 02, 06; Robt., 04; William, 02, 06; Wm., 04
SELL: Deborah, 116, 121; Elizabeth, 116, 120, 121; Enos, 116, 121;
John, 116, 121; Jonathan & Family, 113; Jonathan, 113, 116, 121; Mary, 116, 121; Patience, 116, 121; Sarah, 116, 121; Thomas, 113, 116, 121
SELLS: Thomas, 121
SENIOR: Geo., 04; George, 05, 06, 13
SEXTON: Mary Compton, 124
SHANNON: Charles J., 25; Colonel, 10, 11, 21; Family, 25; Martha Allison English, 25
SHELTON: Ann, 04-06
SHOEMAKER: Thomas, 142
SHUTE: Anna, 142, 143; Elizabeth, 142; Jesabel, 142; John, 142; Joseph P., 143; Joseph, 142, 143; Mary W., 143; Mary, 142, 143; Thomas, 142, 143
SIDEWELL: Nathan, 110
SIDWELL: Amey, 118, 122; Anne, 121; Catharine & children, 113; Catharine, 120, 122; David, 121; Elizabeth, 121, 122; Hannah, 119, 122; John, 121; Joseph, 121; Mary, 120-122; Nathan, 122; Ruth, 121
SIKES: Children (?), 143; George, 143; Isabella, 143; Rachel, 143; Thomas, 143
SIMS: Massey, 121, 122
SINGLETARY: David, 89, 110; Sarah, 97, 110
SINGLETON: --, 25; Harriet English, 25
SINNERD: Margret, 133
SMITH: Aaron, 110; Ann, 95; Benjamin, 96; Buly, 133; Daniel, 46, 95, 110; Daniel, Jr., 110; David, 87, 95, 110; Dinah, 95, 130, 133; Elizabeth Comer, 129, 133; Elizabeth, 95; George, 95; Hannah, 95, 123, 130, 133; James, 95, 110; Jane, 133; Jean, 90, 95, 96, 130, 133; Jeremiah, 95; John, 95, 110; Joseph, 95, 96, 110, 129, 133; Leatitle, 133; March, 95; Margaret, 95; Margarett, 95; Mary, 95, 133, 143; Olive, 95, 123, 130, 133; Rachel, 110; Ralph, 110; Rebekah, 133; Ruth, 95, 133; Sarah, 95; William, 90, 95, 96, 110, 130, 133; Zopher, 110
SMYRL: --, 11
SNELGROVE: Achsah Gilbert, 102; Achsah, 110
SPEARS: Chas., 04; Isaac, 88; Lydia, 88; Mary, 88; Moses Evans, 88; Robert, 88
SPEER: Lydia, 88; Samuel, 88
SPEERS: Samuel, 110
SPENCER: Sarah, 110; William, 110
SPRAY: Abner, 127; Charity Sanders, 128; Dinah Wilson, 128, Dinah, 70, 96, 125, 128; Elizabeth, 128; Esther Cook, 128; Hannah, 96, 127; James, 127, 128; Jesse, 46, 70, 127, 128; Joseph, 128; Keturah Brock, 128; Mary Cook, 128; Mary Wilson, 127, 128; Mary, 96; Massey, 126; Mordecai & Family, 133; Mordecai, 127, 128; Naomi, 110, 133; Rebecah, 96; Samuel & W. & ch., 133; Samuel, 70, 96, 127, 128; Sarah Millhouse, 127; Sarah Saunders, 128; Sarah, 96, 127, 128, 132, 133; Thomas, 127; William, 127, 128
STAFFORD: Garris, 134; Garvis and Family, 139
STANLEY: Thomas, 122; William, 123
STANTON: Borden, 113; Joseph, 50; Mary, 110; Samuel, 103, 110; Sarah Hollingsworth, 103, 110
STARBERT:(?) Charity, 101, 110
STARBUCK: Rebecca Furnas, 126; Samuel, 126
STEDDAM: James, 46, 71; John, 71; Samuel, 71
STEDDON: Ann, 110; Anna, 96; Eunice, 103, 110; Henry & Family, 110; Henry, 96, 110; John, 96; Martha Pearson Steddom, 110; Mary, 96, 108, 110; Rebecca, 124
STEDHAM: Henry, 87

STEDMAN: James, 110; Richard, 110
STEPHENS: Jonathan, 110
STEWART: Gravener, 122
STIDDOM: Anna, 96; Christian, 96; Eunice, 96; Hanry, 110; Henry, 96, 108; John, 96, 110; Martha Pearson, 108, 110; Martha, 96; Mary, 96; Samuel, 96
STIDHAM: Ann, 108, 110
STIDMAN: Richard, 110; Susannah, 110, 111
STRAIN: Adam, 02
STRAWN: Anna, 133; Anne, 133; Mary Hollingsworth, 131, 133
STUART: Elizabeth Dunn, 119, 122; Gravener, 122; Hannah, 118, 122; Robert, 122
STUBBS: Abraham, 116; Deborah & Family, 113; Deborah, 113, 116; Eliza, 116; Elizabeth, 116, 122; Esther, 116; Hannah, 116; Iddo, 116; Isaac, 116, 122; Jacob, 116; Jane Jones, 120, 122; Jane, 116; John & Family, 113; John, 113, 116, 120, 122; Joseph, 116, 122; Margaret, 116; Mary Jones, 120, 122; Mary, 116; Nathan, 113, 122; Newton, 116; Patcey, 116; Rachel, 116; Rebekah, 116; Rhoda, 116; Samuel, 116, 120, 122; Sarah, 116; Tabitha, 116; Thomas, 122; William, 116, 122; Zilpha, 116
STUBS: Mary, 88
STUGGS: John, 113
SUMTER: Thomas, 36
SUTTON: Jasper, 27, 36, 39; Mrs., 27
T.: Squire, 61
TALBOT: Mary, 123
TAYLOR: Ann, 96, 111; Eleneor, 96; Elizabeth, 96; Isaac, 96, 110; Jane, 96, 106, 110; Jonathan, 87, 96, 110, 111; Martha, 96, 111; Mary C., 43; Mary Gilbreath, 101, 110; Mary Pearson, 108, 110; Mary, 96, 105-107, 110; Prudence, 96; Rhoda, 96, 97, 110; Richard, 96, 101, 110; Samuel, 96, 111; William, 96, 108, 110
TEAGUE: Alce, 96; Elijah, 96; Mary, 105, 111; Samuel & Family, 111; Samuel, 46, 70, 96, 111
THARP: Elizabeth, 139
THOMAS: Abel, 46, 76, 96, 109, 111; Abijhal, 116; Abishae, 122; Achsa, 136; Agnes, 136; Agness, 139; Agnis, 136; Agnis, Sr., 136; Ann Dawson, 138; Ann Moorman, 139; Ann Pemberton, 109, 111; Ann, 139; Anna Moorman, 139; Anna Morris, 139; Anna, 136; Anne, 136; Asahel, 116; Benj., 137; Benjamin 136, 139; Benjamin & Family, 139; Betty, 136; Camm, 116, 122; Caty, 116; Charles, 137; Christian, 136, 139; Daniel, 139; Edward, 96, 111, 112; Elijah & Family, 139; Elijah, 136, 139; Elizabeth Pemberton, 109; Elizabeth, 96, 100, 111, 116, 122, 136; Evan, 96; Francis, 134, 136, 139; Gulay, 136; Hannah, 136, 137, 139; Hendley, 136; Hezekiah, 116; Huldah, 136; Isaac & Family, 139;
THOMAS: Isaac, 76, 96, 111, 134, 136, 138, 139; James, 136, 139; Jesse & Family, 111; Jesse, 111, 136, 139; John 2nd & Family, 139; John & Family, 111, 139; John, 136, 137, 139; John, 2nd, 139; John 3rd, 139; John, 76, 96, 109, 111, 134; John, Sr., 134, 136; Joseph, 111, 136, 139; Lewis & Family, 139; Lewis, 134, 138, 139; Lewis, Jr., 136, 139; Lewis, Sr., 135; Lily Dawson, 139; Lilly, 136; Lydda, 136; Lydia, 136; Manlove, 136, 139; Margaret, 121, 122; Mary Wright, 111, 112; Mary, 96, 111, 136-139; Moley, 136; Molley, 136, 139; Molly, 134; Morris, 139;
THOMAS: Nancy, 136; Nanney, 136; Nehemiah, 46, 76, 96; Polly, 136; Priscilla, 116; Prudence, 96;

Rachel Knight, 138, 139; Rachel, 136, 139; Rachil, 136; Rebecca, 122; Rebecca, Sr., 116; Rebeckah, 136; Ruth Pemberton, 109, 111; Ruth, 136; Samuel, 10; Sarah Musgrave, 139; Sarah Pumberton, 111; Sarah, 96, 111, 122, 136, 137, 139; Selah, 137; Simeon, 139; Solomon & Family, 139; Solomon, 136, 139; Stephen & Family, 139; Stephen, 134, 136-139; Susanna, 136; Susannah, 136; Tilden & Family, 140; Timothy, 46, 53; Vildan, 136; William, 76, 96, 109, 111, 116; Zachariah, 139
THOMPSON: --, 39; Ann, 111; Coln., 37; Esther, 132, 133; Hester, 96; Isaac, 96; Jane Laurance, 106, 111; Jane, 111; Joseph, 60, 96, 106, 111, 132, 133; Joseph, Jr., 111; Lydia Randel, 133; Lydia Randol, 132; Mary, 96, 111; Nancy, 96; Richard & Family, 111; Richard, 88, 96, 110, 111, 133; Samuel Brown, 96; Susan, 111; Susannah Stidman, 110, 111; Susannah, 96; Tanner, 79
THOMSON: Isaac, 88; Joseph, 46; Tanner, 47
THORNBRUGH: James, 123
THORNTON: Eli, 111
THORNTOWN: Abraham, 96
TOD: John, 11
TODD: John, 04; Rebecca, 113, 122; Robert, 122; Stephen, 122; Theodate, 122; William, 122
TOLAND: Bryan, 04, 11
TOLLESON: Hannah Harris, 133; Hannah, 130
TOMLINSON: Jesiah, 111; John, 39; Josiah, 09, 10, 12; Marther Coppock, 111; William, 10, 16, 39, 99, 111
TOWNSEND/TOWNSENT: Esther, 111
TOWNSEND: Cole, 133; Elizabeth, 99, 111, 130, 133; Elve, 133; James, 99, 111, 133; John & Family, 133; John, 111; John, Jr., 111; Margaret, 104, 111; Martha & ch., 133; Mary Cook, 111; Rachel, 133; Ruth, 133; Sarah, 130, 133; William, 111
TOWSENT: Esther, 107
TUCKER: Elizabeth, 25
TURNER: John, 71
URDOS: Wm., 04
VANHORN: Benja., 100, 107, 111; Benjamin, 111; Jane Millhouse, 107, 111; Jane, 111; Joanna Demoss, 111; Rebecca, 111; Robert, 111
VARNON: Lydia, 122; Margaret, 122; Nathaniel, 122; Tamour, 122
VERNON/VARMAN: James, 111; Martha, 111
VERNON: Amos, 116, 117, 122; Ann, 116, 117; Content, 116, 117, 122; Elizabeth, 116; Grace, 117, 122; Hannah, 122; Isaac, 116, 122; James, 113, 116, 117, 122; Lydia, 117; Margaret, 117; Martha, 113; Mary McNeal, 111; Mary, 115, 116; Nathaniel & Family, 111; Nathaniel, 111, 117; Rachel, 116; Robert, 116, 117, 122; Samuel, 116, 117; Solomon, 117, 122; Tamor, 117; Theodate, 117, 122; Thomas, 117; William, 117
WADISON: Richard, 39
WADSWORTH: Thomas, 111
WAGGONER: Elizabeth Sidwell, 122; Mary Sidwell, 122
WALLES: Elizabeth, 111
WALTON: Eunice, 124
WATERS: Philemon, Col., 46
WATSON: Archibald, 11; John, 122
WAY: Abigail, 134, 137, 140; Achsach, 134; Achsah Moorman, 139, 140; Agness Moorman, 138, 140; Agnis, 137; Anna, 134; Caroline, 134; Hannah, 137, 139, 140; Henry, 134, 137, 140; John, 137, 140; Joseph, 128; Lydia, 137, 138, 140;

Mary, 137, 140; Matthew, 137, 138, 140; Moorman, 134, 137; Patience, 134, 140; Paul, 137, 139, 140; Sarah, 128; Susannah, 134, 137; William, 134, 137, 140
WEAKS/WEAKES: Benajmin, 112; James, 112
WEBB: Jesse, 122
WEEKE: William, Jr., 111
WEEKS: Abigail Coppock, 112; Abigall, 88; Benjamin, 88, 99, 103, 112; Caron Happock, 88; Clary, 88; Dr., 113, 141; Hannah, 88, 112; James, 103, 112; John, 103, 111; Lydia, 134; Mary, 88; Stephen B., Dr., 87; Susanna, 88
WEISNER: Elizabeth, 112; Isaac, 112; Jacob, 112; Mary, 112
WHITAKER: Wm., 04
WHITSON: Ann, 109, 112, 127, 128; David & W. & Dt. & brother, 133; David, 112, 127, 128, 132; John, 128; Jordan, 112, 128; Mary Milhous, 132; Mary Millhouse, 127, 128; Mary, 132, 133; Phebe, 112, 123, 127, 128, 133; Phoebe, 128; Rowland, 128; Samuel, 112, 128; Silas Willis, 128; Solomon, 112, 127, 128, 133; Willis, 112, 128
WHITTER: John, 143; Mary, 143
WICKERSHAM: Jehu, 112
WIDOS: William, 11
WIGGANTON: Susannah, 143
WILCUTS: Christian, 137
WILKERSHAM: Jehu, 112
WILKES: John, 32
WILKINSON: Mary, 125
WILLCUTS: Christian, 137, 140; Clark, 137, 140; David, 137; Hursley, 137; Jonathan, 137; Joseph, 137; Milley, 137; Milly, 140; Rachel, 137; Tabitha, 137; Thomas & Family, 140; Thomas, 134, 137, 140
WILLIAM: Ann, 112
WILLIAMS: Abigail 122; Amy, 117; Ann, 88; Daniel, 117, 122; Edward, 117; Elizabeth, 117, 122; Ennion, 122; Grace, 122; Henry, 122; John, 04-06, 13, 122; Joseph, 117, 122; Mary, 117, 122; Rebecca, 117; Ruth, 117; Sarah, 117, 122; Sibbilla, 117, 122
WILLIS: Lina, 140; Milley, 137, 140; Thomas, 140
WILSON: Amos, 128; Ann Easterling, 128; Betty, 128; Charles, 128; Christopher & w. & ch., 133; Christopher, 96, 125, 128, 130; Dinah Cook, 126; Dinah, 96, 112, 123, 126, 128, 129, 133; Eli, 128; Elizabeth Spray, 128; Esther, 96, 125, 128, 130, 133; Gideon, 128; Hannah, 96, 126, 128, 130, 133; Huldah, 128; Isaac, 128; James, 128; Jehu & Family, 133; Jehu, 96, 128, 130, 133; John, 96, 112, 126, 128, 133; John, Sr., 129; Martha, 128; Mary Cox, 125, 128, 130, 133; Mary Evans, 101, 112; Mary, 96, 112, 127-129; Phebe, 96, 126, 130, 133; Rebecca, 140; Ruth, 128; Sarah Hawkins, 128, 130, 133; Sarah, 96, 126, 128, 130; Seth, 96, 101, 112, 128, 129; Tamar, 125, 128; Thomas, 128
WITHERSPOON: John, 36
WITTER: Ann, 143; Elizabeth, 143; James, 143; John, 143; Jonathan, 143; Martha, 143; Mary, 143; Norwood, 143; Samuel, 143; Thomas, 143
WORDSWORTH: --, 19
WRIGHT: Ann McCool, 106, 112; Ann, 112; Anthony, 04, 07, 10; Betty, 112; Charity, 112; Hannah, 97, 112; Isaac, 60, 112; James Anderson, 88; James, 112; James, Sir, Gov., 113; Jemima & Family, 112; Jemima Haworth, 102, 112; Jesse, 112; John Mills, 88; John, 10, 22, 46, 49, 60, 61, 96, 102, 112; John, Jr., 112; John, Mrs.,

112; Jos, 46; Joseph, 60, 112; Judith, 102, 112; Leah, 96, 112; Martha, 88; Mary Mill, 107, 112; Mary, 88, 111, 112; Nathan, 88, 112; Rachel, 88, 96, 103, 109, 112; Ruth, 96; Sarah, 88, 103, 112; Sophia, 88, 96, 109, 112; Susannah, 103, 112; Thomas, 60, 112; William, 53, 60, 87, 88, 96, 107, 112, 113; Wm., 46
WYLIE: Samuel, 24; Sarah, 24
WYLY: --, 35; Dinah Milhouse, 10; S., 04; Saml., 04, 18; Samuel, 04, 10-12, 14-16, 22, 27, 34, 40
WYLYS: -- 39
YOREE: William, 122
YOUNG: Ruth Hollingsworth, 133; Ruth Townsend, 133; Ruth, 131
YOUNT: Frederick, 59; Insco, 70
ZEMP: F. M., Dr., 43

www.ingramcontent.com/pod-product-compliance
Lightning Source LLC
Chambersburg PA
CBHW020653300426
44112CB00007B/357